*f***P**

Of
Two Minds

THE REVOLUTIONARY SCIENCE
OF DUAL-BRAIN PSYCHOLOGY

FREDRIC SCHIFFER, M.D.

THE FREE PRESS
New York   London   Toronto
Sydney   Singapore

*f*P

THE FREE PRESS
A Division of Simon & Schuster Inc.
1230 Avenue of the Americas
New York, NY 10020

THE FREE PRESS and colophon are trademarks
of Simon & Schuster Inc.

Designed by Carla Bolte

Manufactured in the United States of America

10 9 8 7 6 5 4 3 2 1

Library of Congress Cataloging-in-Publication Data

Schiffer, Fredric.
      Of two minds : the revolutionary science of dual-brain psychology
   / Fredric Schiffer.
         p.   cm.
      Includes bibliographical references and index.
      1. Dual-brain psychology.   2. Dual-brain therapy.   3. Split brain.
   I. Title.
   RC455.4.D83S34   1998
   612.8′2—dc21   98-23181
                                                          CIP

   ISBN 0–684–85424–4

For Mary Jane

with great love

I desire to conduct the affairs of this administration that if at the end, when I come to lay down the reins of power, I have lost every other friend on earth, I shall at least have one friend left, and that friend shall be down inside me.

—Abraham Lincoln

Contents

Preface

I first saw Ryan sitting on a couch, hunched over, asleep, resembling the sagging duffle bag against which he leaned. Ryan, a freshman at Harvard, had been sent over from the university's health service for a psychiatric admission to McLean Hospital, the flagship psychiatric hospital for the Harvard Medical School. As resident on call, I was roused out of bed that cold night twenty-four years ago to attend to him. The two of us, both emerging from deep slumber, entered a consultation room at 4 A.M., to begin a journey into his mind.

Ryan related that initially he was proud of his smooth adjustment to college life. But a few weeks into the semester, he started to fall behind in his work. He found he couldn't grasp concepts; he was getting distracted and having trouble sleeping. He fell even further behind and started to procrastinate. He was beginning to feel humiliated that this—whatever *this* was—was happening to him. He saw himself flunking out. Where would he go? What would become of him? What good would his hard-earned admission to Harvard be if he left in disgrace? Could he flip hamburgers? No, he would be incompetent at that too, he thought. His only talent was for being a genius, and that was failing him somehow. He felt a sense of doom, and I saw in him a look of despondency.

How was I to understand this young man, who a month earlier was on top of the world, a freshman at Harvard, dating a woman from Radcliffe, liked by his peers, on his way to becoming a scholar, but stopping first at McLean Hospital at four in the morning because he had been thinking seriously of killing himself? And how was I to help him?

He seemed to blame his distress mostly on his pressures at school, battered by his expectation of being exposed as a failure. The idea of the ensuing humiliation terrified and depressed him, making him unable to function adequately. But I observed that his very real expectation of failure and humiliation seemed to be based on something more than the facts and events of his current situation. Surely he had an innate capacity to succeed. It was the *idea* of failure that reduced and then impaired his abilities. Why did he have this idea? "Maybe I'm good at fooling people," he offered, implying some core deficiency that the Harvard admissions committee failed to observe.

Ryan came under my care in 1976, during my second year of training at McLean. Freud was the mainstay of my training, and I found his writings beautiful and rich, but somehow imprecise, with a good deal of poetic license. Freud placed a great emphasis on long-repressed sexual impulses or conflicts, but as I spoke with Ryan, those issues didn't seem apparent, and as we sat together that November morning, the details of Freud's model of the mind only seemed to add to the chill in the drafty corner room, offering neither light nor warmth. I wanted something more tangible, more explicit, closely related to my actual situation—something more like physics than poetry.

It would be a few years before the psychopharmacologists dominated the hospital, and many more years before the managed care insurance companies dominated them, so I was able to meet with Ryan four times a week until he was able to leave the hospital eight weeks later. For most of the sessions, we met in a consultation room on his hall, or later, when he had privileges to leave his hall, in my office. On pleasant days we would spend the hour walking together on the tree-lined paths and roads of McLean Hospital. McLean had been constructed on a verdant site overlooking hills and fields a hundred years earlier, to take advantage of its curative views at a time when neither pills nor theories could rescue the afflicted.

I learned that Ryan experienced his father, a mathematics professor at a small New England college, as aloof and harshly critical. Despite Ryan's lifelong efforts, he could never feel any affection or admiration from his father, a master at finding ways to ridicule or demean even the finest accomplishment. Although Ryan had succeeded in winning acceptance to Harvard College, he had failed to get an early admission, and he had also failed to gain entrance to Brown University, facts that his father's attention and energy lingered on. "I knew Brown had come to outrank it; Harvard's no longer what it used to be," his father commented to Ryan.

Ryan experienced his mother as remote as his father, but in an entirely different way. She came across as somewhat detached, not at all like his father's aggressive, competitive self-centeredness, but rather through a meekness, an anxiety about all of the world and her place in it. Although she doted on Ryan, she seemed disconnected, as if she always held a bit of herself in reserve.

As we walked one afternoon, Ryan said reflectively, "I guess all of my life I felt I couldn't please them, that they were always disappointed with me, and I don't know why, but this was very, very painful for me. It shouldn't have been, I know. But I can feel now that it tore me up inside. It made me feel worthless. I don't know why I cared so much."

Ryan and I had come to believe that somewhere within, a part of him had deduced that if he were not well loved, he needed to strive harder to get that love. This striving in large measure took the form of academic efforts, which seemed the surest way to his parent's approval. Although he had achieved academic success, those efforts repeatedly failed in their true aims, for he had never achieved what he most desired: his parents' admiration. Ryan assumed responsibility for his parents' attitude, and as his college work intensified, he began to anticipate his exposure as an inadequate person unworthy of love or admiration.

One way of viewing Ryan would be to say that he developed his anxiety and depression because he expected, based largely on his early life experience, to be humiliated. We would say that he had this expectation "unconsciously," since at the time of his admission to McLean, he was unaware of the reasons he anticipated failure.

At first I couldn't articulate why I felt this explanation was incomplete. I was confused about what was conscious and what was unconscious and how this all actually led to Ryan's symptoms. And then I noticed the obvious: Ryan was getting better, for whatever reason. Whether it was our walks about the hills with our inquiries into his early life, or simply time, I didn't know for sure. He had by now become an active participant in our discussions. He could wonder aloud about why he felt destined for humiliation. An emerging part of him began to see that he needn't fail or suffer humiliation, that he had a capacity to succeed, and that part of him could now wonder about why he held the conviction that he must fail. I began to see two different parts to Ryan: one side convinced of success and the other convinced of failure.

The thought that came to my mind was that the night he was admitted to the hospital, his personality was dominated by that part of Ryan that saw himself as a failure. Ryan clung dearly to his impostor fantasy, an idea that was destroying his life. Now there seemed to be a second part to his personality, which saw himself as a success. It seemed possible to me that there were two parts battling for control of his mind. When he began the semester, the successful part may have been in control; but under stress, that part came under assault by another part, spewing forth feelings and ideas of his defectiveness. I believed it was the "failure" self that eventually took control.

As his hospitalization progressed, the part of him that believed in his success was clearly becoming dominant, and with that evolution came a complete change in his entire appearance. When he was admitted, he appeared distraught, confused, and disorganized. Now, as he was getting ready to be discharged, two months later, he appeared to be a strong, healthy person with a sense of well-being and confidence.

I felt I had witnessed an amazing transformation. Ryan came in as a psychiatric patient, and he left a Harvard student. When he came in, he had a complete set of ideas, feelings, and behaviors. He knew he was doomed and as a consequence felt overwhelmed with a terror that rendered him unable to function in all but the simplest ways. There was no inherent contradiction in his state. Philosophically, his condition was internally consistent. He was, quite simply, a failed person.

At discharge, he felt his strength in his mind and body. His physical appearance had changed as well. One might not recognize two photographs of him, one in each state, as the same person. He now possessed an entirely different, positive set of ideas about his chances for success. He had been reading and studying in his free time with intense interest and concentration.

At the time I didn't understand how this transformation had been achieved. Although I wanted to assume that I was responsible for his success—that my affection and interpretations on our walks, perhaps even my bad jokes, had somehow facilitated it—I had only a vague understanding of what had happened. I was struck not only by the fact that it had occurred, but also that it seemed as if he had actually changed from one personality into another.

Then another interesting, although disturbing, thing happened. About two months after his discharge, while I was seeing him as an outpatient, Ryan's insecurities, self-doubt, and anxieties returned. His appearance was beginning to deteriorate. One might simply see this as his getting depressed again. He could have had a cyclic depression that was destined to recur, like the phases of the moon. Or I could have seen it as a recurrent abnormality of his brain chemistry, or simply as an alteration in his mood. But that is not how I saw it. To me, it appeared as if he were changing personalities. We hadn't worked out and resolved his problems, as we had assumed. Instead, we had merely pushed his insecure personality to the rear and allowed his confident personality to emerge. And now, I believed, his insecure personality was emerging again and shoving his confident personality to the rear. I began to understand that his success in the hospital wasn't due to Ryan's truly learning to appreciate his own value, but rather to his suppressing that part of him that continued to believe him to be intolerably defective.

I shared my hypothesis with Ryan, and he immediately agreed. We came to see one personality as more mature and healthier. When Ryan maintained that personality, he was confident and functioned well. He knew that his parents were a bit neurotic, but this didn't disturb him. In fact, in this personality, he had compassion for them and was able to understand their own stresses and resulting parental limitations.

In his other personality, Ryan was emotionally immature. He became sullen, withdrawn, and easily upset. He didn't like to go out because he felt he looked troubled and insecure (and to a large degree he did). He had great difficulty concentrating, and as he began to procrastinate and fail to keep up with his massive assignments, he could again imagine his failure. This frame of mind increased his anxiety, and we could easily predict a catastrophe in the making.

It seemed to us as if Ryan was of two minds: one, more adult, more present in the immediate reality, and the other, immature or primitive, seeing the world as little changed from the past and still expecting with certainty that his parents, and therefore any other important people in his life, would disregard and demean him. This part of him still seemed emotionally injured, unable to get beyond the traumas it had suffered.

With this concept in mind, I began to implore Ryan to wake up his healthier half as I saw him sliding fast into a mental abyss from which I could discern absolutely no benefit or profit, only torment and destruction. Something inside him heard me, was awakened, and came to the surface. I had simply (or perhaps not so simply) urged him to arouse the mature part of him, which we had already identified and gotten to know. And right before my eyes his demeanor changed. As if waking from a deep sleep, he said, "What the hell have I been doing?"

This victory lasted only a few days, but we were both impressed by it and were able to repeat it in different ways many hundreds of times over the next four years. We learned how to talk with and negotiate with either his troubled personality or his mature mind. I might say, "Okay, but what does the worried part of you feel about that?" or "Let me speak with the mature side." Gradually his healthier personality became firmly rooted in a position of leadership, and the rebellions by his other side became less intense and less frequent as that side felt better understood and appreciated, as well as more disciplined. Ryan went on to graduate school after he completed his treatment, and today he lives an extraordinarily interesting and successful life.

Was the troubled part of Ryan, which took control of his personality, his unconscious mind? On the night of his admission, his mind seemed perfectly "conscious" to me, with a full set of feelings, attitudes, and behaviors. Nonetheless, I asked myself if the troubled person Ryan became was somehow related to the "Freudian" unconscious mind. How did all the parts of Ryan's mind fit with the superego, the ego, or the id, or the hundreds of other psychological terms being taught during our psychiatric residency—terms like "conflict," "introjects," "self-objects," "self-self-objects," "Oedipal complexes," "projections," and "identifications"? It would take me years to untangle the psychological theory with which I was sent into battle and relate it to what I was actually observing.

Ryan and I did this work before the term "inner child" became popular. With hindsight, I know our work was very different from inner child work, for Ryan had more than an inner child. He manifested an entire overt personality that, though emotionally troubled and relatively immature, was able to take control of his mind. This personality was not merely an image of a wounded child, but a full-bodied personality that could be aggressive and destructive. Whatever name we may give to the inner child, the troubled personality, or the unconscious mind, I believe all have to do with the effects of trauma and how those effects are maintained into adulthood as a covert or an overt part of the personality. I will explore and clarify these concepts through the course of the book.

During my residency, I met regularly with Shervert Frazier, the psychiatrist in chief at McLean. Frazier was my preceptor and as such acted as my mentor and my supervisor on some cases. He was a large man with a deep voice that seemed to boom even when he spoke quietly. At the hospital, he was its center, its unabashed father figure. I felt a deep affection and admiration for Frazier, and when he said to me one day, "I think it's time for you to go into analysis," I felt I was being chosen for advancement rather than remedial care. In 1976, a personal analysis, whether or not one wanted to go on to become a psychoanalyst, was highly prized. It was felt that to be a good psychiatrist, one had to work out one's own issues, to keep them from clouding one's therapeutic judgment. It also was regarded as the best method for learning about psychotherapy. Of the nine residents in my class, six were already in analysis. (Today fewer psychiatric residents are willing to make that journey. Perhaps they cannot justify the time or money. Perhaps they simply do not see the need.)

When Frazier suggested I undergo analysis, I saw it as evidence of his caring about my career and his encouraging me to undergo this initiation into the club of true psychiatrists. I had already been leaning in that direction, and I accepted his advice with appreciation.

Then Frazier went on to say, "I think Elvin Semrad's got some time available. Give him a call. He is a great man, and there are very few of them."

Elvin Semrad was a living legend in Boston with a reputation as the consummate analyst—the analyst's analyst; he was reputed to have trained or analyzed half of the psychiatric community in Boston, he was said also to be able to reach the most profoundly disturbed patients in a single consultation, to make mute patients speak, to make psychotic patients suddenly rational as he gently touched the inner corners of their being.

Semrad worked at the Massachusetts Mental Health Center, a deteriorating state mental hospital that, though drab and dirty, was a major teaching hospital in psychiatry for Harvard. Among the graduates of its program were many of the most highly regarded psychiatrists in Boston, many of whom directed programs or held prestigious teaching positions. But from its physical appearance, Mass Mental, as it was called, resembled any other rundown, underfunded state hospital.

I had a seat by a secretary's desk in the hallway. My appointment was for 4:50; the secretary left me alone at 5 o'clock. At 5:20 there was still no sign of Semrad. In facts there was no one about. I knew because I had been looking all around trying to reassure myself that I was in the right place at the right time. Suddenly a door opened, and about five psychiatrists emerged from an office about thirty feet away. Then at the doorway appeared an unusual-looking man. He was fairly short, about five feet, five inches, and very solid and large, though somehow neither obese nor muscular. His mass was capped by thick, white hair brushed back, and perhaps the total effect was of a small, stout, snow-capped mountain. He said nothing, but with a very thick hand waved slowly across his chest for me to come down the hall into his office.

Semrad motioned for me to sit in a straight-backed wooden chair, the kind every schoolteacher uses. The chair was flush against Semrad's desk, which also resembled a schoolteacher's. Actually, Semrad had once been a schoolteacher in Nebraska. But now, as a full professor at Harvard and a legend in his own time, he sat on his own wooden chair at his desk, covered with piles of books and papers from which he cleared enough space for a stenographer's notebook into which he entered copious notes as I spoke. From time to time he'd look up at me from his writing.

As I had waited in the dingy hallway of a state mental hospital for a man who didn't seem to be keeping our appointment, I had thought of just leaving. "What am I putting myself through?" I asked myself.

And now inside his office, that question resonated louder as I surveyed the space. It was decorated with heavy green drapes from the 1940s, which might have once been in some superintendent's office. Behind my chair, the room was full of tables, each overflowing with stacks of books and papers. To my left and behind me was his analyst's couch, upholstered in tight pink plastic imitation leather. Most disturbing, though, was that the door to his office, which led to the public hallway from which I had just entered, was cut an inch and a half too short. It let the light from the hallway enter his office and, I assumed, reciprocally, allowed the confidential voices from his office to enter the corridor. Offsetting my observations was the fact that this man had a large reputation and had been personally recommended by Frazier, so I decided to play it out further.

Semrad asked me to tell him about myself, and I began relating my life story—who I was, or thought I was, and where I was from. When he'd look up from his writing, he had an expression of profound understanding and respect. I got deeper and deeper into my story. Occasionally, Semrad would interrupt with a question to clarify what I was trying to articulate, but otherwise I continued pretty much on my own, except for his occasional glances up in silence.

At one point, I had been talking about my father and our relationship, which in many ways had been painful and strained. Then I was describing with great pride how my father had from nothing—from less than nothing, in fact from great adversity—fought with pluck and courage throughout his life to succeed and had eventually accomplished what he had pursued. Semrad looked up and with a profound look said simply, "Your father has been very important to you."

I started to sob. And this sobbing kept rising. I felt as if I were being immersed in escalating waves of emotion from deep within. Then suddenly as it intensified even further, I began to feel what I could only describe as strong electrical impulses bursting from my gut. I thought I was in danger. I looked at Semrad, who seemed calm and appreciative, and I said, "I think I'm having an arrhythmia." I began desperately trying to find my pulse, which, of course, was entirely normal.

I began my analysis with Semrad the next day and went four days a week. There was not a session that was not profoundly moving, and my life in many ways changed dramatically. My marriage, excellent to begin with, achieved a great deepening. And in October, a few months after starting my analysis, I made a trip to New Hampshire with my father, and in a canoe alone on a mountain lake we silently repaired our distress. To the day he died, we remained the closest of friends and confidants.

The week I returned from New Hampshire, Semrad died from a heart attack. He was sixty-seven.

Ten years after his death, the Harvard Medical School held a symposium on Semrad's life and work in an attempt to understand and keep alive his contribution, but even there, with so many fine minds who were taught and touched by him, his secret remained intact. A psychiatrist who trained at McLean a few years after me and now worked for a health maintenance organization promoting short-term therapy, commented at the symposium, "Who was this guy? People talk about him as if he performed miracles. This is the mentality of a cult."

As I reflect on my work with him, I have come to believe that Semrad was able to touch a part of me with which I had not been in contact. Why had I sobbed so profoundly? I knew I loved my father. I knew I admired him. I also knew his shortcomings and his limitations. I knew my father all of my life, but I had never sobbed, never articulated or experienced such unbounded love and admiration. My sobbing came as a complete surprise to me. It was almost as if someone else were there in my place. When I took my pulse, I came to full attention and pulled my usual self back into myself. I now realize there was another part of me—an intact part of me that possessed the intense feelings that Semrad was able, seemingly effortlessly, to get me to express. So what are my true feelings about my father? I think it depends on which part of me I focus on.

I understood only many years later that Semrad had helped me to be aware of and to accept and interrelate two parts of me, and that integration enabled me to develop and enjoy a profoundly loving relationship with my father while cognizant of our limitations. My reflections on my work with Semrad led me to the idea that I too have two distinct parts of me. Once a patient, upon discovering a troubled part of himself, asked me, "Dr. Schiffer, do you have an inner person inside you?" With a disdainful look on my face, I replied, "Me? An inner person?" while my left hand waved to him, and we both then roared with laughter.

I was a Freudian in one important sense: I believed in the talking cure. Freud, regardless of the details of his assumptions, powerfully promoted the idea that by talking about one's innermost thoughts and feelings, some sense would emerge and some relief of symptoms would occur. Essential to this talking was a respected psychiatrist who had a genuine concern, curiosity, and high regard for the patient.

Still, though I was a believer in talk therapy, in the therapeutic relationship, and in the patient's ability to resolve his problems, I yearned for a clearer map of the mazes I was in training to explore. I had come to McLean from a fellowship in cardiology. When I graduated from medical school, I had no interest in psychiatry, which seemed too vague and unstructured for my taste. I initially went into internal medicine but found that after I mastered the material, it became rote and boring. I felt more like a cook who empirically followed recipes than a scientist who pondered and puzzled over concepts.

In the little spare time I had during my internship and residency in medicine, I had become interested in the physical effects of emotional stress and began some research, which eventually led to my seeking a research fellowship in cardiology. And so in 1973, I came to Harvard to study the effects of stress on the heart. During the fellowship, in which I was gaining fascinating insights about the effects of emotion on the heart, insights I share in Chapter 10, I became more sure that I didn't want to practice clinical internal medicine or cardiology. I wanted to continue my research, but I saw the need for an in-depth training in psychiatry to round out my education. It was with this reasoning that I went into psychiatry.

This background may explain some of my frustration with the writings of psychiatrists. I was familiar with tangible qualities like the pressures and flows of the cardiovascular system—things that can be easily conceptualized, measured, and manipulated. Thus, it became natural for me as a psychiatrist in the making to try to formulate psychology in more concrete terms, but without losing its humanity.

By the time I had completed my residency at McLean my fascination with the mind and my patients had won out over my passion for the heart. I never returned to research in cardiology. But after many years devoted to my clinical practice of psychiatry, supplemented by consuming armchair theorizing about the psyche, I returned to my roots as a research scientist and turned my sights and energies toward the ineffable, enigmatic mind. This book is the result of my searches and researches.

Acknowledgments

First, I thank my parents, Helen and Samuel Schiffer, both now deceased, for the complex matrix from which I emerged, which set in motion long ago the curiosity that eventually led to this book. As he had done with all of my projects and with all of my brothers' works, my father closely read and enjoyed the entire first draft of the manuscript. I took great pleasure in his delight at the anticipated publication of this book, which his succumbing to ill health prevented him from seeing.

I thank also my two siblings, the esteemed philosopher Stephen Schiffer and the esteemed Shakespearian scholar James Schiffer, both of whom have encouraged and stimulated me in long hours of intense discussion over many years. Their love has been a palpable asset and pleasure.

To neuroscientist and colleague Carl Anderson, I offer my deep appreciation for his consistent enthusiasm and for his close reading of and advice on the manuscript. I also deeply value the research collaboration of Martin Teicher over most of the past decade. Psychiatrist Kenneth Levin many years ago encouraged me to write up my developing ideas, which became articulated in our frequent lunches at McLean where we rediscovered each other on the staff, having first become friends as undergraduates at the University of Pennsylvania decades earlier. In recent years I had the pleasure of getting to know Joseph Bogen and Eran Zaidel. Their hospitality, friendship, and stimulating conversations have added much to this work. I appreciate also the interest and assistance of Frank Pompei and Alvaro Pascual-Leone.

My stepmother, Dolores Schiffer, and niece Tanya Schiffer have assisted me in my attempts to clarify my ideas and writing. Harvard internist Michael Rees has been a close friend and colleague for over twenty years, and I have always valued our close collaboration in many clinical situations over this time. My dear friend Allan Spielman has offered much needed interest and has always answered my late night questions with resounding clarity. To my good friend and colleague Stanislaw Freeman, whose tragic brain injury abruptly interrupted his brilliant mind and career, I express my deep love and appreciation for the hours we and our wives spent vacationing on Cape Cod pondering the plight of the psyche. I continue to miss my friend, colleague, and brother-in-law, psychoanalyst J. Winstead Adams, who like my father died during the past year. In my mind, I easily see and feel his bellowing glee at the sight of this book.

Stuart Miller, "writing coach," was very helpful to me in shaping the book's proposal. I also value the helpful advice of science writer Robert Ross. My dynamic agent, Beth Vesel, and her assistant, Carol Chase, helped to transform my proposal through their editorial advice and their enthusiasm into a contract. Liz Maguire and Philip Rappaport acquired the book for The Free Press, and Philip used his tremendous skill and persistence to help me craft this book out of the uncut stone of the first draft. I am immensely appreciative of Philip's intelligent guidance.

My patients are no less my friends than those I know socially. I have been privileged to share their lives and observe their courage, intelligence, and perseverance.

And finally, I thank the two women in my life: my wife, Mary Jane, and our daughter, Emily. Their constancy in love, encouragement, and wisdom have made this work possible. Mary Jane, a clinical social worker at Harvard, has been a constant source of challenging and stimulating feedback.

CHAPTER 1

Introduction

She is in despair. Her life is a shambles. She can't think straight, and the anxiety she feels seems to bury her. She has spent two weeks in bed, and there she cries most of the time. She doesn't know what has overtaken her. Nothing—not her business failure, not the divorce she sought, not her new relationship—seems even vaguely proportional to her distress.

My first contact with Carol was through her brother, who urged me over the phone to hospitalize her. "She's flipped out," he told me. I asked him to bring her over to my office instead.

Carol seemed to hide beneath her straggly hair, partially covering her naturally pretty dark eyes, now red from crying. She was handsome in spite of her condition. She was no longer crying, and she was cooperative and trying to be pleasant. Carol was in touch with reality. She clearly saw her distress but had no clue about what suddenly brought this great, escalating turmoil into her life several weeks ago. Her life for the past thirty years certainly had been troubled at times, but never before had she been in quite so much distress.

I liked Carol, and I think I had a good sense of the despair she had been experiencing. We seemed to make a good emotional connection. As we discussed her distress, I pushed her to try to see when she had felt this way before, and she discovered to her surprise that as a child she had experienced similar periods of distress.

I asked her to describe her family life in her childhood, and it became clear to us as she spoke that frequently she felt emotionally aban-

doned and betrayed by her parents. There was clearly a connection between her early distress and that perception of estrangement.

I wanted to see if her present despair might somehow parallel that
of her childhood. She began to understand that about a month earlier,
when her divorce became final and her business failed outright, she
started to feel abandoned and unsupported emotionally. And just as she
had as a child, Carol blamed herself, certain she was somehow bad, defective, or at the very least at fault, to warrant the perceived abandonment. Carol's present-day despair seemed related to the anxiety of
feeling abandoned and metaphorically left to suffer a painful psychological death, compounded by the pain of believing she was so repugnant
as a person as to deserve such treatment and its terrible consequences.

Carol was fighting constantly with her new boyfriend, a man she
loved dearly and who loved her in return. She was continually accus-
ing him of not loving her, and her behavior was becoming unbearable
for him. She was effectively pushing him away, which only intensified
her sense of abandonment. Remarkably, Carol was able to see and appreciate all this.

At this point, I said, "But I think there's another part of you that
knows that Mike loves you."

"Yes, I know that."

At that point I explained my hypothesis because I didn't feel I
could wait a few years for her to come to it in her own time. I wanted
to bring some clarity and structure into the session right then. I told
Carol that there was a part of her personality that was immature, troubled, and panicking, and it had been taking control of her life. I explained that she might also have another part of her personality, one
more mature and grounded, but it was being pushed aside now. Carol
told me that she could actually feel that struggle within; she had periods when she felt calm and in control, but then even those times were
disrupted by overwhelming feelings of anxiety.

"I am going to talk with your troubled-sided personality," I told
her. "I can see that this part of you is extremely frightened and upset. I
know you [her troubled side] don't yet understand why you are so distressed, but I and your more mature side will help you to understand
yourself. Right now, I want you to stop attacking Carol. I want you to

let your mature side lead; otherwise your life will continue crashing off course." My tone was caring, firm, forceful.

To Carol's surprise, her symptoms suddenly abated, leaving her calm and in control. Although I didn't expect this remission to last more than a few minutes, its occurrence set out the blueprint for what was to follow in our work together. We interpreted her response as her troubled mind's listening and deciding to cooperate. It was in essence, I believed, her troubled mind's nonverbal response to what I had said.

I explained to Carol that I believe we have two minds, much as Steve Martin and Lily Tomlin are comically portrayed as living and struggling together within the head of one person in *All of Me*. In my view, Carol had a mature part that knew she was essentially safe and well regarded in spite of the business failure—more of an insult to her pride than her pocketbook—and in spite of the divorce she struggled so hard to achieve. But Carol had another mind that knew she was utterly alone and on the verge of a long-awaited destruction. She acknowledged that she had been living in that mind for the past month. Finally, I shared my idea that in life, these two parts of our mind can struggle or cooperate, and that apparently in the past month, her immature part had assumed a dominant role in her personality. In time Carol and I would explore why this switch occurred at this turn in her life, but for now I just wanted to offer a diagram for what had been happening to her and, from that map, a direction back to mental stability.

I next asked Carol to try on a pair of plastic safety glasses taped over the front so that she could see only out of the extreme right side of her right eye. She looked at me skeptically, as if I might need help myself. I simply asked her what she was experiencing. In a moment she said, with some surprise, that the glasses made her feel calmer and safer. I gave her a second pair almost identical to the first, and I asked her to try them on. The second pair limited her vision to the left side of her left eye. She told me almost immediately that she felt trapped and distressed. Her symptoms were recurring. I asked her to switch again to the first pair, and within seconds she was calmed by that pair.

With this strange exercise, which I will explain in great detail as we proceed, I wanted to help Carol see that the idea of an immature personality's taking over the control of her life was more than a metaphor, more than a vague hypothesis; it was a demonstrable, concrete phenomenon. When I suggested that we talk to the immature part of her from then on, Carol knew from her experience that we were not waxing poetic.

I began teaching Carol how to strengthen her mature mind and how to notice her troubled side—how to listen to it, how to talk with it, how to get it to cooperate, how to get it to feel better. By the end of her fifty-minute session, her despair was gone. We had begun a therapeutic relationship, and she left with a new understanding and techniques for taking advantage of that insight. Carol wouldn't need hospitalization after all. Although I knew that her troubled side would reassert itself and that this respite would be brief, we had accomplished something dramatic and would be able to return to what we did.

Over the next month, the course of therapy was turbulent as Carol's immature side showed its strength and determination in fits and starts. But steadily we made progress, and after six weeks, she began, for the first time in several months, to feel almost completely like her old self again. By that time Carol could readily feel what she called "my troubled side," and she had become quite skilled at listening to her, disciplining her, and helping her with her fears. Eventually she easily related to this newly discovered troubled part of her, and she found that her relationship to this aspect of her own self was much like her relationships with other people. She responded to it, and it responded in turn. Over this time, we helped her troubled side feel safer and more a part of her life in a cooperative, constructive way. She improved significantly over the next three months and then dramatically over the following three. By that time she had achieved an emotional stability and balance because the mature part of her personality had firmly established its leadership.

Of Two Minds

From even my early days as a psychiatric resident at McLean Hospital, I noticed that my patients often seemed to have a kind of double personality: on the one hand, very mature and stable, but on the other hand, more irrational, overly emotional, and impulsive. This impression became more complex but clearer as I worked over the next twenty years with patients in private practice. I could see how these different aspects of my patients interacted, with one part often struggling with or sabotaging the other. The troubled part seemed stuck in a traumatic past, and I had begun to see that the object of treatment was to help this distressed part learn that it was more valuable and safer than troubling past experiences had led it to believe. The relationship and the complex interaction between our two minds is the focus of this book: How to recognize them, communicate with them, and, most important, improve their relationship. We will also explore the physical basis for the two minds.

Split-Brain Studies

My clinical impressions led me to reread and reassess the literature on the famous split-brain studies of the 1960s because I had the feeling that the scientists that conducted them had also encountered two minds in one person. The split-brain surgery, a commissurotomy, consisted of cutting the corpus callosum, the large nerve bundle connecting the left and right cerebral hemispheres. It had been performed on patients desperately suffering from epilepsy not relieved by conventional treatments, because it was reasoned that the operation could prevent the spread of a seizure from one hemisphere to the other. The doctors hoped that limiting the spread of the seizures might reduce the epilepsy generally. The results showed that not only were the seizures decreased, but also the patients did not seem adversely affected by the radical surgery. As I will discuss more fully in the next chapter, these operations became famous not as much because of their therapeutic benefits as more because of the subsequent studies performed on the patients after they recovered from the surgery. These studies enabled scientists to investigate the properties of each separated hemisphere, the left and the right brain.

I was, of course, very much aware of the popular belief that there are left- and right-sided personality types with the "left-sided" person being very logical and unemotional and the "right-sided" person perceived as very poetic or impulsive. But I knew also that these ideas were generally held in disregard by neuroscientists.

As I reviewed the entire split-brain literature, I realized that the most striking and dependable finding from the studies was generally underappreciated by scientists as well as laypeople. This most important idea, which I discuss in detail in the next chapter, is that in split-brain patients, there exist two intact, reasonably intelligent, autonomous minds. After these patients had their corpus callosum cut, they each manifested two separate minds. They became, in effect, two people inhabiting one body. In the next chapter, I present extensive evidence and clarification of this incredible statement, but briefly here are some dramatic examples (elaborated on later) to illustrate my point quickly:

- A patient had to wrestle with his left arm (controlled by his *separated right brain*) to keep it from striking his wife against his (left-sided) will.
- A split-brain patient consciously wanted to smoke, but each time he lit up, his left hand (controlled by his right brain) would grab the cigarette and, to his dismay, put it out.
- A split-brain patient was awakened by a hand slapping her across her face. Her alarm clock was going off, and she realized she had overslept and was going to be late for an appointment. The hand that had aroused her was her own left hand! While her left brain was asleep, her right brain awoke and appreciated her predicament.

Each of these is an example of the "post-commissurotomy syndrome," which many split-brain patients manifest for a short time following the surgery. In this syndrome, the left hand, connected to the right brain, acts autonomously and purposefully—but often in opposition to the intentions and actions of the left brain.

My Notions Versus the Popular Notions from the Split-Brain Studies

Although there are similarities between my idea about two minds in each of us and the popular assumption of left- (logical) and right- (poetic) sided personalities, my notion had more to do with maturity versus immaturity. I first expected the immature personality to reside in the right brain, for there is not a long leap from the popular idea of a creative, emotional right brain and my idea of an overly emotional, neurotic side. Similarly, the popular concept of a logical, orderly left brain didn't seem too distant from my idea of a mature side. Yet as I came to understand the dynamics of the two minds, it became increasingly clear that the mature mind might easily be the poetic and artistic one, and the troubled side might tend to be extremely orderly and logical.

The popular notion did not suggest two actual, distinct minds, but rather that some people were more logical and less emotional, like typical computer wizards, and that others were more creative and spontaneous, like typical artists. The popular notion does imply that these personality types might bear a relation to the left and right brains, with one hemisphere—either left or right—tending to have a more important role in shaping the individual's integrated personality. Neuroscientists call this popular notion "hemisphericity," but its scientific validity has not been established. Nor is it disproved. Scientists generally believe that the popular notions about hemisphericity have far overreached the scientific evidence for them. And so while it is obvious that some people are more logical and less emotional, and others the opposite, this categorization has not been well enough studied to determine clearly whether it relates to the hemispheres of the brain.

Although the split-brain findings didn't suggest that one hemisphere was more mature or more emotional than the other, two main, dependable findings from the split-brain studies demanded further investigation. The first was the amazing discovery that two autonomous minds resided in each split-brain patient. The second was that only the left side could speak; the right brain is mute. (The location of speech in the left hemisphere was known prior to the initial split-brain studies, but that fact became more graphic in the split-brain patients.) It appeared that while the left side was superior at most language tasks, the right side excelled at spatial tasks, but whether one side was more intelligent, logical, or mature was difficult to assess. The detailed nature of right mind was not well studied because the right brain, being "mute," was difficult to study psychologically. Recently I collaborated with the California group that did the original split-brain research. Our new studies, described in the next chapter, were designed specifically to explore the psychological nature of the left and right brains in split-brain patients.

Two Personalities?

I wondered how the two personalities I observed in my patients related to the two minds revealed by the split-brain operations. Was what I was observing as a clinical psychological phenomenon supported by the compelling data from these neurosurgical patients? Was what began for me as a clinical metaphor an actual reality? Are there really two minds in my patients? Do these two minds relate to the two cerebral hemispheres in a manner consistent with the observations to come from the split-brain studies? How do these two minds reconcile with classic Freudian theory of the conscious and unconscious minds and to the superego, ego, and id? Do all people have two minds? Is there a relationship between traumatic experiences and the troubled mind's worldview? If these two minds exist, might not both be mature or both immature in some people?

With these and many more questions in mind, I embarked on a deeper review of the literature and a series of neuroscientific and psychological studies, often in collaboration with some of the finest neuroscientists of our age. In this book, I present our results as well as their implications for psychological theory and treatment.

Testing a hypothesis is not limited to collecting and interpreting laboratory data. It extends also to how well it can successfully explain a wide range of clinical observations and to how much its therapeutic methods accomplish. In conducting our research, we attempted to interrelate as much as possible the consulting room and the scientific laboratory.

In and Out of the Lab

In 1990, I approached Dr. Martin Teicher, a highly regarded neuroscientist who had always maintained an interest in novel ideas. I told him of my hypotheses and suggested a protocol that could begin to test my ideas scientifically. Dr. Teicher gave his assent and offered me the use of his laboratory for conducting electroencephalograms (EEGs).* I invited patients with a history of trauma to come to the laboratory,

---

*EEGs, or brain waves, are very sensitive recordings of the electrical activity of the brain and can be use to indicate which areas of the brain are active over a given time period.

where I asked them to recall a neutral memory, such as something routine that they did the week before, and a traumatic memory, which I helped elicit in a brief psychiatric interview. What Teicher and I found was that in most of the patients, their left brains were more active during the neutral memory, and their right brains were more active during their recall of their traumas. The data suggested that traumatic memories might be more often lodged in the right hemisphere. I speculated that each hemisphere had a recollection of the trauma, but the mind in the right hemisphere was more sensitive to it.

In November 1995, I made a completely unexpected discovery that was to advance my ideas and my clinical skills—and drastically alter my hypothesis that it was always the right brain that was more troubled by past traumas.

Dr. Werner Wittling and his associate neuroscientists from Eichstatt, Germany, had developed a technique to show films to one half of the brain at a time in a group of healthy, intact subjects. The German experiment seemed to confirm what a group of scientists working in the United States had already learned: films shown to the right brain often elicited a stronger emotional and physical response than when shown to the left brain. It is commonly known that if something is shown to the extreme left or the extreme right of a person, the image tends to go first to the opposite side of the brain. The German group used an expensive and complicated method for isolating one side of the brain. It was too costly and complex for my tastes and budget, but it inspired me to begin using my hands to block out parts of my vision to see if I felt a little differently when looking out of one side. I imagined I felt some difference, but concluded my brief experience unconvinced.

That afternoon I asked my first patient, Larry, a research assistant at MIT, to hold one hand over his right eye and the other over all but the outside half of his left eye. I was completely surprised when he became a bit agitated and said, "Oh, my God!"

"What's that?" I had no idea what he meant.

"I have all of my anxiety back."

Some months earlier, Larry had entered treatment for profound anxiety stemming from childhood mistreatment. By this time, his symptoms had been substantially relieved.

"Try the other side [right side of the right eye]," I retorted.

"That's better!" he immediately responded, to the relief of both of us.

I asked him to go back and forth, and he repeatedly felt his symptoms when he looked to the left side of his left eye, and he had the complete relief of his symptoms when he looked out of the right half of his right eye. We were both amazed.

I asked all of my patients that day to do the same thing, and the first five all had similar dramatic responses. One patient, a Vietnam veteran, whom I had diagnosed with a severe posttraumatic stress disorder, looked out of one side and developed an expression of intense apprehension as he looked at a large plant in my office. "It looks like the jungle," he said with some alarm. I asked him to look out the other side, and he said, "No, it's a nice-looking plant."

Over the past two years, I have studied this phenomenon extensively, in the laboratory with volunteers and in my office with my patients. To simplify the technique, I taped the front of plastic safety goggles so that they blocked vision in all but the extreme side of the left or right eye.

When I began, I expected that all the troubled views would be associated with the right brain, because that hemisphere had been found more active during episodes of negative emotion. I couldn't understand why Werner Wittling's group in Germany had found in a later study that a second group of subjects, patients suffering from psychosomatic complaints, had more distress in their left brains. However, several of my own therapy patients experienced increased anxiety while looking to the right side, which we believed stimulated their left brains. My unexpected findings in my patients were consistent with Wittling's unexpected findings in his psychosomatic patients. The goggles' effects and later effectiveness in psychotherapy not only supported my long-held hypothesis that we are essentially of two minds, but also confirmed Wittling's reports that emotional distress can be associated with the left hemisphere as easily as with the right.

The New Dual-Brain Science

Dual-brain science is a new field engaged in exploring scientifically the role of the left and right brains (and their relationship) in psychological functioning. Until just a few years ago, it was unfashionable to turn to brain studies for an understanding of emotions. Most of the scientific interest in the split-brain studies focused on cognition. My approach to neuroscience has been grounded in psychology. I have sought to resolve any antagonism that often exists between a biological approach that sees complex psychological syndromes as simply brain or chemical malfunctions, devoid of personal meaning, and a psychological approach that has not been able to relate to the vast amount of information now being generated by technological advances in neuroscience. Indeed, for much of the past decade, I and other scientists have attempted to ally the discrete fields of neuroscience, psychopharmacology, and clinical psychology, to initiate a new understanding of behavior, and to lead to more effective ways of improving psychological balance. I will present compelling evidence from the scientific literature and from my own studies that I believe proves a relationship between the two cerebral hemispheres and the two distinct personalities. I will show that dual-brain science has the power to explain the whole range of symptoms that we humans suffer, from anxiety to psychosis.

Dual-Brain Therapy

The lessons from dual-brain science provide me with the theoretical framework to learn how to access and work with the troubled hemisphere to correct its archaic, destructive ideas and emotions. Dual-brain therapy incorporates aspects of the traditional psychotherapy that I have practiced for over twenty years, as well as strategies from cognitive therapy. Like traditional psychotherapy, it emphasizes empathy and a psychodynamic understanding. And like cognitive therapy, it attempts to help patients correct misperceptions and negative ideas they have about themselves. My new techniques diverge from and surpass these popular therapies because they are better informed by recent advances in brain science and grounded in the idea that we can have two distinct parts to our personality, which allows the therapy to become more active and more concrete. The advance of dual-brain therapy over traditional therapies derives from its demonstration of the troubled side as an interior, complex person. This realization greatly clarifies and simplifies the therapeutic tasks.

One major goal of dual-brain therapy is the care, nurturance, and education of the mind of the more troubled hemisphere. The troubled side is often like a traumatized person who hasn't been able to move beyond the trauma, even when removed from it, because he continues to expect retraumatization.* The traumas can range from the obvious and apparent to the most subtle and inapparent. Initially this mind may have withdrawn from the world around it, making it even more difficult for it to learn that the world may have changed for the better since the traumas. This is especially true for childhood traumas, which are often externally removed with the passage of time and the physical and mental maturity that comes with development. Yet, insidiously, trauma can remain covertly present because the mind on the troubled side fails to notice or trust the improvement. Dual-brain therapy entails a reaching out to the mind of the troubled hemisphere, attempting through patience, persistence, and a loving, mature, and informed attitude to teach it that it no longer has to fear abuse or protect itself with the archaic defenses that have become the source of new pain and problems.

Both right- and left-handed patients respond to dual-brain therapy as well as to the lateralizing glasses. In my studies I found no significant differences between right- and left-handers in regard to the intensity or the side of their emotional responses to the glasses, and I have observed no differences in their clinical responses to therapy.

Some Definitions

Throughout the book we will explore the relation between psychology and neuroscience. The language and vocabulary of neuroscience, although complex, can be defined with some precision. To understand thoroughly the physics of magnetic resonance imaging (MRI) requires a sophisticated grasp of theoretical physics, higher mathematics, and computer science, but we all understand that if the doctor orders us to have an MRI, we will have a series of pictures similar to X-rays taken of the insides of us.

When we cross over to psychology, concepts become more difficult

---

*For ease of reading, I have used the generic *he* throughout this book.

to define precisely. Think about the word "mind," for example. We know that we have one, but few experts have been able to define it to everyone's satisfaction. According to *Webster's Dictionary*, it is "the element or complex of elements in an individual that feels, perceives, thinks, wills, and especially reasons." Our certainty may evaporate when we begin to wonder about the element or complex of elements that does the feeling and perceiving. Still, even if we can't be absolutely explicit, I will state the definition of mind that I use in this book: that part of a person which experiences, thinks, and decides.

But what about the self? How does it differ from the mind? To me, the two terms essentially refer to the same thing except perhaps "self" might imply more of a life history and the added dimension of a human quality. And what of the term "personality"? *Webster's* defines this as "the totality of an individual's behavioral and emotional character traits, attitudes, or habits." Walter Mischel's textbook, entitled, *Introduction to Personality*, states on the first page: "Most thoughtful people have asked the question, 'What is personality?' but few agree on an answer. The term 'personality' has many definitions, but no single meaning is accepted universally."[1]

These three terms—"mind," "self," "personality"—might tend to differ in their temporal implications. If we speak of Joe's "mind," we might be thinking of his mind in a moment of time. We might say his mind was alert or confused. If we speak of his "self," we refer to a lifelong quality, closely related to his personal identity. When we refer to Joe's personality, we are identifying his psychological characteristics, which may change over time. We wouldn't be surprised if Joe manifests changes in his personality over time but we wouldn't expect Joe's self to change. It isn't my intention to stick rigidly to these imprecise meanings. For our purposes, the terms "mind," "self," and "personality" have more or less the same meaning: a part of an individual that has a unique set of memories, motivations, and behaviors.

Compared to the next task, attempting to define mind, self, and personality may seem easy. What does it mean to assert that a person has two minds, two personalities, or especially two selves? Surely Joe hasn't been cloned or twinned. He's one person with one mind and one self. (We wouldn't be too troubled if he had changes in his personality, especially over time.) When I speak of two minds in one person,

I mean that in each person there are two parts side by side, each with its unique (though possibly similar) set of memories, motivations, and behaviors.

This may seem unreasonable and unforgivable on my part. The philosopher Daniel Dennett tells us that we get one self "to a customer."[2] And Nobel laureate and eminent neuroscientist Sir John Eccles and psychologist Daniel Robinson write, "Each soul [self] is a Divine creation, which is 'attached' to the growing fetus at some time between conception and birth. It is the certainty of the inner core of unique individuality that necessitates the 'Divine creation.' We submit that no other explanation is tenable."[3]

But philosopher Jennifer Radden in her book, *Divided Minds and Successive Selves: Ethical Issues in Disorders of Identity and Personality*, argues that a person can clearly have two selves especially in exceptional conditions, such as recurrent psychosis or multiple personality disorders, which she asserts have implications for ordinary people. Radden clarifies what would be required for a person to have two selves in one body. She suggests that each self would have to have a separate, distinguishable pattern of motivation and behavior. They may also have different physical and emotional styles, temperaments, and moral dispositions. Radden suggests that at times, "each [self] exhibits well-rounded and roundly contrary personalities," and that at other times the differences can be more subtle. For instance, Radden quotes a beautiful description by William James of men who are constantly struggling with destructive impulses as an example of more subtle divisions in the self: "Their spirit wears with their flesh, they wish for incompatibles, wayward impulses interrupt their most deliberate plans, and their lives are one long drama of repentance and of effort to repair misdemeanors and mistakes."[4]

Following Radden's definitions, I will present evidence and then argue that ordinary people generally have two selves in one body. In the next chapter, "A New Look at Split-Brain Studies," I will show how split-brain and other neuroscientific research compellingly demonstrate that two separate minds can exist in one person. In Chapter 3, "Looking Right (and Looking Left)," I describe in detail my discovery and research into the effects of the glasses, limiting vision to one side or the other. These findings give graphic evidence from my patients that ordinary people may frequently manifest two distinct personalities, each related to either the left or right hemisphere.

The fourth chapter, "Dual-Brain Psychology," discusses how understanding the many different possible relationships between the two minds, revealed by the research described in the earlier chapters, leads to a much clearer understanding of human psychology. For instance, the two minds can cooperate with each other in a deep, synergistic relationship that fosters creativity and maturity, or they can sabotage each other, leading to a plethora of psychological and psychosomatic problems. Psychological problems often result from injuries to the left or right mind and from the internal struggles and imbalances that such injuries initiate. Many psychological insults of both childhood and adulthood can injure one hemisphere more than the other. Such damage will often enhance or corrupt the power of the troubled side and can often leave the more mature side underdeveloped, which can lead to a destructive struggle between the two minds and to psychological problems.

Chapters 5 through 10 show what the ideas and techniques of dual-brain science really mean for specific areas of human distress: anxiety, depression, posttraumatic stress disorder, psychosis, cocaine abuse, and stress-induced cardiac problems. Each chapter discusses past theoretical explanations and shows how they are improved with the dual-brain approach. Each chapter presents stories of patients that illustrate how they struggled to understand and deal with their problems.

In Chapter 11, "Dual-Brain Therapy to Discover and Assist Your Troubled Mind," I describe how you might improve the relationship between your two minds, how to discover and assist a troubled side to mature further or heal. I explain how a healthy left and right mind with a respectful, cooperative relationship between them can lead you to a life of greater meaning, creativity, productivity, and fulfillment. Only when the relationships *within* yourself are in harmony are you best able to sustain a healthy relationship with another person. Throughout this book I present cases to illustrate my ideas and my work. I have altered identifying information about each patient so that their anonymity will be maintained, but the essential facts of each case are accurate. All the transcripts presented are unaltered except for some minor editing for clarity.

....

CHAPTER 2

A New Look at Split-Brain Studies

I was in Los Angeles chatting with an ordinary-looking man. He was forty-six years old and employed as a printer. He seemed cheerful, content, and perfectly reasonable. If we had been introduced and spoken at a party, I would have noticed nothing remarkable about him. Like most other people, he was right-handed. But there was something exceptional about this man. In 1964, at age fourteen, he underwent a neurosurgical procedure called a commissurotomy in an attempt to treat the epileptic seizures that had tormented him since the age of four.

The operation was performed by Dr. Joseph Bogen, then a young, enthusiastic neurosurgeon, and his mentor and partner, Dr. Philip Vogel. They thought that the new surgical technique they had recently pioneered might successfully treat the fourteen-year-old boy's seizures. They cut the large nerve bundle, the corpus callosum, which had connected his left and right cerebral hemispheres. The forty-six-year-old printer I had traveled from Boston to Los Angeles to meet was the split-brain patient "AA," long famous in the annals of neuroscience.[1]

In the summer of 1996, Bogen and his colleague, experimental psychologist Dr. Eran Zaidel, invited me to join them in a study in Dr. Zaidel's eminent neuroscience laboratory at the University of California at Los Angeles. I had proposed that we test AA and another split-brain patient, known as LB, to learn more about the psychological nature of the two hemispheres in split-brain patients. Drs. Bogen and Zaidel, two of the world's authorities on neurospsychology, have likely

17

performed and published more studies about split-brain patients than anyone else in the world. They both have a deep understanding of the human mind from the special window they helped open.

Joseph Bogen and Eran Zaidel were colleagues of the late neuroscientist Roger Sperry, who in 1981 was awarded the Nobel Prize for the pioneering split-brain studies of the 1960s. The most compelling and important finding to come out of these experiments was the knowledge that split-brain patients such as AA have two separated, autonomous, intelligent minds. This is a strong claim to make about the nature of the human mind. Indeed, some scientists and philosophers call it disturbing, even preposterous. For example, philosopher Daniel Dennett ridicules the idea that split-brain patients could have two autonomous minds by comparing that possibility to the chance that "there could be talking bunny rabbits. . . . There could be, I suppose, but there aren't." But I will present my evidence that split-brain patients do indeed have two autonomous minds, each with its own motivations, behaviors, memories, and temperaments. Perhaps even Dr. Dennett will then be persuaded.[2]

I begin with the essential finding from the split-brain studies. If we sit AA, or any other split-brain patient, in front of a screen and flash pictures to either the left or the right side of the screen (to his left or right visual field), the image will be seen only by either the left or right brain, depending on which side the image is shown to. We know that this involves the neural connections between the eyes and the brain. When AA is shown any object to his right side, he can identify what he sees: a pair of eyeglasses, a pen, a tie clip. An image shown to AA's left side can be seen only by his right brain (due to the neural connections between the eye and the brain). Shown an object to the right brain, AA tells us that he can't see it. But if we ask him to reach with his left hand (connected to his right brain) behind a screen and select from several objects in a box, AA will easily and repeatedly pick out the object that was shown to his right brain, even though he keeps saying that he couldn't see it.

The idea that emerged from these studies is that AA has two separate minds: one in his left brain and one in his right brain. Only the left brain can speak. When AA was shown an image to his right brain, his left brain could not see the image, and it tells us so. The right brain

understands most speech, follows instructions, and recognizes and se-
lects objects, but it is unable to reply verbally to the researcher's questions. AA's mute right brain can express itself with the left hand,
which it controls and consistently picks out the correct items by touch.

To get a sense of the procedure, imagine for a moment that you are
a split-brain patient being tested in Dr. Zaidel's laboratory. First, Dr.
Zaidel tells you where to sit and how to look at the screen. He instructs
you to focus on a dot in the middle of a panel of two screens. Images
flashed on the right side of the screen will be seen only by your left
brain, and images flashed on the left side will be seen only by your right
brain.

Dr. Zaidel then flashes a picture to your left brain, and you see immediately that it is a picture of a banana. As he requested, you tell him
so. Then he flashes an image to your right brain. You can't see it. He
asks you what you saw, and you say, "I didn't see anything." Then he
asks you to use your left hand to reach behind a small curtain into a
box with several items and pick out the object shown to your right
brain. Although you don't know quite what he's talking about, you
place your hand through the curtain. Seemingly acting on its own,
your left hand pulls out a tie clip. You don't understand what is happening. You know you didn't see a picture of a tie clip and you didn't
try to pick one out of the box, yet Dr. Zaidel says, "That's correct, the
tie clip."

The split-brain studies have provided us with wonderful insights
into the mind. We now know that a split-brain person sees and appre-
ciates whatever is shown exclusively to the right brain. The right brain
does not have a speech center and so cannot speak, but *it can understand* Dr. Zaidel's instructions and easily carries them out.

The second finding is that the left brain has a speech center that
enables it to speak, and it can understand and follow Dr. Zaidel's instructions. Each side operates independently. It didn't matter to the
left brain that the right hemisphere was excluded from our conversation with AA. He is a complete person in his left brain and doesn't require a right hemisphere to know who he is and what he sees, feels,
wants, or plans to do. In fact, there are people who do not have a right
hemisphere at all—for example, people who had cancer in their right
hemisphere and had it removed surgically. For the most part, these

people, although often paralyzed on the left side, seem to be able to function and carry on with their lives without a loss of their personal identities.

Just what does it mean to say that AA talks "out of" his isolated left brain only? Technically, brains don't speak, even in intact people. The brain is a hunk of neurons, chemicals, and electromagnetic fields essential to the support and production of a person's mind. When we say, "That's my brain speaking," I think we are wrong. The mind and brain are so intimately connected that some scientists believe they are identical. I don't share this opinion, and so I prefer to say that I was speaking with the mind of AA's left brain. But because it becomes cumbersome to repeat phrases such as "the mind of the right brain," I sometimes refer to that mind as simply the right or left brain or hemisphere.

You might wonder what AA's right brain was up to while I was carrying on a conversation with his left-sided mind. That, in fact, was what I had traveled to California to learn more about. I suspected that his right-sided mind was listening quietly to our conversation, minding its own business. My intention was to learn to communicate with the mute right-sided mind, to gain a clearer sense of what it was thinking and feeling.

In our experiment, we planned to ask AA questions verbally and have him respond simultaneously with both hands by touching two sets of pegs behind a curtain, one set for each hand. Both sets had five pegs lined up in a row. The first peg represented the answer "none"; the second, "mild"; the third, "moderate"; the fourth, "quite a bit," and the last, "extreme." We had him practice, and each hand responded to each practice question. Both hands waited for the question, simultaneously moved over the pegs, and then stopped clearly at the selected pegs. With an assistant to help, we carefully recorded his hand responses.[3]

Before we began the test, I led AA through a brief review of his childhood stresses. He revealed that although it doesn't bother him at all now, when he was a child he was very upset by a group of bullies who picked on him over a period of years. I decided to add this piece of information to the study. We posed a number of questions focusing on his past and current feelings and recollections of the "bully" period in his life.

I asked him forty-nine separate questions, including how much his seizures bothered him and how much his girlfriend annoyed him. I asked him how much he would like to be a movie star, how much he loved his mother, how much he believed in God, in abortion, in the soul. I queried about how much he enjoyed shopping, movies, eating, sex, romance, work, and taxes, and how much he wanted to be admired, to be rich, to be angry. I also asked him fourteen questions having to do with the bullies. I asked how scared he was of the bullies, how frustrated by them, how hopeless they made him feel. I asked how angry he was now with the bullies, how cruel he now felt they were, how painful were their taunts. I asked how much he still hated the bullies, how much the bullies bothered him today.

His right hand, answering for his left-sided mind—the side with which I had been speaking—answered "none" or "mild" to most of the questions that had to do with the bullies. As he told me, his left-sided mind was not upset by the bullies. He had told me that already. But his left hand, answering for his right-sided mind, gave a very different picture. His left-handed answers to most of the bully questions were "quite a bit" or "extreme." On almost half of the bully questions, his left hand pointed to a peg three or four points higher than the one his right hand indicated.

AA's left-handed answers revealed that his right brain remained upset and quite disturbed by what had occurred about thirty years earlier. But his left brain reported both verbally and with his right-hand responses that he was not upset by the bullying. "Of course, I'm not upset by them; that happened so many years ago."

On the questions unrelated to the bullies, the two sides' answers were much more compatible. Both sides disliked paying taxes and enjoyed sex and romance. Both "extremely" believed in God. Both hands pointed to the first peg, indicating "none," when asked how much he believed in abortion. Both sides "extremely" loved his mother, wanted to be rich and a movie star, and enjoyed eating. Neither side wished to be poor, angry, or do puzzles! Both sides indicated that the boyhood seizures bothered him "extremely," and neither found his girlfriend annoying. On 74 percent of these "nonbully" questions, the two sides agreed exactly. When they disagreed, it was almost always by only one point.

Our statistical tests indicated that AA's left- and right-hand answers to the bully questions were significantly different, while his left and right answers on the other questions were not distinct. The left-right differences on the bully questions were also significantly different from the left-right differences in response to the other questions. These statistical tests, plus the overall pattern of answers, confirmed that we had indeed gotten his right brain to "talk" with us through his left hand.

AA, like Ryan and Carol, has two distinct parts to him: one that is adversely affected by a past trauma and still suffers its pain and another part that seems removed emotionally from the injury. In AA we can locate his two parts; the first is in his right hemisphere and the second in his left.

The second split-brain patient was LB. He was forty-four years old and a bit of a prankster. As I tried talking with him, he started flicking some switches on our equipment, and the lab assistant, who knew him well, said, "Cut that out! You're incorrigible." He then settled down and told me that he didn't want to get into any heavy conversation. He was, he said a little leery of psychiatrists. LB, who is right-handed, had his split-brain operation for epilepsy when he was thirteen.

LB also seemed quite ordinary. I would never have been able to pick him out of a room full of people and say, "Oh, him, that person over there, he must be the split-brain patient," even if I knew that one of ten people in a room was a split-brain patient.

But, of course, not all split-brain patients are alike, and LB had his own personality, which was quite different from AA's quiet demeanor. He appeared lively, more of an extrovert, and he seemed very bright and quick-witted. I had to remind myself that in LB's case, the personality we were able to communicate with was entirely "left sided." What his silent right brain was thinking and feeling we would attempt to learn from our study.

At this point, you might wonder what this says about the emotionless Mr. Spock of left brain–right brain lore. Isn't the left brain logical, sequential, and analytic? Yet neither AA nor LB resembles Mr. Spock (or even an MIT graduate student in engineering). In fact, the left-brained personalities of both AA and LB were well rounded and balanced. AA (the left brain of AA, that is) did not seem particularly poetic or creative, but no less so than many other people I know. LB's left side, in fact, seemed very creative inasmuch as he was witty and a jokester, but he also seemed logical and fully capable of reason.

It was perfectly clear to those of us in the room that AA and LB's isolated left brains bore little relation to popular notions about left-sided, logical, analytic personalities. This suggested to me that many of our popular ideas about the left and right hemispheres demanded reconsideration.

Our experimental protocol for LB was a bit more complicated than the one designed for AA. (Remember that images that are shown to the left of the patient are seen by the right brain, and images shown to the right go to the left brain.) Dr. Zaidel suggested we ask the beginning of a question such as, "How much do you feel?" and then finish the question with a different word flashed to the left and right sides of LB. In this way I would say aloud, "How much do you feel ———?" And immediately two words would be briefly flashed, one to the left and one to the right. In one instance, the word "confident" was flashed to the left and the word "anxious" to the right. Simultaneously, we asked LB's left brain, "How much do you feel anxious?" and his right brain, "How much do you feel confident?" Again, as for AA, LB was taught to respond by touching pegs in front of each hand.

In this more complex design, we were able to ask both sides all the same questions but in different orders and at different times. In this way we could ask one side if he liked paying taxes and the other if he liked being loved. Since his answers to questions like these two (with expected responses) came out in the anticipated way (he didn't like taxes but wanted to be loved), this procedure was another confirmation that the left-handed answers were coming from his right brain.

I hadn't questioned LB about the existence of specific childhood memories, so I couldn't devise a series of questions about a traumatic experience as I had with AA. Nevertheless, we found that LB saw himself more positively in his right brain and more negatively in his left brain. For instance, when asked how much he felt he was admired or attractive, his right brain (via his left hand) consistently reported a higher score than his left brain (right hand). And when he was asked about negative traits such as disrespect or dishonesty, his left brain consistently scored higher. In other words, his left brain reported lower scores on positive attributes and higher scores on negative attributes.

These results were significant when analyzed statistically, so we felt confident that we were seeing a reliable result.

These results were unexpected. Generally it is the left brain, in right-handed people, which is believed by scientists to process positive emotions, whereas the right brain is often considered a key center for processing negative emotions. Here, with LB, we were seeing the opposite trend, and we didn't know how to explain the findings. Then I came across an article by two prominent neuroscientists, David Bear and Paul Fedio. They had found in patients with epilepsy in their temporal lobes, an important area of the brain dealing with emotion, that patients whose left brains were more active because of the epilepsy tended to put themselves down. Patients with a more active right hemisphere tended to exaggerate their good qualities. Bear and Fedio labeled the group with more cerebral activity on the left side "tarnishers" and the other group "polishers." Our results were entirely consistent with these findings.[4]

Considered together, these discoveries point to the danger of making generalizations about the character of one hemisphere or the other. At the end of this chapter, I will show how the popular notions about the left and right brains became established in the national psyche. For now, we can be clear that in our study, LB's left brain and his right brain had different opinions, and each viewed "himself" differently. Again, the most important and reliable discovery about the split-brain patients is that they have two autonomous minds. At the end of the chapter, I show why these split-brain studies are relevant to all people, particularly the vast majority of us who have not had brain surgery.

An Earlier Split-Brain Study

The autonomy and interactions of the hemispheres in split-brain patients were demonstrated clearly in a study performed on LB and another split-brain patient and published in 1979 by Roger Sperry, Eran Zaidel, and his wife, Dahlia Zaidel, a renowned neuroscientist. They used a special contact lens, designed by Eran, that could show photographs to only the right brains of these patients. The experimenters talked with the patient while his right brain viewed photographs of himself, family members, entertainers, and world leaders. The patient's left, verbal self could hear the experimenters but could not see the photographs. The experimenters asked the patients, while their right brains were looking at a particular photograph, to rate it by giving a left-handed signal—thumbs up (like) or thumbs down (dislike). That is, the patient's right mind looked at the photographs and then expressed its judgment with a hand signal, while the patient's left, speaking mind sat trying to guess what was going on. Try to imagine this scene as you read this excerpt from a tape recording of a conversation between one of the experimenters and the first patient (LB). Here LB's right brain was shown four photographs simultaneously. His right brain could scan the photographs as you or I could if they were placed on the table in front of us. (All of the following transcripts are excerpted from the published scientific article describing the experiment.)[5]

The experimenter says, "Point to any of these that you recognize."

After fourteen seconds, LB's hand points to a photograph that pictures the only person who is recognizable: a well-known figure who is standing with four other people. The other photographs are of people unknown to him.

Experimenter: "Do you recognize that one? Is that the only one?"

LB again inspects the photos but does not point to any others.

Experimenter: "Well, on this: is this one a thumbs-up or a thumbs-down item for you?"

LB signals thumbs down with his left hand (connected to his right brain).

Experimenter: "Who is it?"

Now LB's left, verbal mind answers (his right-sided mind can't speak), "GI came to mind. I mean . . ."

The experimenter notes that LB's left hand (connected to his right brain) is trying to trace letters on the back of his right hand. That is, his right brain is trying to tell his left brain the name of the person in the picture. The experimenter says, "You're writing with your left hand; let's keep the cues out."

LB's speaking left-sided mind says, "Sorry about that."

Then the experimenter asks, "Is it someone you know personally, . . . or from entertainment, or . . . historical, or. . . ?"

LB's left brain (which did not see the picture) interrupted and said, "Historical."

Experimenter: "Recent or. . . ?"

LB: "Past."

Experimenter: "This country or another country?"

LB: "Uh-hu—okay."

Experimenter: "You're not sure?"

LB: "Another country, I think."

Notice what has happened. LB's left-sided mind was speaking. He did not see the picture, but he apparently had a feeling or an intuition "sent" to him from his right-sided mind because his guesses thus far were correct. These feelings were probably sent through the lower brain levels, which were not cut by the surgery.

The experimenter then asks, "Prime minister, king, president, . . . any of them?"

LB has a ponderous look on his face and says, "Gee."

Experimenter: "Great Britain? . . . Germany. . . ?

LB then interrupts and asserts, "Germany," and then after a pause, "Hitler."

There can be no doubt that LB's verbal self never saw the photos. Yet, prodded by Sperry and the Zaidels, he guessed the correct identity of the person in the picture. How did LB do so well on this test? The implications were fascinating and incontrovertible: LB, and others like him, had a highly developed mind in his right brain. This right-sided mind saw the photographs and recognized Hitler within fourteen seconds of scanning the four pictures. This right-sided mind not only recognized a well-known face, it also had an opinion about the person. With the thumb signal, this right-sided mind definitively signaled that he disapproved of Hitler. And LB's right-sided mind had other political opinions as well: Churchill (thumb up), Castro (thumb down), and pre-Watergate Nixon (thumb horizontal).

It was remarkable how his right-sided mind communicated with his left-sided mind. The right-sided mind apparently was able to send feelings or intuitions to the left-sided, verbal mind. We can see how the left-sided, verbal mind was struggling to retrieve information about the photographs. You may liken this process to what you do when you are trying to remember something on a test or in psychotherapy but can't quite grasp a memory or idea and have to search somewhere inside yourself for clues—clues that may then coalesce, as they did for this patient, into a definitive answer.

Toward the end of the testing session, LB's right-sided mind was shown another four photographs; three of strangers and one of himself. When asked if he recognized anyone in the pictures, he immediately pointed out the correct choice. When asked to rate the person in the photo, he grinned and turned his thumb down. With prompting, his left side guessed the correct identity of the person in the picture. Not only was LB's right brain capable of self-recognition and obviously self-awareness, but it was also capable of humor—and good humor at that.

The other split-brain patient studied with this special lens showed very similar abilities. This patient, a woman, was being tested with a long series of fairly uninteresting pictures. Then she was shown four photographs and was told, "Here are four people. Again, point out the one you like best."

Her right brain scanned the photos for about seven seconds, and then she exclaimed with a burst of mirth and surprise, "Oh, no! . . . Where'd you g . . . What *are* they?" She then laughed and said, "Oh God!" After a three-second pause, she asked, "Dr. Sperry . . . You sure there's people there?"

It was clear that her right-sided mind recognized that these pictures were different from those she had been viewing and that they aroused a strong emotional reaction in the right mind. It is also apparent that her left mind had no idea what the pictures were about. The patient's right-sided mind and her experimenters knew that the four photographs were each different pictures of the patient herself. In that trial, even with prompting, her left-sided mind couldn't guess what or who was in the pictures. But on a subsequent trial of similar pictures of herself, she said, "What do you think, Dr. Sperry? What's the matter with me? . . . I mean, am I thinking or what? . . . K . . . keep pointing to that one, and I don't know why. Whose face is it? Probably me and that's why I like it; nobody else does. Yeah [more definitely], that's a picture of me."

The experimenter said, "Yeah?"

Patient: "Yup."

Experimenter: "Which one is you?"

Patient: "That one [pointing to the one she had picked] . . . and that one, . . . and that one . . . and that one."

Experimenter: "All four?"

The patient responded loudly and firmly, "Yup!"

From these experiments it was apparent that the patients' right-sided minds were conscious, alert, intelligent, emotional, personable, and self-aware. However, their conscious left minds remained unaware of the conscious experiences of their right minds. Both of these split-brain patients clearly manifested two independent, intact minds. One spoke while the other could not, but otherwise there was no obvious or extreme difference between them. Both patients, on both sides, seemed capable of rational judgments (expressing political opinions) and humor. And both sides recognized their own photographs.

How the Two Hemispheres Relate to Each Other

These studies on LB and the female patient tell us not only that the left and right brains have intact, separate minds, but they also tell us something about how the two hemispheres interact. In one instance, the experimenter had to tell LB to stop writing with his left index finger onto his right hand. The passage, or sharing, of information about the photographs from one side to the other demonstrates an attempt at communication.

A female split-brain patient was in Dr. Sperry's laboratory having the vocabulary of her right brain tested with words flashed to the left side of her vision by a tachistoscope (a projector that shows images for a fraction of a second) in a way that allowed only her right brain to view them. Suddenly she began laughing. When asked why she was laughing, she said, "Doctor, you have a funny machine."

Her statement demonstrated that her left, speaking mind had not the slightest idea why she was laughing. Her giggle was precipitated by the very distinguished Professor Roger Sperry, who had placed a provocative picture of a nude woman in among the words being flashed to his patient's right-sided mind.

Her left-sided, speaking mind had no idea why it was laughing; it could only feel that something was "funny." It is interesting that she did not say, "Gee, I have no idea why I am laughing." Instead, she tried to fabricate a reason to gloss over the situation.

Her right-sided mind registered the photograph, appreciated its significance, and responded by evoking feelings of mirth. The impulse to laugh was sent to the left side, but the reason for the impulse was not. Although her left, speaking mind was greatly affected by her right-sided mind, she was unaware of being influenced by a hidden self. Of course, she had no appreciation of that influence or any insight into its cause.

In a similar study, Dr. Zaidel showed a patient's right brain a picture of a funeral procession. The patient's left-sided mind reported feeling very sad and uncomfortable but had no idea why. Apparently his right-sided mind appreciated the meaning of the photograph and sent the appropriate feelings of sadness to the left side, but it sent those feelings without words or meaning.[6]

I have wondered about the origin of anxiety or other feelings that seem to surface out of the blue and are impossible to explain. Perhaps common shifts in our emotional state are not simply due to unexplained chemical imbalances or other psychologically meaningless factors, but rather are due to unexplained feelings coming from our less dominant hemisphere. We will return to this idea in the next chapter.

In another study Zaidel showed a picture to a patient's right brain and asked her left side what was in the picture. The patient, a housewife, said she could not see the picture and did not know what was in it. Dr. Zaidel then encouraged her to guess. After a few moments, she said, "Dumbbell."[7]

Dr. Zaidel had no idea what she meant, and so he asked her what the term meant to her. She said that "dumbbell" was a derogatory name her husband called her when he felt the house was unclean, implying that she was slothful. She did not understand how that might relate to the picture.

Zaidel had shown her right brain a picture taken from a psychological test. It was an emotionally evocative picture of a woman sitting on a bed, appearing grief-stricken or depressed. Apparently her right brain associated the woman in the picture with her husband's demeaning term and then sent feelings or intuitions to her left side that allowed her to guess "dumbbell" without ever having seen the picture.

The Post-Commissurotomy Syndrome

We can also learn about the nature of the mind of the disconnected right brain by considering several fascinating observations that have been made in a number of other split-brain patients. The first is a phenomenon called the post-commissurotomy syndrome, which has been observed in many split-brain patients for a brief period shortly after the operation—possibly before the two hemispheres have learned how to get along with each other. In this syndrome, the patient is shocked to find that his left hand (controlled by the right brain) is acting autonomously, in an obviously intentional manner. For example, one split-brain patient wanted to wear a certain dress and reached for it in the closet with her right hand, but her left hand (connected to her right brain) kept putting it back and tried to reach for another (perhaps more stylish) dress. Another patient tried to pull his pants up with his right hand, while his left tried to pull them down. Another patient's left hand tried to grab his wife forcibly while his right hand (directed by his left conscious mind) tried to rescue her. Another patient struck his wife on a few occasions. Afterward, he apologized profusely, explaining that it was his autonomous left hand, not *himself*, that was the perpetrator. Another patient's left hand tried to strangle himself and had to be restrained.[8]

Not all right-mind behaviors in split-brain patients are destructive. One patient who wanted to smoke cigarettes found that each time he lit up, his left hand would grab the cigarette and put it out. His autonomous left hand prevented him from smoking, something his physician was probably unsuccessful at accomplishing.[9]

The highly regarded neuropsychologist Rhawn Joseph reports a patient whose left hand grabbed food from the refrigerator that the patient consciously did not want to eat. On another occasion, even though he was enjoying a television show, his left hand changed the channel to another show. Once when he was out walking, his left leg refused to move except in the direction of home, even though he consciously wanted to go for a longer walk. At times in the laboratory, he would become quite angry with his left hand and express hatred for it. He even struck his left hand, and both hands were observed in an actual physical struggle.[10]

Perhaps the most amazing story is of a female split-brain patient who was abruptly awakened from a sound sleep by slaps across her face. She awoke to find it was her left hand, acting autonomously and intentionally (it would seem), which was slapping her. The patient had overslept, and the right mind must have awakened, realized the time, and tried to rouse her. Later in the book, I will discuss this case when we look at causes and treatments for insomnia in normal people.[11]

These cases are fascinating—not merely as curiosities, but, more important, as illuminators of the nature of the right-sided mind. They demonstrate purposeful, complex behaviors initiated by the right-sided mind. Even though the post-commissurotomy syndrome does not persist, these behaviors have been observed in many of the split-brain patients.

Split-Brain Patients with Exceptional Right-Sided Expressive Abilities

It is easy to appreciate that a mute right brain must be quite difficult to study. There are, however, three split-brain patients who are quite exceptional in regard to their ability to express themselves. One of these patients could draw pictures in response to questions asked of his right brain. For example, when an image of a horse was flashed to his right hemisphere, he was verbally asked by the experimenter to draw "what goes on it." His left mind said he didn't know because it didn't see the image, but with his left hand (connected to his right brain) he drew a crude picture of a saddle. In this instance, the patient demonstrated not only that he understood that the image was of a horse, but also that he could generate the correct image of an object not shown—an object apparently chosen through a higher level of abstraction than that required merely to match pictures and objects.[12]

The other two patients, studied by the pioneering split-brain researcher Michael Gazzaniga, had expressive language on their right side. Their right brains (as well as their left brains) could speak. You could talk with the patient's left-sided, verbal mind and also have a limited conversation with his right-sided mind, although these exchanges were generally limited to one-sentence answers. That is, you could have two separate conversations, one with each mind. These findings do not mean that every right brain can speak. These were exceptional patients and represent the only two with this capacity in a series of about forty four split-brain patients.[13]

Let's look closely at one of these split-brain patients, a patient named Paul. Initially, his right mind couldn't speak, but it could communicate by spelling words with Scrabble chips. The experimenters would ask questions such as, "What is your favorite_____?" Then they would flash a word such as "hobby," so it could be seen by only one hemisphere. When the experimenters asked his right mind what it wanted to be when he grew up, it spelled out "auto race," which the experimenters interpreted to mean that he wanted to become a race car driver. When they asked his left side what he wanted to become, he replied, "a draftsman." It is interesting that Paul's left side appeared to be more conservative, more reasonable, perhaps more mature than his right side, which seemed possibly more impulsive, unrealistic, and immature.

When his right side was asked, "Who [are you]?" he wrote, "Paul." This shows that his right mind had a sense of himself as a person, a personal identity. His response was consistent with the reactions of Zaidel's two contact lens patients when they were shown pictures of themselves.

In another experiment, Paul was asked how much he liked certain people or things. He was asked, "How much do you like_____?" and the following items were individually presented first to one hemisphere and then later to the other. The list contained: Dad, dope, Fonz, God, home, Liz (his girlfriend), Mom, Nixon, Paul, police, school, and TV. After each item was flashed to his right brain, he pointed, as instructed, to one of five cards, each with one of the following ratings: dislike very much, dislike, undecided, like, and like very much. In this way his right mind could be asked, for example, "How much do you like Liz?" and he could point to the "like very much" card. Over a series of different days, both hemispheres were asked to rate the people or things on the list. Paul appeared to feel better on days when both hemispheres were in general agreement. He appeared out of sorts on days of general disagreement.[14]

Significance of the Split-Brain Studies

The split-brain studies can make us feel uneasy because they challenge our sense of ourselves. We obviously do not experience ourselves as being of two minds. But what makes the split-brain studies so important is exactly that they challenge our intuitive ideas about human nature, even our own personal nature. If we can objectively consider the split-brain studies, we are forced to admit (perhaps against our will) that they definitely demonstrate that these patients do, in fact, have two working, independent minds. Roger Sperry concluded:

> In sum, cerebral commissurotomy [the split-brain operation] appears to divide not only the brain but also the mind. Two separate realms of subjective awareness are apparent: one in each disconnected hemisphere, and each in itself seems to be remarkably whole, unified, and capable of supporting behavior comparable in many respects to that of the combined intact system. . . .
>
> The two disconnected hemispheres of man not only function as if each is independently conscious, but also as if each possesses distinctive qualitative properties not equally shared with the other.[15]

And Joseph Bogen wrote:

> Roger Sperry was awarded the Nobel Prize in 1981 for his work with human split-brain subjects, but the implications of this work have yet to be fully appreciated. The principle of hemispheric specialization [left, language, right, spatial abilities], illuminated by him, has been widely recognized, which has stimulated an immense amount of research. But the principle of cerebral duality [that each hemisphere has its own mind], . . . has so far had insufficient recognition. . . . We all look forward to the day when the implications of the split-brain research emerge in a form that can help guide human society toward an improved understanding of its own internally conflicted creativity.[16]

Patients Who Have Had Their Left Brains Surgically Removed

Another set of observations that substantiate the intelligence and intactness of the mind of the right brain are those of patients who had an even more radical operation than the split-brain surgery: removal of the left cerebral hemisphere (the left half of their brain) because of brain cancer. The findings report that almost all patients, postsurgery, had reasonable emotions and behaviors. Although they had extensive deficits, such as language problems and paralysis, they remained generally functional mentally. For example, a published study of a twelve-year-old girl reported, "Additional observations from the present study indicate that personality characteristics such as humor, boredom, love, and frustration are readily exhibited by the right hemisphere in a pattern reported by the parents to be substantially the same as before surgery." This and similar reports of patients who had their left hemispheres removed demonstrate that a right brain alone has the capacity to support reasonably intelligent human life.[17]

In 1843, the English physician Arthur Wigan published a book entitled *The Duality of the Mind*. Wigan's interest in the subject had begun years earlier when he attended the autopsy of a friend who had died unexpectedly. To everyone's amazement, his friend had only one brain hemisphere; the entire other side of his skull was empty. Yet Wigan's friend apparently thrived with only one hemisphere. For the next twenty years, Wigan pondered the significance of this observation and ultimately concluded that if his friend had an intact normal mind with one hemisphere, then perhaps people with both a left and a right brain have two minds.[18]

The Connections Between the Eyes and the Cerebral Hemispheres

To understand the split-brain studies, it is not necessary to understand the physical connections between the eyes and the left and right brains. The premise is quite simple: Images shown to one side of a split-brain person will be registered only in the hemisphere on the opposite side. But because this and much other research depends on this assumption, I feel it would be helpful to discuss this connection.

Think of the eye as a camera. It has a lens in front that operates much like the lens of a camera. In a camera, the job of the lens is to focus an image of an object in front of the camera onto the sheet of film at the back of the camera. If the camera is not focused properly, the image on the film will be out of focus or blurry. If an object is to the right of the camera, the lens will place the image on the left side of the sheet of film. Similarly, the lens in the eye focuses an image, but in the case of the eye, on a sheet of light-sensitive cells, called the retina, at the back of the eye. An image of an object to the right of a person will be focused on the left side of the retina, which acts much like film or, more accurately, like the light-sensitive computer chips at the back of a video camera. The image on the retina is then sent to the brain via the optic nerve, much the way an image in the back of a video camera is sent via wires to the tape recorder for storage or via another wire to a television monitor for viewing.

Now we come to the tricky part in the human being. The retina is essentially divided functionally into two separate sheets at the back of each eye. As shown in Figure 2.1, in each eye, one sheet covers the left side and one the right side. If we look only at the right eye for a moment, we see, at the back of the right eye, a retina, divided between the left and right sides. Images that fall on the right half of the retina of the right eye are transported via the optic nerve to the right brain for processing. Images falling on the left half of the retina of the right eye are transported via the optic nerve to the left brain. This is true for all human beings. Each half of each eye thus sends its visual information to a different cerebral hemisphere.

Since the optic nerve from the right eye goes to both brains, there must be a point at which it divides, such that one part goes straight back to the brain on the right side and one part veers off to the left to connect with the left brain. This indeed occurs; and the point where the optic nerve crosses the midline is called the optic chiasm. At that point, the optic nerve from the left eye sends a branch over to the right hemisphere. In split-brain operations in humans, the optic chiasm is not touched. In animal experiments, the optic chiasm is often cut, and by doing so the experimenters prevent the images from being sent to the opposite hemisphere. In the case of the right eye, in an animal with its optic chiasm and corpus callosum cut, the optic nerve would go only to the right brain. In that animal, the left eye would be connected only to the left brain. We will return to these animal studies later.

If we close our left eye and keep our right eye open, an image of an airplane in the center of our vision will go to both hemispheres, because there is an area of overlap between the two sides of the retina at

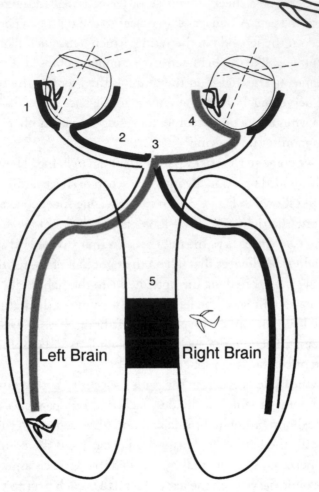

Figure 2.1

This figure illustrates schematically the connections between the eyes and the brain. An object (the airplane) appears to the right of the person. The image of the plane goes through the lens of each eye and strikes the left side of the retinas of both eyes. The retina in each eye is divided into a medial and a lateral aspect. (1) points to the lateral retina of the left eye, which is connected by the optic nerve (2) to the same-sided (left) hemisphere. In the right eye, the image of the airplane is focused on the medial aspect of the right retina (4) which connects to the opposite-sided (left) hemisphere. The point where the left and right optic nerves intersect physically is called the optic chiasm (3). When the object is to the right of the person, the images from both eyes then go to the left hemisphere. Via the corpus callosum (5) the image can then be transferred to the other hemisphere. In split-brain patients, in whom this connection is severed, the image stays on one side. See text for more detail.

the back of the right eye. If we turn so that the airplane is now to our right (the right side of our body), then the image of the airplane will go through the lens and be focused on the left side of the retina only, as shown in Figure 2.1. This is the side of the retina that sends its image to the opposite hemisphere. In this case, the left brain would process the image. After the image is processed, it can be sent (sort of like e-mail) through the corpus callosum to the other hemisphere, so that eventually both hemispheres will be able to appreciate the airplane. In split-brain patients, whose corpus callosum is severed, the image cannot be sent to the other side of the brain. And it is this anatomical fact on which all of the split-brain studies are ultimately based.

The left eye shown in Figure 2.1 is designed quite similarly to the right eye. The only difference is that if an image is focused on the left side of the retina of the left eye, it will be sent via the optic nerve to the left brain. It turns out that if we open both eyes and the airplane is still to the right side of our body, the image of the airplane will go through the left and right lenses and strike the left side of each eye. Both eyes then will send the image of the airplane to the left brain. And, of course, if we focused instead on an airplane located to the left side of our body, we would then send the image to the right brain. In either case, moments later the image can be sent (in ordinary people) to the opposite side through the corpus callosum.

Now suppose we are focused on an airplane to the left side of our body. Its image would go first to the right brain. Because there are delays and limitations in transferring information, even in people with an intact corpus callosum—that is, even in ordinary people—an experimenter can send information preferentially to one side of the brain or the other. In fact, experimenters have shown movies to either the left or the right brain in ordinary people. There also have been many hundreds of studies in which images are flashed to one side or the other of the eyes in ordinary people, and these images go preferentially to one hemisphere or the other depending on which side of the person's vision the image is shown to.

In many experiments, in split-brain patients and ordinary people, it is often necessary to present images very briefly when we want them to be seen by one side or the other. The reason is that if the eyes move even slightly, the image will be seen on the other half of the retina and will go to both hemispheres. This is why many experiments use images that are flashed for only a small fraction of a second. The special contact lens that Eran Zaidel designed was the first procedure to enable split-brain patients to look at an image for as long as they wanted without a concern that the image would be seen by the other hemisphere. In intact people, contact lenses painted over on one side, as well as other methods, have enabled researchers to send persistent images preferentially to one hemisphere or the other.

Do the Findings from Neurosurgical Patients Apply to Ordinary People?

As Joe Bogen pointed out, the duality of mind discovered in the split-brain patients is often dismissed by scientists, psychologists, and philosophers as irrelevant to ordinary people. These naysayers contend that because the surgery is so radical and these patients suffered epilepsy, they should be considered brain damaged in some unspecified way and not related to healthy people. I think this position is taken because the split-brain findings are so unexpected and so often disturbing. The surgery, radical in its concept, creates a specific, limited surgical lesion with no apparent damage to the hemispheres themselves. I believe that the commissurotomy reveals preexisting minds. It is highly unlikely and unproved that the surgery could create an extra mind.

Further, people with epilepsy usually do not have obvious brain damage. The fact that the patient has seizures means that he has some functional abnormality at the time of the seizures, but most seizure patients have normal MRIs, and their EEGs are often normal between seizures. In fact, the task of determining whether a patient is epileptic is often difficult. Even in particular cases when the disorder has been definitively diagnosed, it is very difficult to find its cause or source. Certainly some people who get seizures, such as those who have had a significant head injury, may have an obviously damaged area of their brain, but most people with epilepsy appear to have normal-functioning brains when they are not having seizures. Split-brain patients taken together do not form a homogeneous group; there are very many variations among the types and causes of their epilepsy.

Although it is true that a number of split-brain patients suffered a variety of types of brain damage both before and after surgery, this is not true of all split-brain patients, and it specifically is not true of AA and LB. All split-brain patients have manifested a duality of mind, the presence of a left- and a right-sided mind.

SPLIT-BRAIN STUDIES IN ANIMALS

There is a large body of split-brain studies in animals (without epilepsy, of course), and these studies also show the same duality of mind. Prior to his work on human split-brain patients, Sperry had been experimenting with cats and monkeys in which he would cut the corpus callosum. He also cut the optical chiasm, the point where the nerve tracts from the eyes cross to the opposite side. By this operation, he constructed an animal with not only a split brain but also an eye connected to only one hemisphere. Following surgery, Sperry covered one eye and taught the animal a trick or two. For instance, he could teach the animal that to get a food pellet, it had to push a button with a circle on it rather than the button next to it with a cross on it. What he found was dramatic. He could teach the animal's left brain, and only its left brain would learn the task; its right brain would remain untaught. He could then teach the right side to do the opposite—that is, to push the cross button to get food. Then, depending on which eye was uncovered, the animal would push either the circle or the cross.[19]

Sperry discovered that the split-brained animal acted as if it had two minds, each unaware of what the other had learned. Each mind was capable of perceiving, learning, remembering, and initiating action. This work in animals dovetailed with the discoveries of two minds in human split-brain patients and proved that the phenomena cannot be attributed to epilepsy or some unspecified, undiscovered brain damage.

TESTING ORDINARY PEOPLE

Split-brain studies in themselves imply but do not prove that ordinary people have two minds. Fortunately, there is an abundance of scientific data that demonstrate the relevance of the split-brain findings for ordinary people with intact brains. In studies of split-brain patients that attempted to discover the cognitive advantages of the left or right brains, researchers noticed that the left brains were better at language tasks and the right brains were superior at certain spatial tasks. For example, if you place an unusual-shaped object in the left or the right hand of a split-brain patient and ask him to match that object with a set of pictures, his left hand (right brain) is consistently better at the task, readily able to point to the picture of the object. When the object is placed in the right hand (left brain), the patient has difficulty pointing to the correct picture. In split-brain patients, it seems that the left hemisphere generally uses different strategies from the right side. The left brain can more easily pick out an object placed in the right hand if the object lends itself to a verbal description—say, a cube or a sphere. It has extreme difficulty with amorphous shapes. The left hand (right brain), though, is quite adept at identifying amorphous objects.

Now comes the more interesting point. Scientists have found that ordinary people have the same differences in cognitive abilities between sides as the split-brain patients. If an ordinary person is seated in front of a screen and asked to look forward and an object is flashed very briefly to his right side (his left brain), he will respond faster and more accurately if the task involves language. If you flash a spatial task to the screen, asking the subject, for instance, to tell if a dot is within a circle, he will perform better when the images are flashed to his left side (right brain). Ordinary people also are shown to be better at noticing details if they are flashed to the left brain and better at seeing the overall picture if the image is flashed to the right brain.

These studies and others involving hearing through the left and right ears have been repeated many hundreds of times in ordinary people, and the findings are consistently similar to those in split-brain patients. These findings mean that the cognitive properties of the left and right hemispheres of split-brain patients are similar to those in ordinary people. When all the evidence is sifted and weighed, we are reminded that our "ordinary" minds are more similar to split-brain minds than some neuroscientists would like us to believe.

But What About Mr. Spock? Beliefs That Confuse Us

We need to step back and consider some matters that confuse many people. The idea that the left brain is logical and sequential or analytical and that the right brain is more holistic and more visuospatial comes from the kind of studies I have just described in split-brain and ordinary subjects. For example, the subject is asked to tell whether a face flashed to one side is the same as one being shown in the middle. If the face is flashed to the left side (right brain), the person (split-brain or ordinary subject) will more quickly and more accurately tell if the flashed face is or is not the same as the one being shown directly in front of the person. When the face is flashed to the right side of vision (left brain), the subject is slower and less accurate. But when the experiment was changed so that the subject was required to tell whether the flashed face had a similar specific feature, such as the nose, then the left brain did better. The inference from these experiments is that the right brain is better at analyzing the whole picture—the whole face, if you will—but that the left brain is better at detecting and analyzing smaller details. Also in this research in general, the right brain does not have an overwhelming superiority on its tasks, and the left brain does not have an overwhelming superiority on its tasks. The left brain is better at word tasks than the right brain, but only by a ratio of 1.5-to-1.0. The right brain is better at recognizing faces 1.2 times better than the left side.[20]

Thus, the idea that the left brain is cognitively different from the right is well substantiated, but the idea that those differences are dramatic is not, except for speech, which is only on the left side in almost all people. The right side does have language functions and seems to add embellishment to speech, but in isolation, the right brain cannot speak. In the intact person, the mind of the right brain should be able to use the corpus callosum and control the speech center in the left brain for its own use, so the right mind in intact individuals is probably very articulate. This may seem strange, but if the right brain wants to move the right hand, whose control center is located only in the left hemisphere, it could easily accomplish the movement. For instance, someone who had an injury to his left frontal lobe but whose motor (movement) cortex was intact would not be paralyzed, and his right brain would control most voluntary movement on both sides.

We shouldn't be too surprised that LB's left brain does not seem overly logical and analytical, because this attribute of the left brain refers to rather subtle comparisons with the right brain. Still, there is some merit to the idea that each hemisphere has a degree of advantage at some cognitive tasks. For instance, when LB returned to his high school after surgery, where he was a very good student, he had to drop geometry because he couldn't grasp the spatial concepts with his isolated left brain.

Thus, we are talking about two different things. In one instance, we are talking about LB's personality on his left side, and in the second we are talking about certain cognitive skill that his left brain has, has to a limited degree, or doesn't have. The mind in LB's right brain also has a personality. It tells us with his left-hand responses to my questions that he feels admirable, honest, and confident on that side. That side tells us with his left-hand responses that he "extremely" likes reading, puzzles, math, shopping, movies, and sex but does not like work or paying taxes. If we gave both sides of him cognitive tests, they would score differently, but more important, each has its own mind or personality. In an analogous way, we can find cognitive differences between males and females, with women scoring higher on most language tasks. Still, what is most important to recognize is that males have minds and females have minds. That they may tend to have some cognitive differences is generally of minor importance.

More Evidence of Two Minds in Ordinary People

Another piece of evidence that the split-brain findings relate to normal people comes from a variation of a procedure long used by neurosurgeons prior to brain surgery. In order to locate definitively the patient's centers for expressive language and memory (so they are not removed unintentionally), the surgeon uses a procedure referred to as the Wada test, after the physician who developed it.[21] It consists of injecting sodium amytal, a short-acting anesthetic agent, into either the left or right carotid artery (these arteries support the parts of the cerebral hemispheres most related to higher mental functions). The brain on the side of the injection becomes anesthetized, and the other half remains awake. Actually, for the first three minutes or so after the injection, both sides of the brain become dysfunctional. Then the side opposite the injection recovers rapidly, while the side of the injection remains anesthetized for another ten minutes or so. When the right side is injected, the patient, after the initial brief dysfunction, regains his usual consciousness and can converse fairly normally. The left side of his body remains paralyzed for the fifteen minutes or so during which the anesthesia lasts.

When the left side is injected, after the brief period of dysfunction on both sides, the patient's right brain is awake, even if somewhat groggy, while his left-sided, verbal mind remains anesthetized. Usually the right brain cannot speak.

When the test is conducted in its usual way, it is interesting, but it doesn't tell much about the nature of the right brain. However, an interesting study by Dr. Risse and Dr. Gazzaniga begins to reveal more about this hidden side. They used the Wada procedure to anesthetize the left brain; while the left side was unconscious, they placed objects in the subject's left hand (right brain). When the subjects (left brains) woke up, none of them consciously had any idea about whether anything had been placed in their hands. Yet when they were shown an array of pictures of several different objects, they easily pointed to the correct one. This study implies that the right brain functioned independently of the left brain; it was able to appreciate, remember, and retrieve the object—all without any participation of the left brain. In this study the patients were not split-brain patients, but had whole, surgically intact brains.[22]

Another Wada study lends support to the idea that each hemisphere can possess a mind of its own. Dr. Geoffrey Ahern and his associates reported fascinating results in separate Wada tests performed as part of an assessment for epilepsy in two young men. The patients were unusual in that each had demonstrated two distinct personalities, and in each case Ahern demonstrated definitively that one personality was coming from the left hemisphere and the other from the right.[23]

One patient's usual personality was emotionally withdrawn and sullen, but for an hour or so after a seizure, he became affable and sociable. His family reported that the changes in personality were profound—that he was like a different person.

When the doctors injected the patient's left carotid artery with sodium amytal and anesthetized his left brain, he smiled and laughed and appeared to the doctors to be much more emotionally spontaneous than he was in his usual state. During the test, he was asked if this was what he felt like when he was in his positive personality, and he responded affirmatively.

During a Wada test, the anesthesia gradually wears off after five to fifteen minutes. As the left brain was coming out of its sleep to wakefulness, the patient said, "I think we just got done with the niceness." He then indicated that the drug was wearing off quickly and made a chopping motion with his left hand (controlled by his right brain). He then abruptly had a personality change back to his unemotional, unsociable self. His left brain had apparently woken up and taken control.

The doctors then engaged in the following conversation with the patient:

Doctor: "Did you, I mean the emotional part, like coming out here by yourself today?"

Patient: (turning his head and eyes to the right, indicating that his left brain is talking) "No, not really!"

Doctor: "So you wouldn't want to come out again, by yourself, without the 'talky' [left] hemisphere?"

Patient: "What's that?"

Doctor: "The emotional part of you. I'm talking to that part of you right now. Would you want to come out by yourself again, or do you like being back in there suppressed and quiet?"

Patient: (with very flat affect, suggesting that his left side is speaking) "I'm just naturally a suppressed and quiet person."

Doctor: "You're not going to let him talk, are you?"

Patient: "Who's that?"

Doctor: "Your other side."

Patient: "It all depends on what the other side says." (The patient then smiled, but only on the left side of his face, controlled by his right brain.)

The second case Ahern described was also a young man suffering from seizures who had also been observed to have dramatic personality changes. This patient's usual personality was well adjusted, but after a seizure, his personality became extremely aggressive and disruptive. His seizure activity came from his left hemisphere, and after his seizures, his left brain would be severely inhibited by exhaustion, and his right brain would become dominant. This suggested that his disturbed personality might be associated with his right brain.

During the Wada test, when his right brain was put to sleep with sodium amytal, he remained his usual pleasant, well-adjusted self. When his left brain was made inactive, he again became his belligerent personality. In fact, he became so verbally and physically abusive that the doctors had to inject him with an antipsychotic medication.

The results of these experiments reveal that these two intact people, who had never undergone a split-brain operation, obviously were of two separate minds—one left and one right. In the first patient, the disturbed personality was associated with the left hemisphere. In that patient, an MRI showed some nonspecific scarring, suggesting that his left brain may have been damaged. The doctors speculated that his psychiatric problems might have been related to that possible damage, since his disturbed personality was located on the left side. In the second patient, the disturbed personality was associated with the right hemisphere.

Ahern's study is remarkable because it is a clear demonstration of two distinct personalities, one in each hemisphere, present in two patients not given split-brain surgery.

Much More Evidence for Two Minds in Ordinary People

Thus far the evidence is overwhelming for the existence of two autonomous minds in split-brain patients.[24] We have learned something about how the two relate, and we are beginning to accumulate evidence that ordinary people can have two autonomous minds, each associated with one hemisphere. In the next chapter, we look at new evidence that such minds may exist in all of us.

....

CHAPTER 3

Looking Right (and Looking Left)

oward the end of a therapy session, I asked Tom, a patient with some self-esteem and marital problems, to try something new. I handed him two pairs of strange-looking safety goggles, each unartfully covered with a lot of white plastic tape.

"What do you want me to do with these?"

"Just try them on."

"Which one?"

"Whichever."

"You mean I get my choice?"

"Absolutely. Pick the prettier ones."

With some hesitancy, Tom complied. I asked his consent to audio-tape our session so that I could listen closely to his responses to my unusual therapy aid. (This and all other dialogues with the goggles that follow are transcripts from tape recordings. In a few places I have changed the name of a city or other information that might possibly reveal the patient's identity, but otherwise except for minor editing for clarity the transcripts are verbatim. Each consented to publication.)

"So you're looking out the left side. Tell me what you are feeling about yourself."

"I'm looking out the left side. And I'm . . . I'd say I like myself quite a bit, and I'd describe myself as bright and energetic. And I'm ready to succeed."

"Try the other pair." (He switches to the other pair, allowing him to see to his right side. There is a ten-second pause before he speaks.)

"This is the pair with the right side exposed. I'm feeling anxious, maybe a little scared . . . I would describe myself differently. I would say the way I'm feeling right now, I'm feeling timid and a little inhibited."

"On that scale [which we had discussed previously] how do you like yourself?"

"On your scale: none, mild, moderate, quite a bit . . . moderate."

"And how confident do you feel, now with these glasses on?"

"Less safe than I'd like to feel."

"And how does the future portend?"

"It will have its share of scares, and we'll have to see. Not optimistic, not pessimistic."

"What's your business forecast?" [Tom is an entrepreneur who owns and operates a startup company.]

"We'll hang in there."

"How are you going to do? What are you going to look like in December?"

"Like we look now. Hanging in there okay."

"Would you try the other glasses [allowing vision to his left side]? (Pause) How do you feel?"

"Better. I like these glasses better."

"How's your business going to look in December?"

"Hm, well, I know what I just said, but I'm feeling better. I'm thinking there could be a lot of opportunities, and there could be some large success. So I think we're going to look better than I just said we were going to look. I think we're going to look much better."

"How much better?"

"I think we're going to be a totally different company in December from what we look like now."

"Does that seem like a big difference from where you just saw?"

"Yeah; it does; it seems like a huge difference. It questions my a . . ."

"Try these other glasses." (He switches to the other pair, allowing him to see to his right.)

"These are my forecasting glasses."

"How's the business going to look in December?"

"I'm . . . I don't like to admit that glasses could make any difference, but I don't think . . . I don't feel as confident about what I just said wearing these glasses. (We both laugh.) Interesting."

"What do you think of that? What do you make of that? Do you remember what you just said with the other glasses?"

"Oh, sure, everything. . . . the other glasses; they create an optimistic mood for me. For these, they create a more somber, conservative . . . don't feel . . . don't take the risks, don't think things may succeed because they may not."

Mary Beth is a thirty-seven-year-old divorced woman. For many years she had suffered a form of agoraphobia in which she felt great anxiety when she went to unfamiliar places. In this session, she discussed a strong conflict between her fear of leaving the Boston area and a compelling need, for personal reasons, to travel to San Francisco. During this session, I asked her to wear the special goggles for the first time. As the excerpt begins, she is wearing the goggles with the left visual field occluded, and these have increased her symptoms.

"Now, how would you feel if you were now in San Francisco?"

"Like this? Not too happy."

"What would you feel?"

"Not great."

"Imagine that you were in San Francisco. How would you feel?"

"I would feel lost. I would feel unable to take care of myself, you know, to do what I needed to do."

"I want you to try the other glasses [allowing her to see to the left side of her]." (fifteen-second pause)

"These are much better. (Laughs)

"So now you're looking out the left side."

"Yeah."

"And what are you feeling?"

"Relieved. It's better than the right side."

"How is it different?"

"It's manageable. I can manage this." (Laughs)

"And suppose you were in San Francisco. How would you feel?"

"I would feel like I could cope, but I would feel sad that I couldn't be free that I couldn't be using my whole range of vision."

"It sounds like you'd feel a little differently being in San Francisco. How would you feel differently?"

"Different than I feel now here or different than I would feel were I wearing the other pair?"

"Different from how you felt, imagining yourself in San Francisco with the other pair."

"I feel much less incapacitated, much less handicapped."

"Could you handle it?"

"Yeah."

"With some duress?"

"Yes."

"Manageable duress, or are you not sure?"

"If I'm doing it relative to how I felt with the other pair on, yes."

"As you feel right now."

"Yeah. Yes, because if I don't start thinking about the bigger picture, which is even without glasses, I know I can handle it. . . . This feels certainly better than the other pair."

"Okay, and does it feel better than no glasses?"

"That's interesting. Yeah, it might feel a little safer."

"But the way it feels right now, do you feel you have a reasonable chance?"

"A shot at it."

"You got a shot at it?"

"Yeah."

"And how good a shot?"

"Pretty good shot."

Sitting with patients who have rather dramatic changes in their outlook on their life and the world within seconds of putting on taped safety glasses is an amazing experience. Seeing the patient's entire demeanor change—laughing in bafflement at what is happening, and then witnessing dramatic clinical improvements that occur over a relatively short period of time—is a compelling experience which I want to share with you. Prozac, in the 30 percent of patients in whom it works well, can achieve a comparable transformation, but only gradually. What I was observing in the same percentage of my patients was a vivid, definitive alteration in their mental state.

For a long time, I had difficulty believing that my patients' reports were authentic. Perhaps I was covertly instructing them in some way beyond my conscious intent, or perhaps I was observing a placebo or hypnotic effect. Assuming what I was observing was reliable, I knew that it would be profoundly important, and so I spent two years carefully studying this phenomenon. I want to tell you how I came upon this unexpected discovery, how I have rigorously studied it, and its significance for both understanding our human mind and furthering our ability to deal with a wide variety of emotional or psychological problems.

How It Began

For many years, I had been studying the role our left and right brains might play in determining personality and aggravating psychological problems. I had already published laboratory work on the possible role of the hemispheres in patients who had suffered psychological problems related to childhood traumas. And I had already developed many of my ideas about how the left and right brains affect our psychological status.[1]

One morning in 1995, I was rereading and thinking about a group of scientific papers by Werner Wittling and his associates, the German scientists I mentioned in Chapter 2, who reported that they could show movies to either the left or right brain by showing it to either side of the person. I was most taken with their idea that an experimenter could show a movie predominantly to one side of the brain of an ordinary person. I, like most other neuroscientists, had had the impression that in healthy people with an intact corpus callosum, if you showed something to one hemisphere, it would simply be transferred to the other side via the large connection between the hemispheres. In fact, the whole point of the split-brain studies seemed to be that by cutting the corpus callosum, the experimenters could only then restrict visual information to one hemisphere. But now Wittling's group had reported convincing evidence that they could show a movie primarily to one hemisphere in intact people. If these reports were well founded, the techniques could open an entirely new window into the mind. We might be able to conduct experiments resembling the split-brain or the Wada studies by simply limiting vision to one side, but without any of their discomfort, side effects, or complexity. This was just a thought, and I honestly didn't have much confidence in it initially. But it was an idea that had captured my imagination.

Wittling found that when he showed the movie to a person's left

side (the left visual field), he tended to secrete significantly more cortisol, a stress hormone, than when the movie was shown to the right visual field. Since the left visual field is connected first to the right
hemisphere and the right visual field to the left hemisphere, Wittling's
data indicated that when the right brain saw the movie (which was of
patients getting electroconvulsive therapy), the person had a stronger
physiologic response than when his left brain saw it. In another study,
Wittling and his associates showed a three-minute romantic movie
scene and found significant increases in blood pressure when the
movies were shown to the right but not the left brain. In a later study
they found that both positive and negative films evoked stronger emotional responses when shown to the right hemisphere. Their findings
contained some interesting surprises about which side was more
aroused. They were thus able to show a movie to one side or the other
of a person and subsequently get different physiological and emotional
responses, depending on the side to which the movie was shown.
These fascinating studies demonstrated conclusively that images could
be seen and processed independently by the hemispheres of intact, ordinary subjects.[2]

In the 1970s, the late British psychiatrist Stuart Dimond had led a
group of researchers that used less elegant techniques but also found
that they could show a movie to the left or right brain in ordinary people. They placed a specially designed contact lens over one eye, which
allowed the image to fall on only the left or right half of the retina, depending on where the lens was placed on the eye. The other eye was
simply closed. In general, they found that positive movies were responded to more by the left hemisphere and negative movies by the
right. (We will return later to the discrepancies between the emotional
responses found by Wittling and Dimond.) Dimond's work has generally not been widely appreciated or cited in the scientific literature.
Certainly in the light of Wittling's findings, it now deserves more attention.[3]

How was this possible with an intact corpus callosum? Wittling
thought that part of the explanation is that the transfer of information
through the corpus callosum is slow compared to the transfer of information within a hemisphere. He suggested that the images would remain predominantly on one side. Marcel Kinsbourne may hold a key

to the puzzle. Kinsbourne, a prominent brain scientist at Tufts University, discovered that when one hemisphere is stimulated in an intact person, there may be some tendency to suppress the other side. This suppression could explain how the movie could be viewed predominantly by one side.[4]

Kinsbourne and his associates performed a remarkable study that showed that when asked to perform a verbal memory task (considered a left-brain task), their subjects turned in superior performances when gazing to the right side. Although all of their subjects completed the task looking in either direction, most of them did it faster when looking to the right visual field. Kinsbourne concluded that looking to the right stimulated the left brain, and looking to the left stimulated the right brain. Thus, he asserted that a person could tend to activate his left or right brain merely by looking to one side or the other. Even today his astonishing observation is not widely known or appreciated among scientists. The importance of his point was not that the left side is linguistic and the right spatial, but that one could manipulate which side of the brain would become relatively more active. When Kinsbourne first made this interpretation in 1973, it was a bold and remarkable assertion. Over the years his hypothesis has been borne out repeatedly.[5]

At the University of Colorado, for instance, Roger Drake and his associates found in a series of studies that they could better convince a subject of an argument if they stood to his left side (activating his right brain) than if they stood to the right side. Six separate research groups independently found that subjects could do a spatial task more quickly if they gazed to the left (right brain) and a verbal task faster if they gazed to the right side. These findings, like Kinsbourne's, showed that one could affect which cerebral hemisphere was dominant by simply looking to one side or the other. The differences in performance, while consistent and statistically significant, were not very large. The implication is that looking can influence, if not dramatically affect, cerebral dominance. A subject could still perform a verbal task while looking to the left side, but his performance would be slightly slower than when he looked to the right side. Italian psychophysiologist Patrizio Tressoldi found that subjects didn't have to look far to the left or the right side to attain a lateralized difference in performance. Tressoldi concluded that the image didn't have to go exclusively to one hemisphere to shift the lateral dominance. Apparently what was important was that most of the stimuli went to one hemisphere.[6]

In 1992, University of New Mexico researcher Edward Fouty and his associates used a contact lens, occluded on one side, to test subjects' ability to recognize faces and the orientation of lines in space. Both tasks are known to be better performed by the right hemisphere in split-brain patients and in intact subjects to whom images are flashed to one side or the other. In order to learn if lateralizing contact lenses could affect the balance between the left and right brains, Fouty tested subjects to see if right hemisphere tasks would be performed better when they wore the lenses to the left side of both eyes. They were not disappointed. The subjects performed significantly better when the lens sent the images to the side of the retina connected to the right brain.[7]

More recently, psychiatrist Steve Levick led a distinguished group of scientists from the University of Pennsylvania who performed a series of experiments on twenty-three right-handed men who wore a pair of contact lenses that were painted over except for a small area on one side of the lenses. One pair allowed vision only to the left side, the other only to the right. Levick's group confirmed Tressoldi and Fouty's results. When wearing the lenses so they could see to the right (stimulating the left brain), the subjects did better on a word analogy test. When the subjects attempted a line orientation task (a task known to be performed better by the right brain), they did better when they could see to the left side.

It did seem that all of these research teams were doing a kind of gentle split-brain study, without the surgery. Looking out the right-sided lenses might help to access the left brain more than the right, and vice versa.

I was intrigued by the possibility that the different-sided lenses might provoke different emotional experiences. Levick's group did report that the subjects were asked about emotional changes between looking to one side or the other. The only positive finding was that subjects seemed to feel more fatigue when looking to the left side. But these experimenters didn't distinguish among individuals; they simply reported the average scores on the left and right sides. If some subjects had more anxiety looking to the left and others had more looking to the right, these differences in the group as a whole would cancel each other out, and differences in individuals could have gotten lost in the overall data. Interestingly, they gave one pair of contact lenses to six very disturbed patients who were hospitalized, and one felt so much better with the contact lenses that he didn't want to give them back.[8]

Still, the unexpected element in all of these studies was the finding that one could tend to activate one hemisphere or the other merely by looking to one side. Psychologist Bernard Schiff in Canada reported that by having subjects squeeze a ball in one hand or the other, they were able to increase the relative activity of the opposite hemisphere.[9]

These studies on lateral vision and on hand exercising's affecting hemispheric dominance give support to the work of Wittling and Dimond. They suggest that by merely restricting vision to one side, one might be able to communicate preferentially with one hemisphere or the other in ordinary people.

If this were so, unless my two brains were very similar, it would mean that I should have a different experience looking out one side versus the other. This idea seemed absurd because I have spent much of my life looking from one side to the other (especially crossing streets), and I never noticed any difference. Still, I was eager to give it a try, even if my expectations were low. And the fact that so many groups reported consistent (though usually small) differences made me persevere.

Wittling's work inspired me to create my own experiment. I tried covering my eyes with my hands so that one eye was covered completely and the other was covered so that I could see only out of the side of it. I tried to judge if I felt any differently when looking to one side versus the other. Although I didn't notice much of a difference, I had a sense that I might have been a bit mentally clearer looking to my right than to my left, but as a scientist, I was not impressed with my observations. I was aware also that in the German studies, the subjects were shown upsetting films, and I was only looking around my living room, which though a bit untidy was not emotionally distressing.

A few hours later, I asked my first patient of the day to try using his hands to restrict his vision. His response was clear and dramatic. He almost immediately began to feel intense anxiety, and his whole demeanor changed to an expression of moderate distress. I then asked him to switch his hands, and he quickly smiled and told me that he felt comforted. I immediately felt I understood what I had observed. I believed I had communicated separately with his left and right brains, and I found that each viewed the world quite differently.

Six of the twelve patients I saw that day and the next felt their symptoms intensify on one side and lessen on the other. We could go back and forth, and the differences persisted. We could try to get the view of the world held by one side to consider the view of the other side. By the end of the week, I had constructed two pairs of safety goggles that were taped to allow vision out of the left or the right side. (See Figure 3.1.) The goggles seemed to get a response generally equal to or greater than the hand blocking, and the patients seemed to prefer them. Those patients who normally wore corrective lenses could comfortably wear them beneath the taped safety goggles. I was finding that about half of my patients were having a response to the goggles, and about half of those had a fairly dramatic response.

I began using the glasses frequently in therapy sessions because they appeared to be extremely helpful in treating a significant number of patients. In a patient who had been persistently depressed, I might be able for the first time to get him to see with the glasses, with his own eyes,

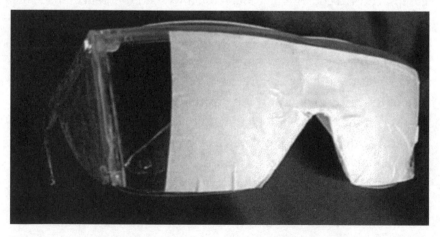

Figure 3.1
A photograph of taped experimental goggles allowing vision out of the right visual field only.

that he was safer and more valued than he had been able to appreciate before. Having two contrary views seemed to be literally mind boggling. It demonstrated dramatically that the patient's negative view of himself in the world was only a perception, not an unalterable fact, for how else could the negative view be changed so easily? Enabling the patient to see this with his own eyes was much more effective than my simply telling him that he was safe and valuable. Often I give a patient a pair of goggles, looking out the comforting side, to take home. They can be very helpful to patients struggling to ward off anxiety or depression.

Evan

I used the glasses in my work with Evan, whom I had been treating for severe anxiety. He was chronically under overwhelming stress, especially at work, and dealt with his anxiety by being hyperalert and supremely efficient. Terrified that he would be caught in error he was motivated to be nearly perfect in his complex work as a financial officer of a large company. He loved his wife and children, but was too stressed to be with them; there were always impending emergencies in his mind that took precedence over them and distanced him emotionally from the people he loved. The sad irony is that he secretly longed for the love and closeness that they longed to give him.

Evan's father was a violent alcoholic, a huge man of remarkable physical strength misguided by an enormous unfathomable rage. Evan explained, "The routine was reenacted almost nightly. I waited for my father's homecoming from the bar. As soon as I heard the car, I pretended to be asleep, my heart pounding. Had I adequately cleaned up the living room? Were my papers or books left around? Were the sofa cushions puffed up? Were my boots put away? My jacket? Did Mom have Dad's supper ready? Was it good enough, or would he toss it against the wall, or, worse, against her? When would their argument start? How soon? Should I try to intervene, risking his terrifying roar, risk being thrown into a wall, into whatever table or mirror or lamp was in the line of fire? Or would he come looking for me because he had tripped over a baseball glove or spotted an untidy corner? Would I live through the next assault?"

Evan and I had been working together for a few weeks, and the taped glasses had become an integral part of therapy. This time I asked his permission to tape-record our conversation.

"So you're looking out the right side [left brain]," I asked.

(Pause of thirty seconds) "Uh huh."

"How does that feel?"

"I feel the same—kind of nervous."

"And how would you rate your anxiety: none, mild, moderate, quite a bit, or extreme?"

"I'd say moderate. The point that I have a stomachache almost. Nervous."

"Do you feel sad?"

"Yeah, I feel kind of grayish."

"How would you rate that?"

"I'd say moderate."

"Ah huh, try the other glasses." (Thirty-second pause) "Now you're looking out of the left side [right brain]."

(Thirty-second pause) "Yeah."

"How do you feel?"

"I feel very relaxed. I feel like I'm calming down. That's how I feel: calming down. Things don't look really bright, but they don't look as gray as they were."

"How anxious do you feel: none, mild, moderate, quite a bit, or extreme?"

"I'd say mild right now. Maybe in a few minutes it will almost . . . it feels like it's just calming down kind of effect."

"And how sad do you feel?"

"I don't really feel sad. I don't feel happy; I don't feel sad."

"Would you say: none, mild, moderate, quite a bit, or extreme?"

"I don't feel sad. I'd say none. I'd say I feel nonemotional at this point."

"And what's your anxiety level now: none, mild, moderate, quite a bit, or extreme?"

"I'd say right now it's none. I don't feel anxious at all."

"Now I want you to try the other glasses again [to the left brain]. (Forty-five-second pause) And how are you feeling."

"A little nervous, but not as nervous as I was before."

"How would you rate it?"

"I would say mild—mild right now."

"And sadness: none, mild, moderate, quite a bit, or extreme?"

"I'd say mild—mild sadness."

"Now which side feels more like you were feeling earlier today?"

"This side."

"Is there a difference between this side and the other side?"

"Yeah, a big difference. This is . . . well, I feel like opposite ends of emotions. I'm sad on this side, and I feel content on the other side. And I feel very anxious over here, and I feel almost relaxed over there. So I feel a big difference."

"Now we were talking earlier about whether this anxiety relates to the past or not. Do you have any sense of that?"

"Yeah, it must."

"Tell me."

"Well, because I'm feeling exactly the way I've felt all day long. I don't know specifically why; I've been feeling this way the past twenty-four hours—but, yeah, I definitely see that it has something to do with my early life.

"How much anxiety are you feeling now?"

"Not as much as I did earlier, but I am still a little anxious."

"Mild, moderate?"

"I'd say mild."

"Try the other glasses [right brain]." (Forty-second pause) "How are you feeling?"

"I feel like I'm just starting to feel calm. That's how I would explain it. More relaxed. I see things more maturely, I think, out of this side than the other side."

"From this perspective, do you have any insight into your distress today?"

"Not something underlying, but I can see that things about which I was getting upset weren't that important. You know what I'm saying? I kind of blew things out of proportion."

"What do you think made you blow things out of proportion?"

"It was my other side of me. I was seeing things the way I felt as a child. Not maturely. I wasn't, you know, saying this happened, and it was this guy's fault, and it's not my fault."

"You say you saw it as a child? How did you see it?"

"As a personal attack on me. I saw it as if I was 100 percent the cause of everything and that it was really all my fault that things were happening at home the way they were. How I should have been looking at it is that now this is not my fault; this is their problem. Instead, I brought it on myself. I thought the reason why my mother was upset was because of me. I wasn't doing what I was supposed to do."

"And how do you feel now?"

"On this side, I can see things a little bit more maturely. These things weren't my fault; they were my parents' fault. And they were just reacting toward me. I take things very personally. It really had nothing to do with me."

"Are you saying that on the other side [left brain] you take things very personally?"

"Yeah, I take things . . . when things happen, I take them as if it's my fault."

"Are you doing this now?"

"No, on this side [right brain], I put things where they belong."

Evan made a rather rapid recovery, and by six months his symptoms had markedly diminished. As part of our therapy, I invited him to write a brief letter describing his experiences with the glasses:

I periodically suffer from extreme anxiety attacks, which stem from an alcoholic father's treatment of me from as far back as I can remember until the age of 15. My father's behavior towards me was physically and mentally abusive but more traumatic was the abuse I witnessed endured by my mother and other siblings. I was constantly told that I was the cause of all the problems . . . whether they existed or not. These episodes occurred three to five nights per week.

This abuse caused me to believe that this routine would always be this way, and that I was a bad person, who could never do anything right. The reason I am explaining my situation in this manner is because a part of me today still feels this way. With Dr. Schiffer's help I realized that this is the root of the problems which cause my anxiety attacks.

Dr. Schiffer has explained to me that there are two sides of our brains that see things differently and that there is a tool that I can use in order to calm my anxiety attack, so I can naturally work myself to a point of becoming calm. The tool we originally used were two pairs of goggles, and currently I use my hands. Basically what happens is that I cover my right eye with the goggle or hand and look out [the side] of my left eye which enables me to become calm, and my mind sees everything in a realistic light. I feel secure, relaxed and comfortable. When I cover my left eye and look out [the side] of my right eye I have an extreme feeling of impending doom. I become very scared and my entire insides feel extremely nervous and nauseous.

An example of this episode: One of the managers in the office told me point blank that I was being extremely negative while conversing with him on issues that involved his department. Within seconds I became extremely anxious, and all I could think was that maybe this manager is right. I began to feel suffocated and felt as if the walls were going to cave in. All I could think of was to get out of the office quickly to make sure that no one sees me in this paralyzed state. I then thought of my sessions with Dr. Schiffer and the tool he gave me. So I sat at my desk and put my hand over my right eye and I looked out [the side] of my left eye and concentrated on the picture in my office and within seconds I became calm enough to maturely rationalize what had happened. I went directly to my supervisor and I explained the issues completely, and asked him if he thought I was being negative, and his reply was no. He explained that it was my job to convey to that manager all the suggestions that I made in the manner in which I made them. My supervisor agreed that it is that manager's job to act upon the information I had given him whether it was negative or not.

This tool has given me the ability to overcome my extreme anxiety in order to maturely rationalize the situation that I am in, so that I can function as a normal individual.

Evan continued to progress, and by nine months from the time we started our work, he was essentially free from anxiety. For the past two years, he has maintained his progress.

Further Explorations

Although I was quite pleased by the progress I saw many of my patients making, after a couple of weeks, I saw the need to test my findings in a series of controlled studies. If my findings had to do with the glasses' enhancing one side of the brain or the other, I needed to have compelling evidence to substantiate that and demonstrate that I wasn't simply placing complex ideas in my patients' heads through suggestion. I began a formal study on seventy consecutive psychotherapy patients. A short time later, I began a laboratory study at McLean using EEGs in fifteen college students who had been recruited for participation in another study in which I was a co-investigator. I also studied Evan and two other responsive patients in the EEG laboratory.

WHAT SEVENTY PSYCHOTHERAPY PATIENTS HAD TO TELL ME

In the study of the seventy patients, I randomly offered each a pair of the taped safety glasses (see Figure 3.1), and after forty-five seconds, I would ask him to rate his level of anxiety on the following scale: none (0), mild (1), moderate (2), quite a bit (3), or extreme (4). Immediately following the rating, I would offer the second pair, which allowed vision out of the other visual field. I included in the study only the patients' first encounter with the glasses. Thirty-nine males and thirty-one females participated. Fifty-nine were right-handed; eleven were left-handed. Their average age was forty-three years.

For the last forty subjects, I added two pairs of control glasses. These were similar safety glasses, taped entirely over one side (as were the others), but on the other side only the bottom one-third of the lens was taped. This meant that the subject could see out of one eye entirely. Vision out of one eye, called monocular vision, sends images to both hemispheres. It in fact sends the images preferentially to the opposite hemisphere, but not nearly as strongly as the experimental glasses. The reason is that the retina at the back of each eye is divided into two sheets: one to the left of the eye and one to the right. The sheet of retina is larger on the side of the eye near the nose than that on the lateral side of the eye (see Figure 3.2). We would expect to find that the control glasses stimulate each hemisphere differently. That is, like the experimental glasses, they would stimulate the opposite hemisphere more strongly, but the differences in anxiety levels between the left and right views should be less pronounced than those of the lateralized safety glasses. If this were the case, we could safely assume that the responses were not due merely to a placebo effect or to suggestion.

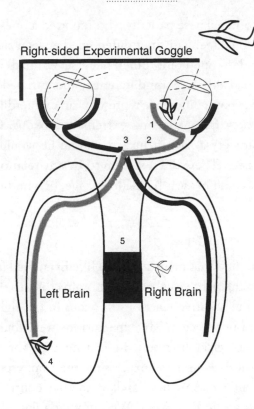

Figure 3.2

Like Figure 2.1, this figure illustrates schematically the connections between the eyes and the brain, but here the person is viewing through the experimental right-sided taped goggles. An object (the airplane) again appears to the right of the person. The image of the plane goes through the lens of only the right eye, striking the medial aspect (1) of the retina of the right eye, which is connected by the optic nerve (2), which passes through the optic chiasm (3) to the opposite (left) hemisphere (4). Via the corpus callosum (5) the image can then be transferred to the other hemisphere.

I found that there were indeed much larger responses to the experimental glasses than the control glasses, and those differences were highly significant by statistical tests. Later, when I describe the EEG studies, I will show that the experimental glasses induced the expected shifts in hemispheric activity, while the control monocular glasses did not.

Of the seventy patients, 60 percent reported a one-point or greater difference on the five-point scale between the two pairs of goggles and 23 percent reported a two-point or greater difference. A person with a one-point difference might feel mild anxiety on one side and moderate

anxiety on the other. These patients who reported a one-point difference said they could feel a distinct difference between sides. Twenty-
six patients had a one-point difference, seven had a two-point
difference, five had a three-point difference, and four had a four-point
difference. A four-point difference represents an extraordinary change,
from being anxiety free to feeling extremely anxious. Overall, the
more baseline anxiety a patient had, the more he would tend to respond to the glasses. There did not seem to be any relation between a
patient's response and his sex, handedness, age, or whether he was on
medication.[10]

TROUBLED LEFT HEMISPHERES

I was surprised to find that many patients, like Evan, had more anxiety
when looking to the right visual field (left brain) than to the left. I had
expected all of the negative reactions to occur in the right brain, but
this was clearly not the case. My expectations were founded on the
persuasive psychological literature indicating that the right hemisphere is better at detecting and expressing emotion, especially negative emotion. But I had in my hands data that contradicted those
assumptions. What did this mean? Were my data flawed? Unacceptable? Or was it possible that we have been making unwarranted assumptions about the right hemisphere?[11]

I have already mentioned that Dimond and Wittling found that
healthy subjects had larger responses to negative films in their right
hemispheres. However, in two repeated studies, Wittling found no
emotional differences between the hemispheres, even though these
studies reported higher cortisol (stress hormone) levels when the negative movie was shown to subjects' right brains. In a subsequent article, Wittling's group reported the results of a study of people with a
high level of psychosomatic complaints. In this population, they found
that the cortisol secretion was higher when the movie was shown to
the subjects' left brains.[12]

Richard Davidson, an experimental psychologist at the University
of Wisconsin, is one of the strongest proponents of the theory that the
right brain handles negative emotion. I have followed his work for
years and appreciate his contributions. Davidson has shown a correlation between fear responses to films and the activity of the frontal as-

pect of the right brain. To measure the brain's activity, Davidson recorded EEGs over twenty different regions of the scalp. His studies indicated that when he recorded baseline EEGs of nursing students while they were resting, he found he could predict the students' responses to films designed to provoke negative emotion. Students whose right hemispheres were more active in the frontal aspect during the baseline EEG recordings tended to verbally report more negative emotional responses when the movies were shown. Further, the EEG measurements over the right frontal areas made during the films correlated with the subjects' verbal reports of negative emotion. These and other studies suggest that the right hemisphere is involved in the processing of negative emotion.[13]

Another method for measuring brain activity is the PET (positron emission tomography) scan. This technique involves injecting a radioactive tracer into the vein of the subject just as he performs a task. The tracer travels to areas in the brain that are active at the time of the injection and is then detected by scanner. The result is a read-out and a picture of the relative activation of the entire brain during the activity. Recently, a group, which included Dr. Davidson, reported a study of twelve right-handed women with a mean age of twenty-three years who were given PET scans while they watched three films. One film evoked happiness, one sadness, and one disgust. The result of the study was that there were no significant differences between the left and right brains in any areas during the three different emotional conditions. This discrepancy with the earlier studies remains unexplained. Further, other PET studies of a similar design have failed to demonstrate a relationship between the right brain and negative emotion.[14]

Still, the preponderance of the scientific literature does point toward the right hemisphere's being more involved with emotion, especially negative emotion, although the differences between the left and right side that are found in most studies are generally fairly small. One way to understand what might be going on is to look more closely at my study of the seventy patients. If I excluded patients who were left-handed as well as patients suffering a diagnosis of posttraumatic stress disorder (PTSD), then we would find that there was more anxiety in the right brain, and the difference between the left- and right-sided anxieties would then be statistically significant. If we had only these limited data, we would have concluded that anxiety was associated with the right brain. Notice, though, even among this limited sample of fifty-two right-handed patients who were not suffering PTSD, eleven still had more anxiety in their left brain (seventeen had more in their right hemispheres, and twenty-four had no difference). My point is that even when the data show a statistically significant difference favoring anxiety in the right hemisphere, there are still a substantial number (21 percent) who have more symptoms unexpectedly in the left hemisphere.

By analogy, it is true that men are taller than women, but a man who measures five feet, five inches tall knows there are millions of women who are taller than he is. Obviously when we say men are taller than women, we mean on average. In talking about the left and right brain, I am concerned that many statements about the properties of the hemispheres are based on averages but are applied to all individuals, and therefore do not give a complete picture.

My unexpected finding that many of the subjects had more anxiety in their left hemispheres should be taken seriously. I pointed out that the group at the University of Pennsylvania reported only average data, and it would be interesting to know if some of their subjects had measurable differences in emotion between sides.

WHY SOME PATIENTS HAD MORE TROUBLED LEFT HEMISPHERES

How do we explain why some people had more distress in their left brains than their right? What factors might predict why someone would be more troubled in his left hemisphere? Among my data, sex, handedness, medications, and age seemed to have had no predictive role. Only a patient's diagnosis seemed to predict the side on which a patient experienced more or less anxiety. A high percentage of patients with PTSD felt more distress in their left brains. Of eighteen patients with this diagnosis, ten had considerably more symptoms looking to the right (left brain), four had more symptoms looking to the left (right brain), and four had equivalent responses on both sides. Thus, among the PTSD patients, 78 percent responded to the glasses, and of these, 71 percent had their symptoms when their left brain was stimulated. In contrast, among twenty-one patients with a formal diagnosis of major depression, 71 percent responded, and of those, 73 percent had their symptoms while looking to the left (right brain). So one factor that seemed to determine whether the patient was more likely to be anxious when he looked to the right (left brain) was a positive diagnosis of PTSD.

Why should patients with PTSD tend to have more symptoms in their left brains? In fact, this result contradicts a study that I performed at McLean with Martin Teicher and Andrew Papanicolaou in which we studied patients with a history of abuse who were not symptomatic. We had the patients remember a neutral memory, such as something ordinary they did the week before. Then we measured their relative left and right brain activity with a technique developed by Dr. Papanicolaou called probe auditory evoked potentials, which uses sophisticated analyses of brain waves. After we took the recordings for the neutral memories, I interviewed the subjects for about fifteen minutes, in which we discussed as in a therapy session the emotional experiences they had suffered. We found that during the neutral memories, the left brains were more active in nine of ten subjects. During the unpleasant memory, the right hemisphere was more active in seven of ten, and we interpreted this to suggest that possibly the traumatic memories were stored preferentially in the right hemisphere. Later, a group at the Massachusetts General Hospital led by Scott Rausch found similar results in PTSD patients using PET scans. And in general, the prevailing view has been that if there is more activity in one hemisphere in PTSD patients, then probably the more troubled side is the right brain.[15]

Nevertheless, other imaging studies on PTSD have contrary findings, and significant new data point to the left hemisphere being the more troubled side in PTSD. My colleagues at McLean, led by behavioral neurologist Yutaka Ito, reviewed the medical records of seventy-seven children around thirteen years old who were admitted to McLean Hospital with a history of abuse. They found rather dramatic evidence of nonspecific abnormalities of their left brains by brain wave and other clinical studies. The problems were not the result of physical injuries. And in another study from this group, a sophisticated EEG analysis was used on fifteen children, eight to twelve years old, with a history of trauma and on a similar healthy group. The EEG analysis indicated that the abused children, but not the unabused, had findings that strongly suggested a delayed or abnormal development of their left hemispheres.[16]

Other studies indicate that under stress, PTSD patients show an opposite hemispheric laterality to that in stressed or unstressed ordinary subjects. For example, PTSD patients under stress do better on language tasks (usually left-brain tasks) when the information is sent to the right brain, and they do better on a facial recognition task (usually a right hemispheric task) with their left brains.[17]

In short, we do not yet know enough about PTSD and the brain to reach the truth in regard to whether it is more closely related to the right brain functions, as such fine neuroscientists as Scott Rausch and Besel van der Kolk suggest, or whether it is more related to the left brain, as Martin Teicher and Rachel Yehuda suggest. Based on my data, I now side more with Teicher and Yehuda, but in fact the truth is likely to be much more complicated. Traumatic memories are likely closely related to a lower brain center called the amygdala which is present in both hemispheres. The amygdala in each hemisphere is inhibited by a high-level cortical center, the orbital frontal lobe, in that same hemisphere. This means that the activity of the hemisphere is related to the interactions of these two components. I speculate that if the amygdala is trying to express itself but is being inhibited by the cortex, we could have a different situation from that of the cortex's being inhibited and allowing the amygdala to have more of an influence. Further, there are a number of other areas that come into the action, and ultimately it all gets very complicated. Moreover, we are dealing not only with the brain but also with the mind. And what the brain does on a given day will depend in part on how the mind feels and thinks; an upset hemisphere is very different from a relaxed hemisphere.[18]

SPECULATIONS ABOUT THE LEFT HEMISPHERE AND PTSD

I feel that to ponder about why patients with PTSD tended to respond to the glasses more to the right visual field (left brain) is permissible so long as we keep in mind that we are speculating. Iaccino cites evidence that when the left hemisphere is stressed, it tends to terminate the emotional reactions faster than does the right hemisphere. Perhaps people who are exposed to extreme traumas use their left brains to try to deal with the stress in order to control the degree of distress, and in this way, the left hemisphere might get more involved with the experience than the right hemisphere. Joe Bogen suggested to me that the left hemisphere may get more involved in traumatic situations because of the linguistic abilities of the left brain. He reasoned that if one can name something or verbally try to understand it, one has a better chance of coping with it.[19]

Martin Teicher offers a possible explanation for his findings of left hemispheric impairments in abused children. He speculates that stress may activate brain neurotransmitter systems that are known to be represented differently in the different hemispheres and that these neurotransmitters might affect brain development differently on each side. It may be plausible that verbal abuse inhibits the development of the left hemisphere because of its tendency to be evoked by language tasks. His argument is similar to Bogen's suggestion but subtly different. Finally, Teicher points to evidence suggesting that the left hemisphere is on a faster developmental track between the ages of three months and six years, and that its advanced development may lead to more vulnerability of the left side in abusive situations. Others, particularly David Galin and Rhawn Joseph, have suggested that the right hemisphere develops first and have used this assertion to explain why emotions are often more associated with the right hemisphere.[20]

THE IMPORTANT LESSON

We have too little information to do more than speculate about why the left brain may be more involved in the traumatic experiences of abused patients. But what the data from the glasses do strongly indicate is that in many patients, there is clear evidence that looking to one side evokes a very different experience from looking out the other side. Patients who have strong reactions to the glasses apparently have two distinct parts of their mind—one that sees the world as threatening and one that sees it as much less so. As with a legal case, some pieces of evidence are more compelling than others. The responses of patients using the glasses were often not subtle but as graphic and compelling as they were unexpected.

WHY SOME PATIENTS DO NOT RESPOND TO THE LATERALIZING GLASSES

These strong data also raise new interesting questions. Why did 40 percent of the patients have no response to the lateralizing glasses? I suggest that in these patients either of two conditions is likely to exist. First, their two hemispheres may be very similar in their outlooks: both sides may be calm and healthy, or they both may be equally troubled and disturbed. The experimental glasses would find little difference in such people. I have tested three patients with stable chronic mental illnesses; none had any response to the glasses. I wonder if both hemispheres are troubled in these patients.

A second, more intriguing possibility is that one side dominates the other so much that, even when the glasses attempt to stimulate the opposite hemisphere, the stimulation is inadequate to overcome the dominance. A number of times in the course of therapy, I have seen patients who did not respond initially, but responded weeks or months later as the subordinate hemisphere became more liberated through the therapy. Conversely, I have seen patients respond to the glasses, but over the course of their therapy, as the troubled side recovered, the glasses no longer elicited a response, probably because both sides then felt well. The majority of patients are consistent in their responses from week to week. I believe that the glasses influence which hemisphere will be more active, but I do not believe they control the brain. The glasses do not have the power of a Wada test and are influenced by the patient's overall situation.

THE GLASSES IN CLINICAL PRACTICE

The patients who significantly benefited from the goggles did not have miraculous cures by simply putting on a pair of goggles. Rather we used the goggles to show that they could manifest two very different views of the world: one very anxious and troubled, and similar to the patient's view from his childhood, and the other a more confident, realistic view. By our work with these divergent views of the world, we could teach the troubled side that the world might be a safer place than it had believed.

This teaching usually was still a struggle. Although some patients recovered rather dramatically, most still required a determined effort. Nevertheless, the work with the goggles made that struggle easier by more clearly defining it and more concretely demonstrating a more positive view of the world. If I told the patient that he was safe and lovable, he would have trouble believing me, but when he could see this for himself through his use of the goggles, then this was more compelling and convincing. Sometimes I would ask the patient to keep switching back and forth between the different goggles, and this often helped to integrate the views. Often I would ask the patient to let his troubled side look out the more positive side, and the patients seemed to clearly understand what I was asking even though I wasn't entirely sure myself. Often I would simply let the patient enjoy the positive view, much like the pleasure of sunbathing. Patients might borrow a pair of goggles for work between sessions; a number of patients constructed their own goggles, and others simply used their hands to block their vision when they were under stress or experiencing unusual anxiety.

Physiological Studies

The next step seemed to be to try to obtain physiological evidence that the taped glasses were indeed affecting the relationship between the two hemispheres.

The group at the University of Pennsylvania did a final part to their experiment in which they measured the brain waves of subjects while wearing the different lateralized contact lenses. From brain wave recordings, a scientist can measure fairly reliably which areas of the brain are active. Steve Levick and his colleagues found, as expected, that with the left-looking lenses, the right brain was more active, and the opposite was observed with the right-looking lenses. In my literature review, I found four other groups that similarly found brain waves to change in the expected direction with changes in the side of vision. I also found one paper with the same conclusion using a PET scan.[21]

I decided to test my goggles with EEGs using a similar procedure. At McLean, my colleagues and I were just beginning a brain wave study of college students while they recalled unpleasant or traumatic memories. Since I was participating in the study and had my goggles approved by McLean for study, it was easy to add my goggles to the first study. When each subject finished the memory study, we let him rest. When each was ready, we first took a baseline EEG recording, followed by an EEG while he wore each of the goggles. In addition to the left- and right-sided goggles, we used the two pairs of comparison or control goggles, which allowed vision out of one entire eye. After each goggle was worn while the EEG was recorded, my colleague, research psychologist Dr. Carl Anderson, asked a series of questions about how the subject felt using my five-point scale. We studied fifteen college students—eleven females and four males.

I also asked three of my patients who had intense anxiety responses to one of the glasses to come to the lab and have their EEGs recorded with the four different glasses. They had very large emotional responses in the laboratory, as they had had in the office. Each had EEG shifts in the expected directions, indicating that the left visual field glasses increased the right hemispheric activity, and the right-sided glasses that of the left hemisphere.

When we analyzed the EEG data for the college students, we found that the subjects' brain activity had robustly shifted in the expected direction. That is, when the patients used the right-sided goggle, their EEGs consistently indicated a relative increase in left brain activity, and the opposite occurred with the left-sided goggle.

More specifically, we found that during baseline recordings without lateralizing glasses, the left hemisphere was consistently, on average, 25 percent more active than the right hemisphere by our measure (theta EEG activity in the frontal and temporal leads that are over the areas thought most important to psychological functioning). With the left visual field glasses, as predicted, the left hemisphere became, on average, only 21 percent more active than the right hemisphere. With the right visual field glasses, the left hemisphere became 31 percent more active than the right. The differences in theta activity using the left and right experimental glasses were highly significant by statistical tests. (Statistical tests take into consideration the consistency of the findings in each condition, the size of the differences between groups, and the number of subjects. The statistical test we used found that the chance of these results being found by mere accident rather than because of an actual cause was less than three chances in a thousand, a highly significant result.) With the left monocular, control glasses the left hemisphere was 26 percent more active than the right, and with the right monocular glasses it was 29 percent more active. These differences between left and right control goggles were not significant by statistical tests.[22]

Figure 3.3 shows a typical theta EEG during a college student's wearing the left and then during his wearing the right visual field experimental goggles. In the frontal and temporal leads we used for our calculations, his left hemisphere was 31 percent more active than the right hemisphere during the baseline recording without any goggles. With the left visual field glasses, left-sided activity decreased to 29 percent of the right. With the right visual field glasses, left-sided brain activity increased to 42 percent of right-sided activity. In the figure, the

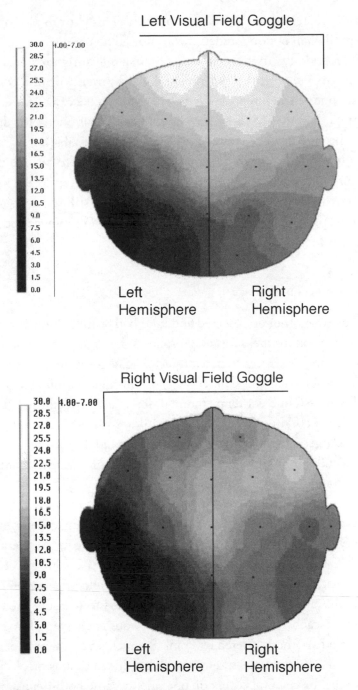

Figure 3.3

A graphic depiction of a typical theta EEG during a college student's wearing the left and then during his wearing the right visual field experimental goggles. The dark areas represent increased brain activity.

dark areas represent increased brain activity. This pattern of response was typical of all but one student, who showed no change.

We found also that the students had significantly greater differences in anxiety with the experimental glasses than with the control glasses. Nine of the fifteen students had more anxiety out of one side than the other, and of these, five had more than a one-point difference. The side of greater anxiety varied between subjects. What is most interesting is that these subjects were unknown to me, were not complaining of emotional symptoms, were not in therapy, were in the sterile environment of the laboratory, and yet they still showed significant shifts in anxiety with the lateralized glasses, and I might add, not with the control glasses.

An Unexpected Finding

We reported another unexpected finding. I had been looking for a convenient method for measuring hemispheric dominance and had been experimenting with ear temperatures. Pediatrician and researcher Thomas Boyce from the University of California, San Francisco, reported that he found ear temperature differences between the left and right sides in children. He found that children with behavioral problems had larger differences than other children did. Boyce found in the troubled children that the left-sided ear temperatures were higher than those of the right.[23]

I wondered if the increased blood flow, expected with a shift in brain activity, might be reflected in temperature changes determined by a very sensitive ear thermometer. I tried measuring my temperature in each ear under different conditions to see if I could detect any changes with different activities. I found some encouraging preliminary results, and so my colleagues and I decided to measure the temperature in each ear while each subject wore each pair of goggles. Based on a hypothesis offered by Frank Pompei, an eminent expert in scientific temperature measurements, we predicted that as more blood was used by the cerebral cortex on one side, because both hemispheres are supplied mainly from the carotid arteries, on the side of more activity, blood would be shunted away from the areas around the ears to the active cortex. In other words, we expected the ear temperature to drop as the hemisphere became more active. We found exactly what we predicted. When subjects wore the glasses looking to the left, stimulating the right hemisphere, there was a relative drop in the right ear canal temperature. The opposite, as predicted, occurred with the right-sided glasses, and the changes we observed were significant by statistical tests. The control glasses did not affect the ear temperatures. We found also a very high correlation between the shifts in ear temperature and the shifts in the EEGs. All of the shifts in EEG and ear canal temperature were in the predicted directions.

A Functional Magnetic Resonance Imaging Study

As one last experimental finding, each of the college students prior to our EEG and temperature studies underwent a functional MRI, the new cutting-edge method of measuring brain activity. Like a PET scan, it gives images of the brain's activity, but faster and without radiation. What we discovered was that college students who had more activity in their right temporal lobes when they had the functional MRIs under baseline conditions tended to have stronger EEG and emotional responses to the experimental glasses.[24]

Implications

The experiments with the glasses offer compelling evidence for the idea that the two hemispheres can each have a separate mind and lend strong support to the psychological ideas I began to develop when I worked with Ryan. In the next chapter, I systematically develop the psychological concepts that follow from the idea that we can possess two minds.

CHAPTER 4

Dual-Brain Psychology

Harold, a rumpled, brilliant fifty-five-year-old newspaper reporter, came to see me because he wanted very badly to marry Jane. It's just that he couldn't. They had been together for two years, and she was quite frustrated by his excuses. "I want to move forward, but my legs somehow won't abide," he explained.

Harold is a non-Jewish Jew. It's not that he doesn't bristle at the rare anti-semitic remark, but he dislikes the idea of Jewishness, an idea that has always annoyed him. He grew up poor in Newark. His father, Harold said, "was a bit of a *schlemiel*," a man who failed in a record number of attempts to earn the living that his wife silently required. Harold's mother was a distant person who, rather than recede into her own unhappiness, stood silently in the center of all of their lives. She was a homemaker in a home that couldn't afford one, a woman who had longed for something more than she had captured in her three-room, fourth-floor walkup, with a man she grew quickly to despise as much as he grew to love her.

Harold remembered joyful errands with his father, helping him make a delivery, accompanying him on a daylong business trip to New York or beyond. His father was a loving man—a kibitzer, a hugger—and Harold could feel his palpable love. Although Harold could cry about missing his father, about how much he enjoyed the hugs, even the embarrassing, sloppy kisses in front of the school, still his father's love was tainted. What use was the love of a failure—a man who couldn't achieve more than contempt from the woman he loved?

Although Harold's mother kept her own counsel, he learned

through some inarticulate gestures or indirect comments that she expected he would find fame one day—possibly a George Gershwin,
someone to make a mother proud, proud to be his mother. "Some
mothers have children that make a mother *kvell* inside with joy," she
would say. But early on, she realized that her ordinary son, who didn't
have Cary Grant looks or Albert Einstein brains, wasn't going to do
much more for her than her dimwitted husband. Eventually she decided that Harold was more related to his father than to her. How did
she get stuck in such a hopeless and painful circumstance?

Most of all, Harold remembers his mother's back. It was her back
that she used to punish him, to reject him, turning from him when he
longed for her face, her smile, her love.

As Harold talked, I appreciated the complexity of his personality.
He knows that he is highly regarded professionally by his peers. His articles are widely read and appreciated. But, he confessed, to me, "I just
know I'm an impostor. People think I'm smart, cultured, and important, but in fact I'm just great at fooling people. They don't see the sim-
pleton, ne'er-do-well inside." With this image of himself, Harold
experienced a profound soul-wracking self-hatred. Lately, the despair
had subsided, in part through Jane's love, which seemed as simple and
straightforward as his was complex and convoluted. Jane had little idea
how tangled in its own debris his mind had become. She expected others to be as clear, uncluttered, and uncomplicated as herself. She had
an inkling of what she was pining to embark on but didn't appreciate
the whole of it.

When Harold would hesitate with Jane, I'd ask what he was feeling
inside, what that feeling reminded him of. I did the same when he felt
self-hatred. And from his associations and our probing, themes began to
emerge. Harold's self-hatred and fear of marriage had the same source:
his fear of his mother's painful rejections. As a child, he felt unlovable,
defective, for why else would his mother—this woman who was the
center of his family's universe—turn her back on him, showing him
utter contempt when she must have known how much he hurt and that
like his father, he needed her love. The only explanation for him as a
child, the only thing that could make any sense to him at the time, was
that he was utterly repulsive. It was exactly this feeling that overtook
him when he experienced his self-loathing, and at times it had driven

him to despair, even the brink of suicide. This was the pain he wanted Jane to relieve, but it was also the pain he feared she would repeat, especially if he let go and allowed himself to love her desperately.

Within a few months of our work, Harold was able to marry Jane, and he began to love and appreciate himself. I want to show how we accomplished this with what I call dual-brain therapy. The path we took was not the only one that could have succeeded, and I will examine how I would have treated him with other approaches, so that we can compare methods and theories. I will also show how the dual-brain model is consistent with many interesting phenomena such as hypnosis, split or multiple personalities, and certain psychophysiological reactions. In the chapters that follow, I will apply this model toward the understanding and treatment of a number of common psychological impediments and problems.

The Dual-Brain Model

The dual-brain model hypothesizes that we have two minds, one associated with each hemisphere. In Harold, there was a part of him that could agree with me that he was a legitimate, worthwhile person and that Jane was a sane, safe, reliable, loving person. At other moments, when he expressed feelings of self-contempt, I asked, "What's all that anger about?" And this would get him to consider his feelings. As we worked on it, he became able to see that in spite of his feelings, he had value and was valued as a person. And when he felt anxiety about Jane—an anxiety that was difficult to articulate—I asked, "Do you feel somehow she'll turn her back on you?" Through our work, Harold grew steadily confident that Jane wasn't a back-turner.

Still, the part of him that knew himself to be an embarrassment and knew that Jane would somehow hurt him persisted. After we could readily get in touch with these feelings, I told him that I believe we have two minds, one associated with each hemisphere. One mind was the part of him that could see his value and Jane's constancy and love. The other mind knew that he was a nincompoop like his father, a faker who would never be able to sustain Jane's love, because after her discovery of his true defectiveness, she would no longer have the strength or desire to bear him.

THE NATURE OF THE TWO MINDS

The second key to the dual-brain model is that often the two minds are different. In one constellation, one mind is more mature, reasonable, and living in the present. The second mind, immature in its cognitive and emotional aspects, is stuck back in an old trauma. It sees the world as it was at the time of the trauma, and like a child, it is dogmatic and overly emotional. It knows, no matter what one tells it to the contrary, that the painful situations it experienced will repeat themselves. For example, the immature part of Harold knew he was worthless and that Jane would reject him.

Harold and I learned to call one aspect "his mature self" and the other "his immature self," and Harold accepted and appreciated this clarification. He saw more clearly what was happening within him. Harold was able to feel both parts and learned to listen to and talk with the immature part. Harold, surprised to see how easily this worked and how clear it was to him, asked me over and over, "Does this mean I'm schizophrenic?" I believe that Harold was embarrassed to carry around this distinct immature personality. Repeatedly, I explained that the dichotomy of mind he had discovered within himself is entirely normal—that it is, in fact, the way we human beings are made. Harold wasn't crazy in any sense at all; he had simply become aware of his true nature. (Technically, "schizophrenia" does not mean "two minds," even though when the term was first used almost a hundred years ago, the "schizo" part of the word did have to do with a poorly defined splitting of the mind, referring to a poorly defined disharmony of mental functions. Today "splitting of the mind" is not considered in any way a part of that severe mental illness.)

Harold was surprised to see how powerful the immature part of him was, how it got him to procrastinate and play computer games instead of meeting his deadlines. It made him turn away from Jane and even made him question his attraction when his other part knew that he was deeply attracted to her physically and mentally. Harold marveled at all this: "I can't believe this. If someone heard our conversation about this immature person and this mature person, they would think we were both nuts." Nonetheless, Harold eagerly addressed his troubled mind, "Let's get our work done, and then I'll let you play on the computer." And surprisingly, he would feel the other part of him settle down and become calm.

Harold was typical of many of the depressed or anxious patients I see, in that his two personalities were getting to know each other and learning how to communicate in a healthy way. Harold appreciated how hurt that part of him had been; he felt its pain, its longing for his mother's love, and the utter distress that her persistent rejections had caused him. With my encouragement, Harold comforted that immature person inside and eventually learned to love him deeply in much the way he had hoped his mother would. Harold described the burgeoning relationship between his two sides as one that would eventually heal his distress and enable him to enter his relationship with Jane fully. He would not be able to commit to Jane until he had the safety of a solid relationship with himself. Once Harold had established this healthy relationship within, he was able not only to commit fully to Jane, but to forgive and love his mother, because she was no longer blocking his growth and mental integration.

THE IMPORTANT MESSAGE IN DUAL-BRAIN THERAPY

Harold responded well to the lateralized glasses. Looking to the left (right brain) called up his immature view of the world, and looking to the right (left brain) consistently evoked the mature view. Although the lateralized glasses are therapeutically beneficial when they work with a particular patient, they aren't indispensable. In almost all the patients I have worked with, whether or not the glasses achieved a response, the dual-brain hypothesis of two distinct minds is helpful. When they work, the glasses are an important adjunct to the tasks of dual-brain therapy, the discovery of these different parts, and the establishment of a healthy relationship between them. But with or without the glasses, the essence of dual-brain therapy lies in teaching the troubled side that it is safer and more valuable than it had learned through some archaic experiences.

DIFFERENT CONSTELLATIONS OF THE DUAL-BRAIN MODEL

In Harold, I observed the most common constellation of the two minds in the dual-brain model: the presence of a mature mind and the presence of an immature mind. But in other people I have found what I believe to be two troubled minds—that is, an unquiet mind in both the left and right brains. I tend to see this more in patients who have suffered chronic mental illnesses such as chronic schizophrenia or severe manic depressive illness. It is possible, in a particular instance, that there is a mature mind buried deep inside, and that I am unable to find it because it is so dominated by a troubled side. But I suspect that in some people, both sides have become very troubled.

In other people, I've observed two sides that are both healthy and somewhat similar. Such a person is likely to be in touch with a part that may be less mature, but is not dramatically different from the other, more focused side. For instance, one side might be very tuned to the world and the other part more of a worrier. If such a person has trouble sleeping, it is always this worried part that remains wide awake and distressed. But in general the two parts are allies, working together in life. One part may be more sensitive and intuitive, but in a healthy state, this part won't keep him from flying, make him depressed, or prevent him from yearning for his lover.

At other times, I have worked with patients who clearly had one side dominate the other such that it was only over time that the other part (which I suspected existed inside) could come to the surface and express itself. I have seen this, for instance, in a person who for years repressed a verified traumatic memory. Simultaneous with the recovery of the memory, an immature part of the person's personality became more apparent. Perhaps both the memory and the immature personality were repressed.

Other times I have seen a patient whose life has been dominated by a troubled personality, which suppressed its healthier but weaker partner. I often see this constellation in patients who abuse drugs or alcohol. We have to dig to find the more mature part and then nurture it, so eventually it can take on the position of leadership. This constellation is different from Harold's in which a mature mind predominated but was interfered with by an immature side.

Understanding the many different possible relationships between the two minds leads to a much clearer understanding of human psychology. The two minds can *cooperate* with each other in a deep, synergistic relationship that fosters creativity and maturity, or they can *sabotage* each other, leading to a plethora of psychological and psychosomatic problems. I am suggesting that the roles and activities of the hemispheres are dynamic and changeable. Sometimes the subordinate hemisphere influences a person in the background, and sometimes it comes out and takes over the personality, as when we suddenly lose our temper and then later say, "I don't know what came over me." When a patient recovers quickly from an acute depression or psychosis, it may be because his more mature side has regained control. When, after years of intensive psychotherapy, a patient of mine has achieved a true resolution of the illness, I consider his improvement and stability largely due to the maturation and healthy development of the more troubled hemisphere that our interpersonal treatment facilitated. I remain optimistic about the treatment of psychological problems because I see that the major requirement for success is simply that the injured troubled side recover through the process of therapy (often assisted by medications). In my view, drugs alone do not repair an injured side.

DUAL-BRAIN PSYCHOLOGY AND THE SPLIT-BRAIN STUDIES

The properties of two minds in my patients (including the relationship between them) appear remarkably similar to the properties of the two minds found in split-brain and Wada studies. We observe that the two minds constantly interact. As Harold's situation demonstrated, his conscious mind was covertly, though strongly, influenced by his inner mind, an interaction that was initially inapparent to Harold. This mirrors the relationship between the left and right sides of the female split-brain patient (described in Chapter 2), who was shown a picture of a nude to her right brain. Asked why she was laughing, she replied, "Doctor, you have a funny machine." Her left-sided speaking mind in fact had no any idea why it was laughing; it could only feel that something was "funny." She did not say, "Gee, I have no idea why I am laughing." Instead, she tried to fabricate a reason and gloss over the situation.[1]

Another patient of mine, who had grown up in an intense, dysfunctional family, had a highly developed though disturbed inner immature mind. At times she felt as if this inner mind were trying to kill her. As a child, she was continuously threatened and rejected in sadistic ways by her severely disturbed mother. When my patient was about eight, her mother, crazed and enraged, threaten to throw boiling water at her. This patient, a woman in her thirties, came to therapy because of a profound depression. Her mother, still intense and troubled, continued to hurl outrageous, inappropriate insults at her daughter. Intellectually, Margie understood that her mother was extremely disturbed, and she could often laugh about her mother's aberrant behavior.

But when Margie was very depressed, she could feel an inner, troubled self attacking her just the way her mother would have. I once listened with great anxiety as she described how she felt that some part of her had tried to grab the steering wheel and drive her car off the road. She physically struggled with herself and survived. Over the course of her therapy, this and similar struggles repeated themselves. Through dual-brain therapy, Marie realized that her immature self at times copied and behaved like her hostile mother.

This patient reminds me of the split-brain patient I described whose left hand tried to grab his wife but was restrained by his right hand. She also reminded me of a split-brain patient who went out for a walk and found his left leg trying to pull him in another direction. His doctor, who knew the patient's neighborhood, realized that the patient's right brain (controlling his left leg) apparently wanted desperately to walk in the direction of his ex-wife's apartment. She had spurned him because she could no longer tolerate his medical problems.[2]

One split-brain study has shown that the two hemispheres can compete for dominance on experimental tasks. In a complex experimental design, the experimenters found that if they encouraged either hemisphere, they could get it to control the person's behavior, even when the other side was better at the particular task. In a similar way, Dr. Ahern's dialogue with his patient during the Wada study, described in Chapter 2, showed that the patient's left mind was actively and thoughtfully suppressing his right mind.[3]

My point is that not only have we discovered two intact minds in split-brain research and in psychology, but we have found that in both cases, the two minds seem to interact in similar ways. Psychologically, the relationship between the two minds can be one of dominance-submission, sabotage-alliance, or harmony-disharmony.

Beginning with the psychiatrist David Galin in 1974, a number of authors, including myself, have turned to the split-brain studies to advance the notion that the right hemisphere is the site of the Freudian unconscious. In 1988, Galin reconsidered the accumulated evidence and appreciated that the reality was far more complex than he had first realized. I too have altered my own views over the years. Although I no longer closely associate the right hemisphere with the unconscious, I continue to believe that the basic idea emanating from the split-brain studies—that of mental duality—offers a profound foundation for any psychological thinking.[4]

Dual-Brain Model as a Possible Explanation for Distinct Mood or Personality Changes

PREMENSTRUAL SYNDROME

When the two minds are of similar strength and power, they often vie with each other for dominance. Try to imagine a tug-of-war between the minds. One side leads but then is thrown by the other side, which will then come to dominate the person's overall mind. Dual-brain psychology accommodates both subtle and significant personality or mood shifts. Awakening from sleep full of anxiety may not simply be a result of brain chemicals randomly scrambled, but may signal a change in hemispheric dominance. On the other hand, brain chemicals may act, in part, through evoked changes in hemispheric dominance. I suspect that premenstrual syndrome (PMS) may be such a situation. Perhaps the change in hormones alters the hemispheric dominance. A group of prominent scientists from Edinburgh have reviewed findings demonstrating that estrogen levels, which are altered during the menstrual cycle, affect brain neurotransmitter systems, which are known to be asymmetrically distributed between the left and right brains.[5]

MANIC DEPRESSIVE ILLNESS

Manic depressive illness, which has recurrent dramatic shifts in personality from healthy to depressed to manic, has been hypothesized by a number of authors to be related to lateralized problems in the brain. I speculate that these switches in mental state might relate to struggles between the two minds. I address manic depressive illness more closely in Chapter 8.

DISSOCIATIVE DISORDERS

There are a number of interesting examples of a mental duality that come under the heading of dissociation, a state in which a person manifests clear evidence of two or more fairly distinct mental aspects or personalities.

One of these is multiple personality disorder (MPD), which entails often dramatic shifts in personality and is frequently associated with evidence for changes in brain laterality. Substantial, but not conclusive, evidence, mostly from EEG studies and neuropsychological testing, suggests that the different mental states found in multiple personalities relate to shifts in hemispheric dominance. Neuropsychologist Polly Henninger has suggested that in MPD patients, the more mature, dominant personality is related to the left hemisphere and the alter personalities, of which there may be several, are associated with the right hemisphere. Some have argued that since MPD often involves more than two personalities, it cannot be associated with the cerebral hemispheres, of which there are only two. But in many cases, there are only two major personalities, and in other cases the lesser personalities, as suggested by Henninger, may be subdivisions of the alter personality.[6]

Many cases of dissociative phenomena are of historical importance, yet remain useful for demonstrating the presence of two intact minds in one person. In 1889, Freud's contemporary, Pierre Janet, presented this fascinating case history:

> This young person was brought from the country to the hospital of Le Havre at the age of 19 because she was considered insane, and the hope of seeing her cured had almost been given up. The facts were that she had periods of convulsive attacks with delirium which lasted for days. . . . At the time preceding her menstruations, Marie's character changed; she became gloomy and violent, which was not in her habits, and suffered pains, nervous spasms, and shivering in her entire body. . . . At times, she would utter cries of terror, ceaselessly speaking of blood and fire, fleeing in order to escape the flames; at other times she would play as a child, speaking to her mother, climb on the stove or on the furniture, and create havoc in the ward. The delirium and the violent bodily contortions alternated with short periods of rest during 48 hours. The attack ended with vomiting blood several times, after which everything

came back approximately to normal. After one or two days of rest, Marie would quiet herself and remembered nothing of the episode.

After she had been hospitalized for eight months, Janet decided to hypnotize her:

It then occurred to me to put her into a deep somnambulic condition, a state where (as we have seen) it is possible to bring back seemingly forgotten memories, and thus I was able to find out the exact memory of an incident which had hitherto been only very incompletely known.

At the age of 13, she had had her first menstruation, but, as a result of a childish idea or of something she had heard and misunderstood, she imagined that there was some shame in it, and she tried a means of stopping the flow as soon as possible. About 20 hours after the beginning, she went out secretly and plunged herself into a big bucket of cold water. The success was complete; the menstruation was suddenly stopped, and in spite of a violent shivering, she was able to come back home. She was sick for a rather long time and had several days of delirium. However, everything settled down, and the menstruation did not appear again until five years later. When it reappeared it brought back the disturbances I observed. Now, if one compares the sudden stopping, the shivering, the pains she describes today in waking state, with what she describes in a somnambulic condition—which, incidentally, was confirmed from other sources—one comes to this conclusion: Every month, the scene of the cold bath repeats itself, brings forth the same stopping of the menstruation and a delirium which is, it is true, much more severe than previously, until a supplementary hemorrhage takes place through the stomach. But, in her normal state of consciousness, she knows nothing about all this, not even that the shivering is brought forth by the hallucination of cold. It is therefore probable that this scene takes place below consciousness, and from it the other disturbances erupt.[7]

First, Janet realized that the patient had "fixed subconscious ideas" or an intact, inner mind that operated on archaic, unrealistic premises. Second, when she was in her so-called delirium, Marie apparently would lose contact with her usual conscious mind, and her whole being would come under the conscious control of her inner mind.

HYPNOSIS

It is well known in psychology that certain highly hypnotizable people can be given a suggestion to not consciously remember a command and yet carry it out. This phenomenon strongly supports the notion of the subject's having two minds: one that hears, remembers, and carries out the hypnotic suggestion, and one that performs the command without knowing the real reason for its own actions. A number of EEG studies performed on hypnotic subjects suggest that different levels of activation of the hemispheres are involved in hypnotic phenomena.[8]

Stanford University psychologist Ernest Hilgard in the early 1970s performed a now-famous experiment. He hypnotized a number of highly hypnotizable subjects and had them put their hands in ice water. He gave the hypnotic suggestion that they would not experience the procedure as painful. He also suggested that they could perform what is called automatic writing, in which a person's hand writes in legible English while he is consciously fully engaged in another task and is consciously unaware of what is being written. As the subject's hand remained in the ice water, Hilgard at intervals asked if he were experiencing pain. The subjects consciously reported minor discomfort, but their automatic writing expressed that they were feeling intense pain. "Hidden observer" is the term Hilgard gave to this phenomenon. His subjects had an unconscious awareness of the pain that they were able to express through automatic writing.[9]

PSYCHOPHYSIOLOGICAL REACTIONS

Psychologist Matthew Erdelyi offers an interesting example of another situation demonstrating the existence of an inner autonomous mind. By way of a completely spontaneous experiment, Erdelyi saw how physiologic responses reveal complex and sophisticated thinking that is consciously inapparent to the person:

> Elizabeth, at this time a first year graduate student, was strikingly pretty. She had wavy blond hair, her eyes were deep blue, her skin was utterly free of blemishes. On a previous occasion, however, she had complained of a tendency to break out into a peculiar rash when intensely angry: First her neck and eventually her whole face would develop pink blotches that soon darkened into spots of red and scarlet.

The event of interest transpired during one of our weekly research conferences. She had been making rather poor progress, and I had invited a more advanced graduate student (who happened to be male) to our meeting, in the vague hope that he might be induced to join our project. This graduate student, who had just returned from a year's leave of absence, had never before seen Elizabeth. As soon as he entered the room it was clear that he was very taken with her. Unfortunately, he did not know how to handle the situation and attempted to make an impression on Elizabeth by adopting a superior, overbearing manner. He criticized Elizabeth's proposed experiment in altogether abrasive terms. . . . He interrupted most of her efforts to explain or defend her work, taking every opportunity to show off his expertise.

Some twenty minutes into the meeting, during which he ignored several attempts on my part to defuse the atmosphere, I suddenly noticed Elizabeth's neck, and then her face, turning into a mottled mass of pink, red, and scarlet splotches. I decided to put an immediate end to the research conference, suggesting to the graduate student that he summarize his major points in writing for future discussion. He had clearly noticed Elizabeth's dermal reaction, looked uncomfortable, and took his cue to leave eagerly.

But for Elizabeth's rash, it would have been impossible to deduce any untoward emotion; in every respect, in her overall demeanor, her expression, and her speech, she exuded a cheerful calm. I tried to smooth matters over and urged her not to be unduly angry at the graduate student. Elizabeth looked at me in surprise: "But I wasn't angry!"

I was unsure whether to drop the matter at this point or to pursue it further. Finally, curiosity compelled me to retort: "But Elizabeth, you have your famous rash all over your face and neck; you look like a pink leopard!"

"You are putting me on," she said. With a hint of annoyance, she reached into her pocketbook, took out her compact, and looked at herself. She started shaking her head and giggled in embarrassment. A normal blush lit up the pale rest of her face. "That's amazing," she said, "I was completely unaware of it!"[10]

There are many other examples from psychosomatic medicine that demonstrate a relationship between an inner mind and involuntary physiological functions. We discuss these more fully in Chapter 10, on heart disease.

Role of Trauma in the Dual-Brain Model

Psychological problems often result from the emotional injuries to one hemisphere and from the internal struggles and imbalances such injuries initiate. Many psychological insults of childhood and adulthood can injure one hemisphere more than the other. The damage often enhances or corrupts the power of the troubled side, while leaving the more mature side underdeveloped. This can lead to a destructive struggle between the two minds and to psychological problems.

We speculated in Chapter 3 about why one hemisphere might become more injured by trauma or abuse. Although scientists disagree about the rate at which the two hemispheres develop from birth to adulthood, it is likely that the two hemispheres develop on different timetables. It is also likely that the two hemispheres manifest different cognitive and emotional capacities at various stages of development. We can speculate that the developmental achievements of the hemispheres at the time of the trauma will influence how each hemisphere will be affected by the trauma. How and to what extent the hemispheres process and respond to the traumas seems dependent on the nature or type of traumatic experience. There appear to be exceptions when both hemispheres are adversely affected by the trauma, but the most common experience is for one hemisphere to be more mature emotionally and cognitively than the other.

Is it possible, as suggested by Martin Teicher, that if one side becomes injured, the other becomes "parentified"—much like children of alcoholic parents who must assume the role of the parent. Or could the hemisphere that deals actively with the trauma become injured to the point that its development is delayed or interfered with? In time, the other hemisphere may be able to proceed with its own development and achieve adult cognitive and emotional maturity. A traumatized child who was unprotected and alone during his childhood years may discover at some point, perhaps in early adulthood, that a new, mature mind has materialized. Some of my most rewarding moments in therapy come from teaching a person that not only has he survived and been removed from the old traumatizing circumstances, but also he has a strong, new ally within himself that has developed, even if not yet consciously recognized. This new ally is his more recently acquired mature mind.

In my clinical practice, I work closely with the inner minds of people who are troubled by their unresolved and often unacknowledged trauma. When a child is traumatized, the hemispheres may tend to disconnect emotionally to some degree. The troubled side then can remain isolated and stuck in the trauma. The abuse might stop the natural maturation and development of one hemisphere and cause it to remain immature to some degree. That hemisphere can continue to resemble an unhappy person, one who constantly lives in the past and comes to believe only in the worst (perhaps so as not to risk disappointment by expecting better). As this traumatized, immature mind stews for years cut off from current realities, which have often improved over the past, its intrapsychic power and influence can grow.

Martin Teicher has suggested that early stress can affect the functioning of the corpus callosum, the large bundle connecting the two hemispheres, which leads to decreased hemispheric integration and a pattern of unusual hemispheric dominance. Teicher and his associates hypothesized that early abuse might adversely affect the development of the corpus callosum, and they embarked on a study to examine the size and structure of the corpus callosum in fifty-one consecutive pediatric psychiatric admissions to McLean. Each of these children had had an MRI as part of their hospital workup, and Teicher had each of these MRIs reviewed by an expert (unaware of the study's intentions) to determine the size and physical structure of the corpus callosum. From the medical records, colleagues unaware of the MRI results were able to determine the presence and extent of physical, sexual, psychological abuse, or neglect. They found that in males, either neglect or physical abuse was associated with a 25 percent reduction in sections of the corpus callosum. Females who suffered neglect had large increases in the size of the corpus callosum. Teicher suggests that these increases may also represent an abnormality, perhaps due to tangled fibers. We can only speculate about the meaning of the gender differences and why all forms of abuse were not associated with abnormalities of the corpus callosum. This study is a first important step in exploring the possible effects of abuse on the corpus callosum, and it lends support to the idea that a traumatized hemisphere may in some circumstances become relatively isolated from the effects of the nega-tive experience on the development by the corpus callosum.[11]

Most of the traumas to which my patients were exposed occurred in childhood, when we are most vulnerable and therefore most easily traumatized. Children rarely have the power to avoid trauma and are poorly equipped to tolerate it when it does strike.

Let me offer an analogy. Suppose I am watching television with a six-year-old child, and suddenly the program depicts graphic violence. I am used to seeing such violence on television and am an adult with a few good coping skills, but the child is unable to deal with what she has seen. I will sleep well that night, but she will have nightmares that may linger for months. We both viewed the same scene, but it had very dif-ferent meanings to us. To me it would probably be ordinary; to her it might be catastrophic.

But trauma does occur in adults, of course, and severe trauma in adults can have devastating psychological consequences. I have treated a number of Vietnam veterans and have come to appreciate the effects that the war had on their inner minds.

HOW TRAUMA AFFECTS THE BRAIN

Perhaps the first step in trying to identify how trauma affects the brain is to clarify what we mean by trauma. Some psychologists describe two kinds of trauma: life-threatening, such as extreme physical abuse, vio-lence, or disasters; and critical incidents, which cover such common events as the death of a grandparent, school-related anxiety, or a play-ground incident. The most common trauma that I see in my practice is from the psychological effects of being a child in a dysfunctional fam-ily. I prefer to keep the definition of trauma related to ordinary life ex-perience, and I think we generally mean by trauma any event that hurts or harms us—an offhand comment we possibly took the wrong way (or possibly the right way); a shove, a punch, a stabbing, a shoot-ing; a look, a statement, a series of looks and statements. If we cope well with the trauma, we may grow from it and may not be harmed by it. But traumas that are more than we can deal with (and what we can deal with will depend on our age, health, allies, and other factors) will harm us. Some traumas, like rape, incest, or a bludgeoning, are always severe and harmful, although the degree of harm depends on the relation between our coping abilities and the severity of the trauma. We should not forget that we are often injured (and therefore traumatized) by neglect, rejection, or humiliation, assaults that are often difficult to detect, especially when we are children. The effects of profound trauma (war or incest) are qualitatively and quantitatively different from those less dramatic, such as neglect and rejection, but I believe that they all share enough common characteristics to discuss them together here.

When we are traumatized, our brain registers the pain. In response to the pain, we develop two types of responses: cognitive and emotional. Cognitively, we decide to try to avoid hot stoves or pointed people—whatever has hurt us. Emotionally we may be showered with a variety of affects, from anger to sadness to despair. With cognition, we have a sense of being active. With emotions, they seem to happen to us, and as Goleman points out, they may erupt with great speed.[12]

One of the most common emotions to follow trauma and pain is fear or anxiety. Generally we refer to this emotion as fear when we believe we understand its source and as anxiety when we don't. Fortunately, fear (or anxiety) is one of the best-studied emotions from the neurophysiological perspective. In his book, *The Emotional Brain,* Joseph LeDoux of New York University gives an excellent review of this well-developed field, in which he has led much of the research. LeDoux has shown that fear responses involve largely three brain structures: the orbital frontal cortex, the hippocampus, and the amygdala. When trauma occurs, essentially two types of memories are laid down—one in the amygdala and one in the hippocampus. The memories in the amygdala are called *implicit memories,* because they are beyond our consciousness. When after a trauma we return to the scene, we are likely to feel nausea or other physical feelings of emotional distress, and we will feel these even though we know we are now safe. This is an example of an implicit memory of the trauma, and such memories are stored in the amygdala. Interestingly, the amygdala not only retains a covert memory of the trauma but is connected to the autonomic nervous system and is capable of evoking the adrenaline-mediated "flight or fight" response. A part of that response is the release of adrenaline, which comes back to the amygdala and acts to reinforce the traumatic memory. The amygdala also stimulates the release of the stress hormone cortisol. LeDoux believes that memories set down in the amygdala may be indelible, an assertion we will return to.

The hippocampus, a structure physically near to the amygdala, helps to form long-term memories and is associated with conscious or explicit memories. Both the orbital frontal cortex and the hippocampus tend to try to calm the amygdala. The hippocampus tries to reduce the release of cortisol. When the amygdala cannot be calmed but rather overpowers the other centers, then the person is likely to enter a state of panic. In this state, cortisol release continues; over time, it can cause damage and even physical shrinkage to the hippocampus.

The orbital frontal cortex is more related to cognition and to the interaction of emotion and cognition, and will attempt to inhibit the excited amygdala. LeDoux points out that cognition allows us to turn from reaction (emotion) to action (decision). When the cortex learns that safety has been achieved, it tries to override what the amygdala has learned through suppression of the lower center.[13]

THE DUAL-BRAIN MODEL AND THE BIOLOGY OF FEAR

Both cerebral hemispheres, left and right, have a cortex, an amygdala, and a hippocampus. The dual-brain model accommodates the biology of fear by appreciating that each hemisphere can physically respond separately to a perceived danger. Each hemisphere has a cortex closely connected and related to its lower centers. On each side, for instance, the cortex and the amygdala can struggle for control.[14]

Neurosurgeon Pierre Gloor, of the Montreal Neurological Institute, has placed electrodes in patients who are undergoing brain surgery for temporal lobe epilepsy, and he has been able electrically to stimulate the amygdala on both the left and right sides in thirty-five patients. In about half of the patients, stimulating an area of the amygdala elicited experiential phenomena, such as an old memory or an emotion. Interestingly, stimulating the same patient on both sides almost always elicited different results. In one dramatic case, a twenty-year-old man whose right amygdala was stimulated, a memory of a traumatic event on a cliff by the seaside and associated fear were elicited. When his left amygdala was stimulated, he hallucinated odors and felt "exasperated," but did not experience a memory or fear. Another patient had an experience when his left but not his right amygdala was stimulated. Although we cannot be certain how to interpret data from brain stimulation, stimulation of the amygdala almost always is associated with negative emotions, especially fear, and in the same person the two sides appear to respond differently, with the side of the greater fear varying among patients.[15]

LeDoux pointed out that the hippocampus can be damaged by high chronic levels of the stress hormone cortisol. Usually the damage, which results in shrinkage of the hippocampus (detected by MRI), is asymmetrical, and in different studies, on different groups of patients, the side of the shrinkage has varied. For example, one study showed an 8 percent shrinkage on the right side in twenty-six Vietnam veterans. But another study of Vietnam veterans found a bilateral reduction in hippocampal size, with slightly more on the left side. And seventeen patients with PTSD from sexual abuse had a 12 percent shrinkage on the left side. Thus, studies in patients with PTSD have shown shrinkage of the hippocampus as LeDoux pointed out, but interestingly the shrinkage was on different sides in different patients.[16]

Think back to my interview with AA, the split-brain patient. On one side, he was still upset by the bullies, but the other side treated the childhood experiences as a mild annoyance that he barely registered. Could this suggest that his amygdala-cortical interactions are different on his two sides? We do not have enough information to determine if the differences are in the two amygdalae, cortices, or hippocampi, or even in combinations and interactions of these structures. In both hemispheres, each mind is an emergent property of all the brain structures on that side, and important among those brain structures surely are the cortex, the amygdala, and the hippocampus.

If we reconsider the Vietnam veteran who thought my plant was the jungle, it seems that we have a few struggles going on. One is perhaps between the orbital frontal cortex (and the hippocampus), trying to calm the amygdala on each side, and the other struggle is between the entire left mind and the entire right mind. In dual-brain therapy, I emphasize the struggles and relationships between the left and right

minds, realizing that both emerge from the workings of many underlying brain structures.

The Location of the Unconscious Mind

Not only is the *nature* of the different minds important in the dual-
brain model, but also their *relationship* is critical to the expression of
the person's total personality. In Harold's case, his immature mind
functioned as an "unconscious mind," inducing neurotic behaviors and
anxieties and sabotaging his more mature mind. Harold was completely unaware of his immature mind, and yet it had a great impact on
his life. It was this mind's suffering from his mother's mistreatment that
made him depressed, self-loathing, and unable to commit to relationships. This mind was simply doing what it believed it had to do to survive in the kind of world where contempt and rejection were the rule.

When I say that Harold was upset by his mother's behavior, I
should be more specific and say that Harold's inner mind felt very rejected, but his more adult mind for the most part did not. His conscious mind came to see me not because he was upset by his mother's
past behavior, but because he could not achieve intimacy and had periods of depression. He was unable to achieve intimacy because his
inner mind had the power to interfere covertly with his feelings and
behavior. That is, his conscious mind was affected by inhibitions and
painful feelings sent to it by his inner mind.

I call the ideas and feelings in Harold's immature mind "neurotic,"
meaning that they were based not on a present reality but on a past experience that was no longer present except in the constructs of his
inner mind. If a person is anxious and doesn't want to get married, but
has a cogent, realistic reason (perhaps the partner has repeatedly acted
abusively), I would not call the behavior or emotion neurotic. And if
he chose to end the relationship, I would not see that as an imperative
reason to embark on psychotherapy.

When an immature mind dominates a person's whole personality,
I would *not* refer to it as an unconscious mind. For example, if Harold's
immature mind took over, and he became chronically irritable, anxious, sullen, and cantankerous as a result, it would be difficult to call
his immature mind *unconscious* because it would be in full control of

his conscious personality. We can say that he wasn't conscious of being motivated by past traumas with his mother. In this sense, his immature mind was motivated by factors beyond his awareness and hence was unconscious. But in this latter case, we should not call his "dominant" immature mind "the unconscious mind"; rather, we should call it his immature mind affected by unconscious factors. That is, to call anything that is not held in conscious awareness "the unconscious mind" would be a serious mistake. For example, when my doctor strikes my knee with his reflex hammer, my lower leg gives a kick. This is a reflex. I am not consciously causing the reflex, but to refer to it as occurring in my unconscious mind would be meaningless. The reflex arc is not a mind; it has no thoughts or feelings. As we work our way up the nervous system, we find more and more complex reflexes, but we have to get to the cerebral hemispheres before we can find an area of the brain that could definitely support a mind. There are lower brain centers, such as the thalamus, hypothalamus, or the amygdala, that perform complex functions, but they probably do not by themselves constitute a mind—an integrated center with intentions, feelings, and actions. Harold's immature mind could be dominated by his right-sided amygdala, which may retain vivid, archaic traumatic memories of his mother's rejections, but I would not consider the products of his right amygdala as a mind, and therefore I would not call it "the unconscious mind," even though it probably plays an important covert role in producing the immaturity of his right-sided mind. For me, the unconscious mind should be an intact mind that acts covertly, but in an integrated manner with well-developed thoughts and feelings.

What is the difference between an intact mind and a lower brain center, such as the hippocampus or amygdala? In the first instance, Harold has a mature mind that is being troubled by his covert immature mind. His immature mind is a complete mind. It has cognition (thoughts) and feelings (emotion), and like an immature person has a tendency to overgeneralize and obsessively hold onto ideas. A lower brain center like the hippocampus or amygdala can contain memories and perform mental functions that affect mentation, but they are not minds in and of themselves.

Do children have unconscious minds? Consider young children who tend to be more emotional than mature adults; their emotions more easily overpower their thoughts. A five-year-old child, heart-broken over his mother's attitude, may have difficulty making the connection between his mother and his pain, and yet his pain is real and it affects his life dramatically. The roots of his pain are not understood and in that sense are not conscious, but I don't hypothesize an intact, even smaller child inside him, and so I would not refer to his inarticulate pain as coming from his "unconscious mind." I would see it as coming from elements in his mind and brain beyond his awareness. The mental properties of the two hemispheres in children are unstudied, but I suspect both are similar (less differentiated) and both childlike.

Freud's Unconscious—and Mine

THE PSYCHOANALYTIC VIEW

Psychoanalyst Ruth Munroe has written on Freud's concept of the unconscious:

> Freud does *not* conceive of an "unconscious mind" as a separate, unchangeable entity somehow inhabiting our mortal flesh. . . . It is mentioned here as a common misinterpretation of psychoanalytic doctrine, understandable because in all psychoanalytic literature conscious and unconscious processes are informally contrasted and goal-directedness is ascribed to each with some separateness—in fact, often with complete antagonism. The popular dichotomy, however, is far too simple. . . .
>
> . . . For all schools the unconscious is a process—or better, processes—conceived within a dynamic (motivational) theory of human behavior. It is *never* thought of as an isolated entity which can be studied independently of the total personality, according to its own peculiar laws.[17]

Freud, in his later years, saw the unconscious as essentially consisting largely of the id, a seething caldron of primitive drives and emotions. He also discussed an unconscious aspect of the ego that acted as a censor, keeping some painful ideas from becoming conscious. But Freud was never clear about the boundaries between the conscious and unconscious aspects of the ego, or about their specific properties or relationships. And certainly Freud never described the unconscious aspect of the ego or any other aspect of the unconscious mind as an intact, inner being.[18]

Freud saw repression as necessary to the construction and maintenance of the unconscious. He felt that people often had sexual or other unacceptable impulses, which needed to be repressed from conscious awareness. But who or what instructs the unconscious to repress or censor some ideas? Does the censor decide what material must be repressed? If the unconscious can make decisions and can oppose the conscious mind, why can't it be studied in isolation? How could the analysts describe the unconscious, tell us it was primitive or childlike, had wishes, memories, fantasies, and yet say it did not exist in actuality, but existed only as processes?[19]

A psychoanalyst may have diagnosed Harold as suffering neurotic symptoms such as his fear of intimacy and his self-loathing. These symptoms would be conceptualized as coming from unconscious conflicts. The analyst would try to establish an empathic relationship and would encourage Harold to free-associate—that is, say whatever came into his mind. From his free associations, connections are made (called associations), and from these the analyst may make interpretations. The relationship between the analyst and the patient is also examined in the light of how Harold will tend to view it as similar to his relationships with his parents. The relationship with the analyst thus contains this transference, and by examining the transference relationship, more is learned about the unconscious mind.

Ultimately the analyst would come to see Harold's unconscious as a primitive id or drive state that intensely wants to be gratified by a loving mother and becomes desperately hurt and angry by her failures in this regard. These emotions are overwhelming in Harold's present unconscious and lead to depression and regression of his ego, or conscious executive mind. Since his mother was hostile, a part of her was internalized in his unconscious, and it is her introject (the internalized image of his mother) that becomes a part of Harold's superego and violently criticizes him, producing his self-loathing. In psychoanalytic terms, Harold's hesitancy about marriage would be interpreted as his unconscious fear of and rage at his mother, his conflicted need for her love, and his fear of her rejection. A further interpretation would describe his fear of his mother's accepting him and moving him into com-

petition with his already partially spurned father. All of this is unknown to Harold because an unconscious part has repressed it in order
to protect him from this knowledge, which is too distressing to face.
Unconsciously, Harold fears defeating his father and winning his
mother's love, but he also unconsciously longs for this. This is a classic
unconscious conflict.

As the primitive contents of the unconscious slowly become revealed and are worked on and integrated, Harold's symptoms would be
expected to decrease as his insight increases, and he should emerge a
more integrated, mature, healthier individual.

THE DUAL-BRAIN CONCEPT OF THE UNCONSCIOUS

My work with Harold, in many ways similar to a psychoanalytic approach, in other ways takes a much different conceptual path and therapeutic course. In either approach, Harold should be treated with
profound empathy. The quality of the therapeutic relationship is critical to both forms of treatment. That is, in both, Harold should feel well
regarded, respected, liked, even loved in the therapeutic sense—
deeply and genuinely cared about and appreciated, in the healthy
brotherly or sisterly sense. This solid relationship should anchor the
treatment and lay the foundation for the trust that is essential for any
substantive treatment.

The differences begin with the concepts around the nature of the
unconscious mind. In the dual-brain model, the unconscious is an intact mind (albeit immature) with its own thoughts, feelings, and actions (either urged or taken), a mind we physically associate with one
of the cerebral hemispheres. In the psychoanalytic model, the unconscious is a vague process, as Ruth Munroe described it, rather than an
entity or actual mind.

I believe that my idea that Harold has an immature mind, which is
evoked by a lateralized pair of glasses, can encompass and clarify the
psychoanalytic concept of the unconscious mind. I see free associations as feelings or ideas coming from the immature side. The analysts'
"interpretations" are actually the deciphering of the thoughts of
Harold's immature mind. The "transference" is the relationship between Harold's immature mind and the therapist, and I agree that understanding and interpreting and working on transference issues can

be extremely valuable for understanding and communicating with Harold's immature side. I don't believe Harold has an "id" per se; rather, I believe that his immature side is simply immature, childlike, and therefore primitive. I believe that the immature part of him does copy some of his mother's negative, abusive behavior and does attack him, but to call this an "introject" or a part of a "superego" seems to me to miss the point. We all have a tendency to copy powerful figures, especially when we are children. Harold's immature side is merely copying his mother because she is so powerful and important to him. And like a child, Harold has a tendency to blame himself. Children do this all the time. I don't think we need to invoke the idea of a punitive superego as the punisher. I think Harold's immature mind can punish himself very well all by itself. And I don't believe that the term "repression" properly captures the struggle between Harold's mature mind and his immature mind. His mature mind is trying to suppress his immature side, but he does so with varying success.

The aim of dual-brain therapy is to mend the archaic, destructive ideas and emotions of the mind on the troubled side, to teach it that it is safer and more valuable than it learned during some traumatic experiences, and to help it appropriately grieve and come to terms with its actual losses and disappointments so that it can appreciate its abundant gains. I teach patients how to recognize and listen for the mind in their troubled hemisphere, and then how to speak to it—out loud! I show patients also how to strengthen their more mature minds and, most important, how to improve the relationship between the two sides.

The troubled side is not an ill-defined confluence of id, superego, and introject; rather, it is an intact mind that can't get over the trauma, even when removed from it, because it continues to expect retraumatization. Initially, this mind may have withdrawn from the world around it, making it even more difficult for it to learn that the world may have changed for the better since the traumas. This is especially true for childhood traumas, which are often externally removed with the passage of time and the physical and mental maturity that comes with development, but can remain covertly present because the mind on the troubled side fails to notice or trust the improvement.

Dual-brain therapy often entails a reaching out to the mind of the troubled hemisphere and attempting, through patience, persistence, and a loving, mature, informed attitude, to teach it that it no longer has to fear abuse and no longer has to attempt to protect itself with the archaic defenses that have become the source of its new pain and problems. The advance of dual-brain therapy over traditional therapies derives from its demonstration of the troubled side as an interior, complex person. When it operates covertly, it becomes an unconscious mind—not a vague construct, but rather an intact though often troubled mind.

In the chapters that follow, I apply the ideas of dual-brain therapy to several major, common emotional disorders. With a number of stories in these chapters, I include transcripts of interviews I had with patients while they wore the lateralized glasses. These transcripts are not typical of therapy sessions per se, but rather are intended to demonstrate that the unusual findings with the glasses occurred in many patients and in many different disorders.

CHAPTER 5

Apprehension

Joe came to my office sweating, wringing his hands, and pacing. He had a new job and felt a lot of emotional pressure there. Joe had trouble thinking clearly and trouble performing his work. He avoided meeting people because he felt it is apparent to others that something was wrong with him. (He was right. His emotional discomfort was apparent, though perhaps not quite as apparent as he felt.) He had become so apprehensive about being called to task for poor performance, about being humiliated, about being fired that he had trouble noticing that something made him anxious in the first place, before it began to feed voraciously on itself. "I've been feeling this way for two months, and as far as I can tell it is only getting worse," he told me on his first visit to my office.

Everyone knows what it's like to be scared. Some of us have been very scared, perhaps after an automobile accident, perhaps during an examination for which we were ill prepared, perhaps on a date when we seemed to care more than the other person. We all know the sickening feeling in the gut, physical clumsiness, mental cloudiness, and general sense of distress that we call anxiety. Some people seem to experience this frequently, while others feel it only when they fall off their white horse. But there can be little doubt that this emotion is pervasive throughout the human species. For those of us, like Joe, who experience this feeling with an intensity and duration that becomes distressing, this ordinary feeling can become a problem of catastrophic proportions.

Is it a chemical imbalance that first made Joe this way? A genetic

defect, perhaps passed on by a long-dead ancestor? Was Joe simply suffering castration anxiety, id anxiety, separation anxiety, or superego
anxiety, any one of which is posited as the outcome of repressed, unconscious, sexual, or aggressive drives? Had he been covertly condi-
tioned to be fearful, much like Pavlov's dogs learned to salivate
whenever a bell rang, even when it rang without the food with which
it used to be paired?

How could I help Joe? His primary care doctor had already tried
him on Prozac, Zoloft, Effexor, Klonapin, Xanax, and Ativan. There
was behavioral therapy to teach him to relax, but relaxing only made
him more agitated. A cognitive therapist could teach him to recognize
his negative, defeating thoughts, but those seemed to be the only
thoughts he had. As for psychoanalysis, Joe's managed care company
expelled all of the analysts from its panel. And there's psychotherapy,
but the nature and quality of this enterprise varies so tremendously
from therapist to therapist that it's hard to define what it is or what to
expect from it.

How Dual-Brain Therapy Can Help

In our first session, I learned from Joe that his father had been a tough
man in public, but at home he felt nothing but disrepect from his wife,
whose approval he desperately sought. Joe's mother favored him
among her three children, but his father had developed a harsh, con-
descending, even belligerent attitude toward his son. Joe responded in
part by copying his father, growing into a bully at school. Toward his
father, Joe expressed defiance through mischievous behavior at home.
Predictably, Joe's father responded to the childish acting out with severe physical punishment. Although Joe tacitly assumed that the
ridicule and physical punishment were warranted, he could not articulate why. Joe had never connected his father's attitude and treatment
as possibly related to his adult symptoms. When I suggested such a
connection, Joe laughed and said, "You sound like a typical shrink
wanting to put the blame conveniently on my parents." He felt no
connection between his past and his symptoms. Yet halfway through
his first session, Joe commented, "I think the way I feel at work is a lot
like the way I felt as a child when my mother sent me to my room to

wait for my father to come home to punish me." He explained that he had not realized how painful still was his father's continuing disapproval, couched now in an appearance of helpfulness. His father still ridiculed Joe. His hair was too long or too short, or too messed or too combed.

The humiliations Joe felt were devastating, echoing what he anticipated at work. His longing for his father's approval was similar to his longing for acceptance at work. Joe began to sob, though he said, "I don't understand why I'm crying." When he pulled himself together, he expressed bewilderment at his crying and skepticism about the connections he had just made between his father and his anxiety.

"How are you feeling right now?" I asked.

"I'm doing a lot better than I was earlier today, but I'm still anxious, and the emotions are just beneath the surface. I'm afraid they could come out at any time. That's basically how I feel. My emotional state is high right now."

"And how do you feel you'll do with the job right now?"

"I can do well with this job. There's no doubt about it. Obviously I have normal anxieties about walking into a place with new people and stuff like that. I've always felt inferior in some ways and superior in other ways. It's nervousness—natural anxiety."

"Joe, I want you to try on these special glasses. They're going to be the rage in Paris."

"You want me to try these on?"

"Yes. Just pick either pair."

"What are these?"

"Just try one of them on."

Joe put on a pair of goggles taped so that he could only see out of the left side (right hemisphere). Almost immediately he took a deep sigh.

"How do you feel now?"

"I'm definitely very nervous, and when you look out this side, there's an optimism, a certain life affirming. You've got a chance, you know. You can go in there and do the job."

"How do you feel you'll do?"

"Well, I think I can do well on the job. I'll go to work and work hard at it. I'm gonna do my best. I can do the job."

"Try the other goggles [left hemisphere]."

There was a thirty-second pause, then he sighed and said, "Ah, man. This is a, ah . . . I wouldn't want to go to work wearing these."

"What do you feel?"

"Well, I feel a, I feel more. . . . the longer you wear them, the more you get subdued. I'd like to say I think I could still do the job, because I just said that before, but you don't have as optimistic an attitude from this spectrum."

"What do you feel?"

"I just feel sadness on this side. I mean, this kind of brings up the feelings of how I felt earlier today."

"Tell me."

"Just pain and fear and insecurity, and a lack of confidence, and then sadness. Turned to sadness."

"What's the sadness about?"

"It's about . . . just about [he's crying and having difficulty speaking] ah, it's never doing what I could do, never achieving any goals, running away from things, never . . ."

"Not being good enough?"

"Well, knowing you're good enough, but being lazy, self-centered."

"Is that how you feel, or how you feel you're being accused?"

"Ah, that's tough to say."

"How sad do you feel?"

"I felt very sad there for a while. The crying actually helped a little bit, I think; it's kind of a release. But out of this side there's a . . ."

"How much sadness are you feeling at the moment?"

"I'm sad."

"How would you measure it: none, mild, moderate, quite a bit, or extreme?"

"Moderate."

"Moderate now?"

"Right. Quite a bit before. I mean, in talking to people you just . . . Obviously this all stems from my parents [crying] really. I mean, when I think of them, that's when it comes up."

"You feel it right now?"

"Yeah, now I do."

"You feel it quite a bit?"

"Ah," he sighs deeply in pain. "Yeah."

"Switch to the other pair of goggles." There is a thirty-second pause. Then I ask, "What do you feel?"

"Hey, I feel better a little bit, right away. Now let me just try to think of my parents. (ten-second pause) It blocks out certain wavelengths of pain, which is interesting."

"What are you feeling now?"

"Oh, I feel better now like this, definitely. I mean, I just tried to shift gears into thoughts about my father and stuff like that. If I were wearing the glasses on the other side, I probably would be weeping right now."

"And what do you feel right now?"

"Just a bundle of nerves, but I feel better with these on. I just feel I could be in more control like this. I could deal right now. Before, it kind of obliterates your ability to function. I could be sad and deal with it now."

"Can you think about your parents now?"

"Yeah, I can actually. I can think of them in a more reasonable way, and I can constructively criticize them. I don't know if that makes any sense or not."

"How do you understand the sadness on the other side?"

"That's a mystery to me."

"What is that part of you saying?"

"It just comes up to the depths, and it's so hard to explain to other people—you or my mother. When she called today, she was very kind. She wanted to take me out to lunch. She was very worried about me. When I called, when she called . . . tremendous concern. I just didn't know how to explain it to her."

"Do you feel that anxiety now?"

"I just felt it big time."

"Just now?"

"Yeah, but in a way, I could talk about it more than the lugubrious other side. I still felt the emotion. It's an emotional thing. I just don't know. I don't know where it comes from. I just know what the fuck happened to me to where I'm just so prone. I mean kids get beaten all the fuckin' time, ya know. Why am I so prone to fuckin' depression? Why does it hurt me so much. I think I'm a fucking phony. Well, (laughs) at least I can laugh a little on this side."

"You feel like you're a phony or something?"

"Yeah. [He sobs] I think there's a tremendous part of me that just thinks it's never going to be truly at home with other people in a warm, loving environment, where I'm not a little bit uncomfortable, unless I'm drinking with them or something. There's a part of me that maybe will always feel things a little different—maybe sometimes a little better, maybe a lot of times a little worse. I don't know. I know that I'm gonna be able to come to grips with this thing. I think the stress of the new job and the old job and my father—maybe it's bringing something to the surface that was here a couple of times before. I just know I want to be able to come to grips with it and just be able to walk out of my house and jump in my car and just do what I want to do and not be driven by thoughts of what other people want me to do or what—you know, not be my own person, not be driven by other people, like a constant search for love and acceptance, which basically I've done in a lot of ways . . . as bizarre as that may sound."

"Hm, I think that's true. I think that's what happened. Is there a part of you that can see your value?"

"Yeah, there is. I know that; I have a lot of friends, and they're wonderful, and we have wonderful times together. Yet sometimes I'm still uncomfortable with them."

"How are you feeling now? Is there a difference with the glasses?"

"Yeah. I feel a little more laid back and relaxed. Once again, that huge swell of emotion calmed me down. I remember when I was depressed in the past, I would sit there and bring on the tears because there would be some kind of solace to the pain after . . . there certainly is now."

"How do you feel about yourself right now? Do you feel a legitimate person, or do you feel illegitimate? How do you regard yourself?"

"I feel like there's a thousand volts of electricity running through my body. But I am a legitimate person—there's no doubt about it."

"Do you feel that on the other side?"

"It's tougher on the other side. It's definitely tougher on the other side. There's no doubt about it."

"What do you feel on the other side?"

"The other side is lugubrious; it's down in a hollow somewhere. The longer you have them on, you are kind of being sucked down inside there. Over here, you can still have the emotion, but I'm a little more pumped up on this side."

"Do you feel more approval of yourself on this side?"

"Yeah, I do. I feel more approval, but I'm still extremely anxious. I don't feel I could get up and go wild right now, but I definitely do feel . . ."

"And how about going to work after the weekend?"

"Yeah, but I'll be very nervous there. I know that."

"You feel nervous now?"

"Yeah, I feel edgy."

"How will you do at the job?"

"Well, I'm gonna go in there and give it my best."

"What do you predict?"

"I predict success. I know I can go in there and do it. I know this is something I can do."

"Okay, can you let the other side [his troubled left brain] look out this window?"

"Well, that side is kinda looking out this window. That's why I'm not as upbeat right now. That side is definitely pushing over to this side right now. There's no doubt about it, which is causing doubts. I don't know if that's something that makes sense to you or not."

"It does."

"Because this guy's definitely coming out here. I can definitely feel it."

"Can you let him look out and see? Can you hold your confidence while he looks out?"

"That's very hard. But I'm trying right now."

"Why don't you try the other glasses."

He puts on the pair of glasses that stimulate his left hemisphere, and thirty seconds later, I ask, "How do you feel about the job, about going back to the job?"

He sighs, "Um, similar to the other side—about nervousness, anxiousness. I mean, I don't want to walk into the job with this kind of heightened anxiety when I walk in to meet my boss."

"Is the anxiety the same on this side as on the other side?"

"No, it's fuckin' movin' on up! As we speak, it's movin' on up!"

"What's it about?"

"I don't know. It's comin' up right through here" (pointing to his gut).

"Is it about feeling humiliated?"

"No. You know what it's about? It's about the nervousness of meeting someone who's my boss and about meeting people."

"And why does meeting people, meeting your boss, make you nervous?"

"I really don't know. It just does."

"Is there a threat there?"

"Yes."

"What's the threat? What's the harm?"

"The threat of not being liked."

"Yeah, right."

"And being . . . and failing."

"And being humiliated?"

"I don't feel the threat of humiliation. I feel the threat of . . . I have to go there in a couple of days, and I don't want to be like this. This is what's freaking me out right now because now I gotta go in there. I don't want to fucking feel like this."

"What's the thing that you're afraid of?"

"Just the simple fact that I'm unworthy."

"Yeah, you're unworthy, right, and they're gonna see that."

He laughs, "Yeah."

"And they're gonna blow smoke in your face, right?

"Yeah."

"Are we hitting it? Is that what it is?"

"Yeah, I mean, it's doubt. Basically, it's doubt."

"They're gonna criticize you. Your tie's crooked, and you've got the wrong pants on, and you're no good. Are we hitting it?"

"Well, yeah, tie's crooked and no good, that's not basically it, you know. That's something my father said to me. I know what you mean."

"But is it the same sort of thing that you expected?"

"It's more deep rooted. It's more like they could see through me, into my phoniness."

"Right, but remember on the other side. Let's check the other side."

He changes to the left-sided goggles, which stimulate the right brain.

"What are they gonna see?" I ask.

"This guy's awful strong over here. No, now that you say that, I got more of a chance out of this side than I do out of the other side. A much better chance. I wish I could just isolate this side."

"What are they gonna see when they look at you?"

"Well, they're gonna see a guy, a good guy, well spoken, who's extremely nervous."

"Are they gonna see right through you?"

"No. I understand what you're saying. No, they're not gonna see right through me, 'cause there's nothing . . .'"

"Nothing to see through?"

"Right," he laughs.

"You're a substantial person."

"Right."

"You're nervous, right?"

"I'm nervous to a fault."

"But you're nervous because you feel they may see through you."

"But they're not gonna see through me because if I sit down to talk like this, I feel I could carry a conversation with anybody. If they ask me a question, I can respond to it."

"On the other side, you don't feel that way?"

"No, on the other side, that was different."

"So what do we make of that?"

"This side goes through the world and functions and goes down and works out at the gym and gets along with people and stuff like that in a substantial way. But there's also a huge side that is keeping me from anything that I would consider. Playing basketball is what little kids do; I can do that. This other side can cripple any efforts to try to improve yourself."

"What we're saying is that one side is very nervous and expects to be ridiculed."

"Yes, no doubt about it. One side is so sad it's unbelievable. It almost killed me today."

"The other side?"

"The other side. This side can be sad too; it's sad for the other side. That's what's going on right now."

Joe was much improved after our first session, and his symptoms were largely alleviated by his third. Our work was not finished, although he had become essentially asymptomatic; we still had work to do on the underlying problem to keep it from recurring. When his managed care company wouldn't support his care after ten sessions because of the reduction in his symptoms, he had to cut back to monthly sessions, and his symptoms erupted again. With renewed authorization from his insurance company, we resumed our work and again quickly got on top of his symptoms. We continue to work toward resolving his underlying problem. Essentially we continue to teach the immature side of him that he is now safe and valuable, and this side of him is slowly but continuously assimilating our message.

Causes for Anxiety Disorders

In my practice, I have seen many people with anxiety disorders, and each has resembled Joe in most important aspects. Each attributed his anxiety to his "nature"—in other words, to a personal weakness, be it moral, chemical, or genetic.

It is possible that Joe and my other patients suffer chemical imbalances or genetic deficiencies, but the capacity to become anxious is universal. Recall the frightened, haggard, and depressed appearance of the U.S. Air Force pilots captured and put on Iraqi television during the Gulf War. These well-trained, highly selected, brave men were reduced to obviously terrified, defeated souls, as would any other person subjected to torture. Anxiety is a response to a significant threat of danger; it is part of our biological nature. Joe and my other patients who have suffered persistent anxiety are exercising this same universal capacity. The difference between Joe and the pilots is that the threat is obvious in regard to the pilots but not to Joe. (At times psychologists refer to this emotion as "fear" when the source is known and as "anxiety" when it is not. But the pilots suffered anxiety even though they had an obvious reason for their emotional state. The term "anxiety" implies a greater level of impairment than fear.)

Initially Joe's anxiety appeared spontaneously generated, much as bacteria in broth were thought before the microscope was invented to spring spontaneously from nothing. But Joe had a reason for his anxiety. In part of his mind (his left brain) he believed he would always be humiliated, just as he was throughout his life by his father. This is the danger he anticipated. A struggle within him began as the more adult part of him (in his right brain), which does not experience such humiliation, became prominent.

Dual-brain therapy, aided by goggles, helped Joe to learn that his anxiety was a natural response to danger perceived in one hemisphere of the brain. We learned that the perspective on life that the troubled hemisphere harbors often mirrors the perspective it had as a traumatized child.

EEG studies confirmed that the goggles stimulate the hemisphere opposite to the side out of which we can see. It is also apparent that with each pair of goggles, Joe's personality and view of himself in the world were altered. Accordingly, as in most of the severely traumatized patients in my study, the mind in his left brain saw himself as vulnerable and insubstantial. The mind of his right brain was more adult, more reasonable. Thus, the origins of Joe's anxiety were obscured because he tried to understand it with his right brain, while the problem existed in his left, and there was poor communication between the two sides.

Joe and many of my other patients were anxious because a part of them associated with one hemisphere was frightened; they saw the world as they had seen it as a child—as much more dangerous than their capacity to protect themselves. In Chapter 8, we will learn about patients who have distorted views of the world in both hemispheres. This condition can make patients more difficult to help with dual-brain therapy.

In many important ways, Freud was wrong when he suggested that neurotic anxiety is usually a signal to the conscious mind that the id manifests sexual or aggressive urges in conflict with the superego's moral standards. Although Joe was caught in a triangle between his parents as a child, he didn't appear to be significantly troubled by repressed desires for his mother or rage against his father. He became troubled in one hemisphere by the effects of real events: his father's ridicule and beatings. In Joe's case, this hemisphere cannot be called an unconscious mind because it is often dominant and indeed very conscious, even though Joe could not at first understand the reason for his anxiety. His left-sided immature mind, motivated by hidden fears, responded to the world almost reflexively with anxiety. Joe simply put on the wrong pair of goggles, and his distress soared.

A Chemical Imbalance?

Joe wondered whether his anxiety was the result of a chemical imbalance, a natural question for him to raise. We seem to hear all the time about chemical imbalances in the brain. Indeed, the brain has chemicals, and when we are frightened, our brain chemistry is going to be different from when we feel relaxed and secure. Other than this reasonable hypothesis, we know frightfully little about brain chemistry. We know that chemicals injected into the body can induce feelings of anxiety, especially in people prone to panicking, and we know of alterations in hormone levels in patients with posttraumatic stress disorder. Moreover, animals that are threatened show heightened activity of certain brain systems. And we have gained some insights from brain imaging studies of patients diagnosed with anxiety disorders. But in general, the results of these studies are inconsistent from one study to the next, and it is difficult to synthesize a consistent picture. Another problem is that if we see heightened activity on an imaging study, we do not know the nature of that brain activity. The area that is more active could be one that is busy inhibiting other areas, or it could be the area causing the anxiety. Nor do we know if the areas that show heightened activity are causing the anxiety or simply responding to anxiety induced elsewhere.

The brain is so complex that we are only at the edge of the frontier in many regards. If I ask you how fast a car is going and tell you the time but not the distance it traveled, then no matter how smart you are or how much you know about the specifications of the car, you will never be able to solve the problem. It's impossible. And with the brain, there are many factors that remain unknown and many questions that remain unanswered. Neuroscience has to be commended for its efforts and its honesty in reporting its uncertainty in many areas.

But we do know that a pair of glasses can calm Joe's anxiety; whichever of his chemicals are imbalanced, they seem to right themselves easily, at least temporarily. Because the anxiety symptoms of most of my patients resolve with psychotherapy, the chemical states associated with anxiety can often be altered psychologically. This fact would not be possible if the chemical changes were generally inalterable. Of course, anxiety can be markedly reduced with medications, but this does not prove that a chemical disorder is the primary cause (medications help many medical and psychological problems). More likely, anxiety is caused by an interaction of brain states (including chemical states) and psychological factors. It appears that Joe has different brain states in his different cerebral hemispheres.

Genetic Factors?

Our genetic makeup is undeniably important. Let's consider tennis. Surely there are genetic traits that enhance one's ability to play tennis. But we do not generally think that there is a gene for tennis. We inherit thousands of characteristics that might affect our ability to play tennis. Further, some of our genes will be activated (or inactivated as the case may be) only if we are put in an environment at the right time in development that stimulates those particular genes.

What we begin to see is that the relationship between genetic makeup and the ability to play tennis is very complex. If we play poorly, we can't simply blame our tennis instructor, but we cannot blame our genes either. I believe each of us can play tennis. Our range of abilities will vary, but unless we suffer some debilitating condition, we each can put on a pair of sneakers and stand at the baseline with a racquet in our hands. Thus, like anxiety, I see the ability to play tennis as a universal characteristic. Most people who begin lessons early and practice regularly should become competent players eventually. Some people grasp it quickly and excel at each step of their development; others find it more difficult; and some remain lousy players no matter how hard they try. Do genetics play a role? Certainly. Does the environment? Certainly.

Let's suppose that there is a tennis school for small children, and suppose that, unknown to the parents, the instructor is extremely threatening and humiliating toward the children. He tells them that he will harm their parents unless they give glowing reports about the tennis school and attend class regularly. We can predict that out of one hundred students, most, if not all, will become poor tennis players (as well as trauma victims). We can acknowledge that each child has genes that affect tennis performance, but we wouldn't think of the problems of these children as genetic disorders.

Of course, there are some genetic defects that are profound. Down's syndrome is a genetic problem that causes mental retardation regardless of the environment in which the child lives. Could some people inherit strong tendencies to be anxious? Certainly. Do we have any scientific evidence for this? Not so far. To date the best studies on anxiety and heredity have been done on patients diagnosed with a panic disorder. Here the scientific evidence is inconclusive.[1]

Behavioral Approaches to Anxiety

The group of psychologists called behaviorists theorize that behaviors especially, but also emotional states, are determined largely by learning experiences. They called their discovery "learning theory." J. B. Watson, who enthusiastically brought Pavlov's ideas to America in the 1920s, discovered that when Albert, an eleven-month-old "experimental subject," was given a white rat to play with, he enjoyed the animal and showed no fear. But when Watson made loud, unpleasant noises whenever the rat appeared, Albert not surprisingly became afraid of his former pet. He also became afraid of anything that remotely resembled the rat, such as cotton wool or sealskin. Watson discovered that we learn from our experience and apply what we learn to other objects, in a process learning theorists call "generalization." Some behaviorists have suggested that experiences such as Albert's could underlie anxiety disorders in adults, but that hypothesis remains underdeveloped.

Watson was followed by Edward L. Thorndike, who was to lead American psychology in the first half of this century. Thorndike discovered from experiments on cats that we learn from trial and error. B. F. Skinner, building on Thorndike's work, proposed that we learn from rewards and punishments (positive and negative reinforcements). Skinner believed that all behavior is the result of the combined effects of a person's cumulative rewards and punishments throughout life. Skinner and many other behaviorists objected to discussions of emotions or the unconscious mind because they felt such concepts were less reliable scientifically than observable behaviors. Today cognitive psychologists, the successors to the behaviorists, appreciate some of the importance of emotion and admit that many mental processes are beyond consciousness; for these, they have applied the term "the cognitive unconscious." The cognitive unconscious does not relate to hidden psychological issues, as in the psychoanalytic unconscious mind, but rather describes how mental processes, cognitive and emotional, can occur outside of awareness. Cognitive psychologists are particularly interested in covert learning and implicit memory (memory not easily available to language) when they discuss the cognitive unconscious.

You might wonder how anyone could argue with such a compilation of obvious observations as those obsessively detailed by the behaviorists. But I find an important defect in thinking behind learning theory. It failed to appreciate that each of us has two minds, each of which learns differently from the same experiences. All of the principles about learning are true. Certainly we learn from trial and error and from rewards and punishments, but what we learn and how strongly we learn depends on which mind we are talking about and the condition, developmentally and physiologically, of the brain areas supporting that mind. Joe's mature side can grasp in a few minutes that he is a capable, admirable person, but his immature side, the mind of his left hemisphere, will keep him in therapy for a while yet. What the behaviorists have failed to appreciate is that the person is the product of the interactions of both minds. Because the struggles that go on within a person are not easily observable, they were missed by the behaviorists.

Am I Anxious?

Most people have or eventually suffer some form of anxiety. Many of my patients have had episodes of panic. Some feel self-conscious in public (the essential symptom of agoraphobia); some have obsessions or compulsions; almost all have been traumatized by some form of stress, acute or chronic. Symptoms are dynamic and fluid; they are responses to a person's circumstances, either internal or external, and they cannot be easily captured in an enduring diagnostic label.

Nonetheless, mental health professionals use the specific criteria of the *Diagnostic and Statistical Manual of Mental Disorders*, now in its fourth edition. This latest edition of the DSM-IV, as it is called, lists over a dozen major disorders relating to anxiety. One of the unfortunate outcomes of the hegemony of DSM is that patients are meant to have one specific disorder that can be corrected with a specific treatment. But in practice, this goal is often elusive, and the same medications and treatments are used, as they should be, to treat a wide range of problems.

I believe that anxiety and depression are natural biological states that one enters when threatened (anxiety) or defeated (depression). Some people are more severely threatened or more chronically defeated than others, but fundamentally such states are fluid and dynamic and depend on which hemisphere is dominant. Dual-brain therapy applies knowledge about hemispherically based intrapsychic differences to clinical practice. Often I prescribe medications to assist my patients, but I do so as a partner with them in an ongoing uncontrolled experiment of sorts, in which we both watch carefully for possible medication effects and side effects. For patients experiencing distressing anxiety, I may offer a benzodiazepine such as clonazepam, or an antidepressant such as imipramine or Prozac if the first session or two has not brought enough psychic relief. In my experience, it is relatively easy to move patients off psychotherapeutic drugs when anxiety is well treated psychologically. This is especially true when a patient is able to help his emotionally healthier side convince his troubled side that together they are safe.

CHAPTER 6

Despondency

Celia, an attractive woman in her early forties, is a literature professor at a local college. In spite of her obvious intelligence and considerable accomplishment, she had always felt deep within that she was hollow. Celia diminished her accomplishments and held out little hope of doing anything interesting with the rest of her life, for she "knew" herself to be neither attractive, nor intelligent, nor worthwhile. She avoided or rejected professionally successful men, and she intimidated those who weren't. After the last breakup, several months before beginning her treatment, she found herself feeling long periods of despondency. She felt very alone and pined for a relationship, but was afraid of getting injured if she sought one. She also felt stymied in her career by a department chairman with whom she could not relate amicably. Celia seemed so depressed that I prescribed Prozac in the first session. She came to feel that the medication was helpful to her as we continued our work over the next few months.

Celia felt her mother was extremely critical of her, especially during her adolescence. Her relationship with her father had always been very strained. Celia described him as a man who couldn't express love, but only unwarranted and unnecessary precautions and admonitions about sexual promiscuity. Her parents always appeared to her to be in an unhappy, painful relationship with each other. Celia discovered that she could escape the family's pain through her academic work.

Although her mood improved and Celia seemed clinically less depressed, I felt that her therapy was moving slowly. Celia struggled to avoid looking deeply into her psychological nature because she was utterly convinced that she was unalterably, intolerably "defective." Confronting her ugly essence, she felt, could be devastating.

It was at this point, two months into our work, that I suggested she try on the lateralized glasses.

"So you are looking out the left side [right brain]. How do you feel?"

"Well, I feel anxious, nervous."

"How would you rate your anxiety on a scale of none, mild, moderate, quite a bit, or extreme?"

"Moderate."

"And how do you feel about yourself as a person?"

"I feel as if I have a lot of things I need to work on."

"You mentioned earlier that you were feeling 'defective.' Could you use that same scale to measure your sense of defectiveness?"

"I don't know—more than moderate."

"On that scale."

"Quite a bit, I guess."

"You have a sense of quite a bit of defectiveness as a person? And can you elaborate on that a little bit? What do you feel is defective about you?"

"I don't think I do as much with myself as I should. I don't think I'm as good as most other people as a person in terms of being a good person, in terms of going out of my way to help other people. I think I could be more ambitious, and I could do more with myself. I'm not as creative as I'd like to be."

"Do you feel, if you're in a room full of people, that you're as good as the other people?"

"No."

"You feel that you're not as good?"

"No. I will, in fact, find the person that I'm convinced is what I consider to be better than myself, and that will be the person I compare myself to."

"And if you are on a subway, how do you usually feel?"

"On a subway, I'll tend to look at the different people, and I'll do the same thing even in a subway."

"How do you rate yourself on the subway: as good as other people or less than other people?"

"Less than, I would say, because I would feel self-conscious."

"I want you to try the other glasses." She switches glasses, and then there is a pause of twenty seconds. "Now you're looking out the right side [left brain]."

"Right. I feel more comfortable for some reason. I'm not sure. Not quite as anxious, maybe mildly anxious, and I feel a little calmer. Hm, not so critical. I know I've just been critical; I know what I've just said."

"Just looking at what you're feeling now."

"My feelings are more complacent—more at ease."

"And suppose you were on a subway and you were looking around. How would you feel you were compared with other people?"

"I think I'd see myself more as someone who's just an observer rather than someone who's being observed. And I go back and forth with that."

"How do you mean?"

"Sometimes I feel very self-conscious, and other times . . ."

"I mean right now."

"Right now, I would feel more like the observer."

"Would you feel less than other people on the subway?"

"No."

"Would you feel superior to people on the subway?"

"No. Equal."

"And if I ask you to measure your sense of defectiveness, would you say none, mild, moderate, quite a bit, or extreme?"

"Ah, mild."

"Now, do you remember how you felt when you had the other glasses on? Do you notice a difference?"

"Yeah. I guess I feel a little more secure with these on."

"And is there any difference in terms of how you feel about yourself, your self-worth?"

"Well, I think I feel that I'm okay."

"With these glasses?"

"Hm."

"And with the other glasses?"

"I tend to think of being a little more not okay, I guess."

"Right. And do you notice that difference?"

"Hm."

"What do you think of that difference?"

"Well, it's a little strange because obviously I can remember what I just said. I'm going back and forth with these feelings. I guess it's maybe the way I tend to view myself."

"I'm only asking, Do you notice any difference between the two ways in which you view yourself with the glasses?"

"Yeah."

"Would you say it's a big difference or a small difference?"

"Well, I think it's a noticeable difference. I think it reflects the conflict I always have in myself."

"So this a conflict you've always observed, but now it's kind of made more concrete?"

"Yeah."

"And you can see one piece of yourself with one pair of glasses and another piece of yourself with the other pair of glasses? Is that what you're saying?"

"Yes."

"How does that feel to see these two views and separate them?"

"Well, I'm not sure. It makes sense to me, but I not sure why it's so, why it would be different—I mean, not different, but why this situation would be so clear-cut with the two glasses. This struggle is a familiar one to me."

"Right. It's a familiar struggle. Which view do you feel is more real?"

"That's hard to answer. I would say the anxious one."

"And you feel that even with the glasses that you have on right now?"

"Yeah."

"So you sort of trust the other side more?"

"Hm."

"But with these glasses on, you can see this other view of yourself."

"I can see the two."

"Has that changed at all? If you were on the subway, how would you view yourself right now?"

"I would be calm, and just . . ."

"Would you be as good as other people?"

"Yes."

"So that's a pretty stable view of yourself."

"Uh-huh."

"So I want to say that this negative view of yourself could be questioned—not by a factual debate, but it's just interesting that out of another side you just see yourself differently. And nothing else besides switching the glasses has changed. It's just that your view is different. Isn't that interesting."

"Well, I think the thing that is annoying for me about all of this is that one side dominates the other."

"Right."

"And it's not just a balance. It's a struggle, and one seems to get the better of the other."

"More that the insecure part seems to dominate?"

"Right."

Celia's sense that she was worth less than other people is a common symptom of depression. She also suffered a sense of hopelessness, loneliness, alienation, meaninglessness, and despair. She was inhibited and withdrawn in both her work and her social life. All of these factors were interwoven into her general condition that psychiatrists call depression.

What became clear through the magnification of the goggles is that it was only Celia's right hemisphere that viewed herself as inadequate; her left side viewed the same person as adequate, and (from my further observations) was not depressed. In Celia's case, as in the majority of my depressed patients, her right brain harbored the disparaging view.

The Role of Trauma in Depression

In the next chapter, we will discuss the syndrome of posttraumatic stress disorder, in which traumatic experiences seem to implant themselves deep within the person and evoke symptoms such as flashbacks or nightmares that clearly represent a residue of the traumatic experience. But, in fact, all of the stories here are really about trauma victims. The differences among them are in the timing in the person's development and the duration and severity of the trauma. These factors influence the person's response to the experiences and shape the symptoms he is likely to develop.

All of the injurious experiences described so far occurred in patients' childhoods. Childhood is the time people are the most vulnerable, the least capable of protecting themselves. In order to traumatize a healthy adult, we may need an extreme condition such as war or torture, but René Spitz, studying infants neglected in an overcrowded nursery, found that profound psychological injuries, even death, resulted from the lack of loving care.[1]

The fact is that small children are defenseless on their own. They are small, and their brains are not fully developed. They own nothing and have few legal rights; even their few rights and protections are a mystery to the young. Children are completely dependent on the adults who are expected to care for them. When those adults, through lack of education or psychological disturbance, do not look out for a child's needs the child will suffer. Siblings and peers can also do great damage to children. Small children perceive bullying and ridiculing as serious forms of torture, even when they are physically unharmed. Adults often do not appreciate the damage that children can do to one another. Even worse, the child-victim often doesn't appreciate that he is being assaulted, but rather assumes that it is he who has been bad and deserving of mistreatment. One major psychological consequence of trauma is depression.

Depression as a Natural Biological Process

Depression, like anxiety, is the natural biological consequence of experience. Anxiety comes from a sense of threat. Depression comes from a sense of defeat. Anxiety and depression are both emotions, which psychologist Daniel Goleman defines as "a feeling and its distinctive thoughts, psychological and biological states, and range of propensities to act."[2] Emotions are part of our biological makeup, evoked by our brains in response to certain stimuli. When an emotion such as despair becomes persistent, it interferes with our functioning and leads to the pathological state called clinical depression. Any condition that leaves us feeling utterly defeated will eventually lead us into the state of despair and hopelessness that we call depression. When we are in this condition, nothing works right. Our body betrays us; we become clumsy, jittery, unattractive, often incompetent. Working or socializing in a depressed state can be impossible, and not understanding his condition, the depressed person will often become severely embarrassed on his own, trying to hide or withdraw from the world around him. A depressed person can become very angry with himself, experiencing the same self-contempt that he believes others feel for him.

Why would mother nature provide us with a biological mental mechanism for self-destruction? From nature's perspective, the victim's destruction is good for the species. Imagine that a female moose is in a valley, and two strong males want to approach her and mate. First, the males must confront each other. They go off to the mountaintop and fight. The winner gets the rewards and produces offspring. Right? Wrong. These moose will fight to the death, and by the time the fight is over, both will be severely injured and exhausted, including the winner. Along will come a skinny moose, and since he's the only male left, he gets to mount the female and beget weak, skinny offspring. In order to guard against such a natural catastrophe, nature, through evolution, came up with the solution: anxiety and depression.

These two strong moose go off to fight, but as soon as it becomes clear that one is superior, nature makes something happen. The one who's doing well becomes more emboldened; his adrenalin gets pumping and everything functions well. He's having what we could call a success syndrome. The other moose, who senses that he is going to be defeated, begins to go into a depression. His energy ebbs; he becomes uncoordinated and confused. He has all the symptoms of a depressed person. In fact, he is depressed. In this condition, he has no choice but to submit. The two moose no longer have to fight to the death. So as soon as one moose gets the upper hand, nature assists him, and he can win without serious injury. It is he who gets to mount the beauty. The defeated moose, like his human counterpart, gets depressed and wanders off despondent. His human equivalent will not only feel despair but is prone to any of a long list of lethal diseases associated with depression, including heart disease and suicide.

We don't have to go to the northern woods of Maine to prove my theory. Just watch the Super Bowl on TV. When one team gains a substantial advantage, it gets fired up and plays better, while the other team begins to fall apart. What you are watching on national television is the early stage of the formation of depression. Notice, too, that this happens even in the most successful, best-trained, world-class athletes. It's biology—the same behavior we would observe in the jungle.

Psychoanalytic and Dual-Brain Explanations for Depression

Psychoanalysts have long recognized a relationship between painful childhood experiences and depression. They saw traumas such as loss of a loved parent or the loss of a parent's affection as especially important. The renowned psychoanalyst Karen Horney saw a connection between the loneliness and insecurity of depression and parental rejection. Freud's colleague, Sandor Rado, linked depression with the child's sense of helplessness. More recently, British psychoanalyst John Bowlby emphasized the importance of problems with the emotional bond between the mother and infant for the development of depression in later life. In Chicago, psychoanalyst Heinz Kohut founded the school of self psychology on the principle that a lack of emotional nurturance early in life is the basis for most psychological problems. Analysts Elizabeth Zetzel and Charles Brenner also wrote about the relationship between early psychological traumas and later life depressions.[3]

My addition to all of this research on depression is that the traumas of the past get retained in the mind of one hemisphere. All of these analysts saw childhood psychological insults as predisposing to depression, but none had a clear explanation for how this happened. Each asserted that a link existed, but the nature of the link was always a bit murky because they mistakenly viewed the person as having one mind. Heinz Kohut, for example, would say that the patient was depressed because his early needs for admiration and approval were not met, leaving him unfulfilled as an adult, frustratingly searching for the missing approval. My subtle correction is that Kohut's hypothesis is accurate for the mind in one hemisphere, but wrong for that of the other hemisphere.

The mind in Celia's right hemisphere suffered exactly what Kohut described. When she looked out the extreme left side of the glasses, she experienced herself as less than other people. This was the image she developed in her right mind, in response to the rejecting attitudes of her parents. This archaic view persisted in the mind of her right brain. On that side, she felt inadequate because, in accord with Kohut, her parents were poor at providing the emotional nurturance she needed. In her left hemisphere, however, she had developed a more realistic sense of her value. Her problem can be more clearly understood as an injury to the mind in her right hemisphere, which then tends to dominate her left-sided mind.

Sometimes when the defeat is persistent and overwhelming, both hemispheres will feel defeated and manifest depression, but this is the case only for extreme circumstances. In that situation, the analysts would be correct to speak of the whole person's becoming depressed over a massive loss or trauma. But in most people with intermittent depressions or depressions of varying degrees, I believe that the depression results from the negative side's gaining the upper hand in its constant struggle for power and control over the other side.

There are a few other interesting hypotheses from psychoanalysis about the genesis of depression. Freud and Karl Abraham suggested that depression stems from anger turned inward against the self in a very complicated scheme. The child's mind first feels his mother's slipping away in their relationship, and so he tries to internalize an image of the mother inside his own head. He then becomes so angry with the inner idea of the mother because she abandoned him that he attacks her image. Because the image is actually located inside himself, he unwittingly winds up attacking himself, and not his mother, at whom he is really angry. Freud also came to feel that an image of a critical parent could be lodged in the patient's mind in the superego, and from that position could torment the patient with a lifelong barrage of criticism.[4]

I would reinterpret both of Freud's hypotheses using my schema. Indeed, the child does get angry about the lack of fulfillment he is experiencing. Children can protest quite well, especially after a certain age. But if the parents become threatening or unresponsive to the child's protests, the child will become anxious (threatened) and then depressed (defeated), and the protests will eventually stop. This is why many, but certainly not all, depressed children have difficulty expressing anger outwardly. The troubled hemisphere of adults who are depressed is an immature mind that feels anxious and defeated. When this troubled mind has a strong influence on the adult's personality, the adult may have trouble expressing anger because his troubled mind believes that such an expression would be too dangerous.

The troubled hemisphere in Celia's mind often attacked by making her feel insignificant and inadequate, turning the anger inward. Celia's troubled side was treating her exactly as her father had. Sometimes she would have the feeling that she was sexually promiscuous—something her father accused her of, but nothing that could ever be attributed to her actual behavior. Depressed patients have troubled, defeated minds and as a result have difficulty expressing anger outwardly because they do not feel empowered; they express it against themselves because that is what the troubled mind has been taught to do.

The Dual-Brain View of Depression

The reasons the troubled minds of depressed people attack themselves are the same reasons immature people become belligerent. First, we have a biological tendency to get angry with those who are failing. We don't like losers. Again consider the Super Bowl. The fans get angry and disgusted when their team plays poorly. The fans of the losing team may even feel a bit of depression after a loss. We humans are enamored of winners and repulsed by losers. The troubled mind of the depressed person is no different. When he sees himself losing, he can become quite critical, beating up on his other side. This is one reason why depression is likely to worsen after humiliation.

But here is an additional, more interesting, and complex reason that the troubled hemisphere might pick on its partner. Sometimes when a person feels overpowered by someone else, there is a human tendency to try to befriend that person. It is plausible that the mind of an abused, mistreated, troubled hemisphere would try to "join" the powerful person. We often identify with powerful figures, and so could a troubled hemisphere.

Since the tormentor sees him as lowly or evil, he must assume this same view to maintain the identification. To join the tormentor, the troubled mind must begin to attack himself. Paradoxically, the troubled hemisphere is too concerned with joining the tormentor in order to survive to be concerned with the fact that he must attack himself. Psychologists call this mental process *identification with the aggressor*.

The mind in Celia's right hemisphere acted much like her father in its condemnation of herself. Because it is on the inside, the troubled mind can attack with a ferocity rare in the external world. This is why many of my depressed patients say to me, "If you've never been depressed, you have no idea how terrible it is."

A Person in the Troubled Mind

The picture of the mind of one hemisphere's acting autonomously and attacking the other side is astounding to witness. One of the poignant examples of this is that often I have *spoken* to the troubled mind, *and I have had it answer me!*

An example of my talking directly with a patient's troubled mind occurred in a recent session with Don, a forty-seven-year-old electrician who was severely mistreated as a child and for most of his adult life has suffered severe depressions. The right-sided glasses (left brain) readily evoked his more troubled side, which, for convenience, we call Earl (his middle name). The left-sided pair draws out his mature side, which we call Don. He has been in treatment with me for two years and has made excellent progress, but at times his depression breaks through in spite of our work and the medications I prescribe. The following dialogue began at about the middle of our session when he was describing his current feelings. He was wearing the right-side glasses (left brain), which evoke his troubled side.

"What do you feel?" I asked.
"Anxious. Nervous. Depressed."
"What's the depression like?"
"I'm sitting here and contemplating the anxiety I have. I can't quite get out of it. I'm stuck. Don't know exactly how to turn it around."
"Does Earl feel angry?"
"He's always angry."
"Tell me about his anger."
"Anger is just anger. It can come out at anyone, at any time."
"Does he get angry at Don?"
"Yeah. He's not doing his job."
"How's that?"
"I still like Don, but I feel bad for him."
"How do you feel bad for him?"

"Because he's weaker than a woman to me, because Earl, he's a strong son of a bitch."

"Does Earl get angry with Don?"

"Yes."

"Do you feel angry with him now?"

"Yeah. A little."

"How so?"

"Earl is pissed. He don't like too many people. He don't even like himself."

"Who's he most angry with?"

"Well, Earl is just fuckin' pissed off, 'cause he just can't figure out what's right and what's wrong."

"So he's not particularly upset with Don?"

"Earl, he's jealous of Don. He doesn't like it when things are fuckin' good. He likes to be a little on edge, no matter what. Earl's not really mad at Don. But he likes to take a bite outta Don every once and a while, for sure—just to keep him on track. This is the way it is. Earl, he keeps on turning wild. Don don't want it that way. They're pissed off at each other."

"Does your anger relate to your depression?"

"Yes."

"How?"

"Well, when I get depressed, I get angry because I'm fuckin' depressed."

"And who's gettin' angry: Don or Earl?"

"Well, Earl's gettin' angry."

"And what's he do when he gets angry?"

"He tries to make Don angry; he tries to get Don in the same fuckin' boat."

"What's he do to Don?"

"He aggravates him; he throws him off kilter. He makes him mad; he wants Don to join his side. And when I'm depressed, I'm angry because I know he's fuckin' workin' on me."

"And what's he doing when he's working on you?"

"He's not accepting reality; he's seeing things that aren't really there. He's frightened."

"When you get depressed, is he biting you?"

"Oh, yes, definitely."

"How's he bite you?"

"Just like a thing I feel: pain, guilt."

"And is he doing that now?"

"Yes."

"Now I want to talk to Earl. Can I talk with him?"

"Yes."

At this moment I change the tone of my voice, speaking firmly and with authority.

"Earl, I want you to listen to me. I want you to stop biting yourself. I want you to stop biting Don. I want you to cut it out. I want you to relax and let it go. I want you to stop this biting. I want you to stop this depression, stop this picking on yourself. I want you to stop this abuse. You've had enough of that. What do you feel?"

"I feel like a six-year-old who just got a spanking for acting up."

"How about your depression?"

"I'm eased off a little bit now."

"Tell me."

"I listen to you, Doctor. Earl listened to you. It's funny. It's not funny. See, I take what you say seriously. Earl, he'll listen, but he doesn't seem to retain the thought or the advice, the knowledge, the right thing too long. He listened to what you said. He listened, and he responded."

"Is he still responding? Or has he stopped listening?"

"No. He's responding."

"He's not biting you now?"

"No."

"And how do you feel?"

"I feel more comfortable."

"And how about nervous and depressed"?

"More comfortable, Doctor."

"Less depressed?"

"Oh, yes. Earl's there. He was attacking me. It was like you pulled him off me."

"He listened to me?"

"Yes, he did."

"What do you think about that?"

"Well, I wish the fuck he'd listen to me more. I think he takes me for granted. See, I have more faith in you than you realize. I think Earl does too. In fact, I know he does, 'cause he might not want to come here; he might not want to get well. Well, this motherfucker is gonna get better whether he likes it or not. Your talking was like a good flick on the back of the ear in second grade, and it got his attention. He's not roughhousing with me now."

"He'll listen to me?"

"Yes, he will."

Again, I assumed my firm tone. "Now I want Earl and I want Don to listen as well. I want you to listen to me, and I mean it. But I want you to listen also to Don. Don is more important in this. And all three of us are going to work together. I want you to listen to Don the way you listen to me. I want you to follow me, and I want you to do what Don asks you to do. I want you to cooperate with Don."

"Now he's agreeing with you. Son of a bitch. Sorta strange. It's the first time that I've gotten a downgrade on his performance level on me, listening to you. He's calmed down tremendously. I was at an eight [on a ten-point scale we have used] and was getting next to a fuckin' nine."

"What feeling was an eight or a nine?"

"Anger. Depression. Both."

"And can we get Earl to treat you nicely?" I again assume my firm tone. "Earl, I want you to treat Don nicely—not just not bite him. Be his friend. Make him feel well. Earl, I want you to make Don feel well, welcomed, loved, valued. He's working hard for you; I want you to comfort him. Can you do that, Earl?"

"Yeah, Earl can do that. Earl can do that. It's just a matter of him doin' it."

"What do you feel now?"

"Feel a little anticipation because that would be great to have a partner that's not bitin' me."

"Ah. A partner that's not bitin' you. That sounds good to me. Huh?"

"Yeah, it does."

"And how about a partner who's loving? How's that sound?"

"That would be icing on the cake."

"How would that feel?"

"I don't know?"

Again in my firm tone: "Earl, do you hear me? I want you to love Don. Earl, do you hear me? Love Don. Let it come. I know you've got that love. Give it to him. Share it."

Don cries. Tears flow down his cheeks. "I think Earl's feeling sorry for me now. Well, he's beaten me up so fuckin' much. Seems I wonder if he's even capable of loving."

"Can you feel his love now?"

"I can feel his caring, his concern. It's definitely weird. He's come over. I feel rested. I feel like I've won. I feel stronger with him, of course—more than I do without him even though he's a fuckin' asshole at times. I want Earl to learn to love. I haven't had these feelings. I don't know what a real capacity of giving love, sharing love, receiving it is like."

"Are you beginning to? Are you beginning to discover what it's like to be loved? Can you feel Earl's love?"

"Yeah, because I think Earl can learn to love me. I'm gonna be lovable."

"And can Don love Earl?"

"Oh, sure, even though he's treated me like a fuckin' goddamn bastard.

"See, the abuse wasn't Earl. It's that Earl was abused. Earl can love; we just simply need to teach him. Earl suffered, and he also gave out a lot of abuse, but he can love. And we feel that now."

"Yes."

"And that's what's gonna make you better."

"Hm. That's when it hurts me at times, thinking that I wasn't capable of loving."

"He's gotta learn how. He's learned about abuse; now he's going to learn about love."

"That's right. I just got a lot out of that. Earl did. Thank you Doctor."

Don was abused as a child. His troubled mind, Earl, is a victim of that trauma, but he has also become a perpetrator. We see that when we see Earl "biting" Don. When I talk to Earl, I try to address both aspects. I try to let Earl know that I appreciate his suffering—his own anxiety and depression—but I also let him know that I want him to stop attacking Don.

Parents do this all the time when their children need discipline for negative behaviors that stem from insecurities and hurt feelings. The parent needs to say, "No, you can't kick me, but why do you want to?" or "No, you can't use drugs, but why do you want to?" I also believe that the mind on the troubled side can have changes in mood. It is not always attacking, and this is why depressions seem to cycle, to come and go.

The Troubled Mind Can Recover

One of my patients who was very responsive to the goggles had a troubled and depressed right hemisphere. The patient had been severely ridiculed as a child by other children. When his depression was at its worst, his right-sided mind was very strong and very certain that it was about to be ridiculed. It dominated his left-sided mind, which did not share this frightening view of the world. When the patient wore the right visual field goggles (stimulating his left brain), be felt much better, but as soon as he took off the goggles, he returned to his depressed, frightened state.

The patient made a fairly rapid improvement over the next few weeks in his therapy. Interestingly, the goggles continued to work, but now his right side was not so frightened. And even without the goggles, he was beginning to feel well, though not as well as when he wore the goggles that stimulated his left brain. His left hemisphere was having a greater influence on his overall state and the mood of his right side.

As he progressed, he was no longer clinically depressed, and in fact was beginning to do groundbreaking work in his field. Nonetheless, when he wore the goggles activating his right side, he was untrusting, and that side wanted to stop his therapy. What became clear was that the right side wanted to stop the therapy because it was afraid of being ridiculed—first by me possibly, but also by others if it ever became know that he was seeing a psychiatrist. To his troubled right hemisphere, anything that might provoke ridicule in the school yard needed to be urgently avoided, and seeing a psychiatrist was something his troubled side saw as potentially dangerous in that regard.

His left side, however, was not at all afraid that I might ridicule him and wanted to continue his therapy because he saw that his right side still had work to do. It had to learn that it was truly safe from ridicule. When the patient came into his session (without any glasses), he wanted to stop his treatment because his depression had been resolved, and he was functioning extremely well. He didn't have the time for therapy, and he could not justify the cost. But after seeing that his right side was still troubled, though no longer so powerful or so troubled as to cause a clinical depression, the patient decided to continue his therapy with the aim of helping his right side further. A few months later, when his right hemisphere was feeling secure and trusting, we both decided that he was ready to terminate his treatment, for we had accomplished our goal: we successfully taught his right side that he was now truly safe.

There appear to be two ways a person can resolve depression. The first and more successful is when both sides become healthier, and the troubled side is no longer troubled. The other is when the healthier side becomes able to dominate the person's mental life, and the troubled side, though still maintaining its archaic ideas, recedes into the background.

Cognitive Therapy

Learning theorists have contributed the other major psychological explanation for depression. Aaron Beck, of the University of Pennsylvania, who led their charge in the clinical aspects of this area, discovered that persons with depression have negative thoughts. He categorized three types of negative thoughts, which he called a "cognitive triad": thoughts of helplessness, interpretations of events in an unfavorable light, and thoughts that the future is hopeless. Beck developed cognitive therapy, which attempts to help people discover, clarify, and then work to change their negative, depressive thoughts. I would venture that the excellent results that cognitive therapy can achieve stem from the therapist's correcting the negative thoughts in the troubled hemisphere.[5]

The Biology of Depression

For the past few decades, neuroscientists have studied a large and increasing number of neurochemicals and hormones to determine a relation between them and depression. Candidates being investigated are norepinephrine, acetylcholine, serotonin, cortisol, and thyroxine, among others. Since the selective serotonin reuptake inhibitors (SSRIs)—such as Prozac—have become useful medications for depression, a great deal of research is under way to understand how serotonin may relate to depression. One hypothesis is that a low level of serotonin does not by itself cause depression, but low levels permit either mania or depression, depending on the norepinephrine level, which tends to be higher in mania. Some researchers believe that serotonin is an inhibitory chemical that reduces arousal and decreases norepinephrine secretion. Another hypothesis is that an imbalance between acetylcholine and norepinephrine, such that the acetylcholine exceeds the norepinephrine, might contribute to depression. What is clear is that the neurochemical systems in the brain are quite interrelated, and a change in one chemical leads to complex alterations in its related systems.[6]

There is much speculation about whether chemical changes precede or follow the psychological changes wrought by depression, but easy, clear answers are not available. Quite possibly the complex interactions between mind and brain are inseparable. The fact that many patients can recover quickly and permanently suggests that many of the neurochemical changes associated with depression are not inalterable.

Research into the genetics of depression has not yet yielded clear results. There has been no research on the inheritability of ordinary, everyday depressions. Research has been conducted on patients with major depression, a profound depression often requiring hospitalization, but the evidence does not suggest much in the way of inheritability. For instance, when identical twins (with identical genes) were compared to fraternal (nonidentical) twins (with different genes, as in any other pair of siblings) in regard to depression, there was little difference between the two types of twins. One study involving over a thousand twins showed that if one identical twin was depressed, then so was the other 48 percent of the time. If one fraternal twin was depressed, then so was the other 42 percent of the time. A larger difference between the two types of twins would be expected if major depression were an inherited disorder.

Geneticists often use this type of twin study, in which the similarities between identical twins are compared with those between fraternal twins, but these studies have certain inherent problems. For instance, identical twins probably have more similar environments than fraternal twins; they may be dressed identically and are constantly mistaken for one another, and so one might find differences between the groups on the basis of environmental as well as genetic factors.[7]

Better twin studies are obtained by examining identical twins who were adopted and reared apart, but there are no such studies. What we do have are two studies of adopted children who were not twins. The first study looked at how many biological parents of fifty-six depressed, adopted children living separately were also depressed. They found that five of the biological parents suffered depression, in contrast to three of the adoptive parents. This study suggests that depression is not inherited.[8]

The second adoptive study looked at eight depressed biological parents and found that 38 percent of their adopted-away children suffered depression. Of forty-three biological parents who were not depressed, only 9 percent of their adopted-away children suffered depression. Although 38 percent is much larger than 9 percent, because there were only eight depressed parents the results could be due to chance alone since they did not meet the requirements of statistical analysis. These authors did report that known environmental factors were very important in inducing the depressions in these children. I think this study leaves open the possibility that inheritable factors are important in depression, but it certainly proves nothing of the sort.[9]

Another serious test of hereditability would be to see if we could find the actual genes that cause depression. But this has not been the case. The next best thing would be to see if known inheritable traits, such as eye color or blood type, could be consistently associated with depression. Such known inherited traits are referred to as *genetic markers*, meaning that if an association between a known trait such as eye color and depression can be established, then eye color would become a genetic marker for depression. Over the last few decades, a plethora of studies have attempted to find such genetic markers for depression. On many occasions genetic markers have been found, but in each case so far, the findings were not confirmed by repeated study. No accepted genetic markers for depression have been discovered.

There is considerable evidence reported by psychiatrists for the hereditability for manic psychoses, which often alternate with depression in bipolar illness, commonly known as manic depression. The data demand continued examination, particularly because we know that about one-quarter of patients with a diagnosis of major depression are eventually reclassified as manic depressive.

I remember in 1987 being very impressed when Dan Rather announced on the CBS *Evening News* that a group of scientists had located the gene for manic depressive illness by finding that it was linked to a specific known gene on a specific chromosome. I found this incredible since it contradicted all I had observed about psychiatric illnesses, including manic depressive illness.[10]

Over time, nine different attempts by different groups of scientists were made to replicate these amazing findings. None could. Two years later, the group that had originally announced the breakthrough discovery retracted its claim.[11]

Some neuroscientists have suggested a relationship between a "physically defective" right hemisphere and depression. These scientists base their hypotheses on studies involving neuropsychological testing, EEG analysis, imaging studies, and clinical histories of patients with brain injuries to one hemisphere. Most of these workers have not yet conceptualized the right hemisphere as psychologically troubled, and I would not generally classify the emotionally immature nature of one hemisphere as a brain disease, although certainly this psychological nature could relate in part to the hemisphere's physical structure.[12]

Neurotransmitters (brain chemicals) are not free floating in the brain but are secreted locally in small amounts by discrete systems of neurons with specific paths and locations in the brain. It is intriguing that a number of the neurotransmitter systems that are considered possibly related to depression are physically located more in one hemisphere than the other. In most people, the norepinephrine and the serotonin systems appear to be more concentrated in the right hemisphere than in the left. Further, a number of recent studies have indicated that many medications appear to have more effects on one hemisphere than the other.[13]

These findings lead to the possibility that popular SSRIs such as Prozac have their effects by enhancing the dominance of one hemisphere over the other. Although Prozac is widely believed to be a cure for depression, in the only large controlled study comparing it to placebo, the differences were not impressive. Prozac lowered the level of depression 40 percent compared to a lowering of 29 percent for the placebo. Psychopharmacologist William Appleton points out that while 70 percent of patients taking Prozac achieve some benefit, only 28 percent manifest an excellent response. Is Prozac likely to work by helping to shift the hemispheric dominance to the healthier side?[14]

The New Magnetic Stimulation

Recently a new treatment for depression was announced by the National Institute for Mental Health and by a group from Spain led by neuroscientist Alvaro Pascual-Leone. Both groups reported treating depression using a pulsating electromagnet held over one side of the head. The electromagnet has a powerful localized effect on the underlying brain. Depending on the rate at which the magnet is set to pulsate, it can either enhance or inhibit the area of the brain being treated.

Recently I met with Pascual-Leone at his new laboratory at Harvard. He has found that by placing the electromagnet over the left side of the patient's head—in other words, over his left hemisphere—and setting the pulse rate so that it enhances the left brain activity, he is able to reduce the depressive symptoms significantly in 60 percent of his patients. I speculated that the healthy hemisphere of each improved patient was physically enhanced by the electromagnetic stimulation, allowing the more mature side to become more dominant. Possibly the patients who did not respond would have benefited from stimulation on the other side. Of my patients with major depression, 60 percent responded to the glasses in a manner that indicated that their left hemisphere was the healthier side. I suggested to Pascual-Leone that perhaps the lateralized glasses might predict which hemisphere is more mature and more likely to benefit the patient from its stimulation. I sent him a set of the two lateralized glasses, and he and his associates are using them on his patients as part of their pretreatment workup. So far many of his patients have had lateralized emotional responses to the glasses, and we are planning a study to see if the side and intensity of the responses to the glasses correlate with the clinical responses to the electromagnetic stimulation. I have also suggested that following my method of combining the goggles with psychotherapy, the electromagnatic stimulation treatment, in concert with psychotherapy, could prove helpful

Why Therapy Succeeds or Fails

Depression is often difficult to treat, and I welcome advances that can be made from the neurosciences. When therapy fails, I feel it is because we have failed to win the confidence of the troubled side. Often the frightened, troubled side is so dogmatic and determined that it defeats me and, with me, the patient, even aided by Prozac. Fortunately, the troubled side usually learns through its trepidation to accept the help it pines for. The goal in dual-brain therapy is to help the patient's healthier side to teach, comfort, and discipline his more troubled side, and eventually to convince it of the reality that it no longer has to be defeated.

CHAPTER 7

Extremes

*L*yle waits with his head down. He hears the shouts to "move on the fuck out." The firefight erupts. Bullets rip in from cross directions from an impenetrable jungle on both sides of the rice paddy. The lieutenant goes down, dead. Lyle fires aimlessly at the jungle and tries to run forward, but his feet slip and he's back in the water. He hears bullets all around. He knows it's the one he doesn't hear that will kill him.

Lyle is in Vietnam. He has been on this mission for several days and is exhausted and spent. But he is alive. Half the men in his platoon are dead or so badly wounded they wish they were. The leeches don't bother him as much as they used to. He wonders if he'll get out of this one—something he's wondered a hundred times before.

Lyle survived. He wants to attribute his survival to his grit and courage, for which he has been decorated, but he knows his real debt is to dumb luck, blind statistics and probabilities. He survived only because he survived, only because some bullet or some mortar round didn't happen to land exactly in the small space his body occupied.

When he returned from Vietnam to Fort Benning, Georgia, he learned that his fiancée was four months pregnant. He was always a mild-mannered man of southern gentility. Now he found himself intoxicated, screaming at the woman whom he felt betrayed him, the woman he didn't have the strength to leave. He was becoming chronically angry. He never slept much. He couldn't function at work. And he always felt scared and jumpy. He couldn't trust anyone. He was alone and terrified. At night, in the dark and in his dreams, he was back in the rice paddies and the firefights. He woke up drenched in sweat. He needed a drink or he'd kill some motherfucker.

Lyle's drinking became more intense and more frequent. When he was not picking barroom fights, he was driving his pickup truck around the town as if he was in a stock car derby. Eventually he was arrested. By the third arrest, the army suspected he needed a psychiatrist. He was hospitalized uncaringly.

I met Lyle twenty-seven years later, after he had had Thorazine, Stelazine, Prozac and Valproate and three more hospitalizations, all for conditions with which he was labeled but only vaguely fit—from character disorder, to reactive psychosis, to manic depressive illness. And somewhere back there, he's not exactly sure where or when, he was given a series of twelve electroshock treatments. Lyle had been referred to me because his last psychiatrist became too frightened of Lyle's anger, too frightened that Lyle's rage would erupt in his direction, too frightened to treat him any longer. And this psychiatrist was right; Lyle was dangerously angry with him. In fact, Lyle's anger embraced much of the world. And he was about as terrified and depressed as he was enraged.

Lyle and I knew almost immediately that we would work well together. I understood that he was injured profoundly—initially by his experiences in Vietnam. His rage, terror, and despair were the distant sequelae that evolved from his war experiences and from the error upon error that followed in attempts to address his misunderstood symptoms.

Although Lyle suffered the classical syndrome of posttraumatic stress disorder (PTSD), his condition had been misunderstood from its beginning, just as the syndrome itself as it relates to Vietnam was not widely recognized until the mid-1980s. For twenty-seven years, Lyle had been regarded as a genetically deficient, character-disordered, mentally ill patient, unresponsive to the modern treatment bestowed upon him. Lyle had slipped through the cracks when the mental health profession made the connection between the effects of war trauma and the thousands of broken Vietnam vets being treated at veterans' hospitals nationwide. Neither he nor his caregivers considered his war experiences central to his problems. One of the reasons is that patients with PTSD suffer profound anxiety, depression, and impulsive behaviors, any of which can capture the attention and concern of health providers and overshadow the distant roots of the problem.[1]

Psychiatrists have been leery about letting in the Trojan horse of PTSD, lest it contaminate all of the psychiatric diagnoses that are seen by many as biological disorders unrelated to the environment, and they have worked hard to delineate it clearly from all other psychiatric syndromes. To have a diagnosis of PTSD, a patient must have experienced or witnessed an actual life-threatening event. The emphasis here is on the word "actual." A person threatened as an inarticulate child with humiliation by a dysfunctional family would not qualify for PTSD since his trauma would not be "actual" as this word is intended by the committee of anonymous authors of the DSM-IV. To have a diagnosis of PTSD, one must have experienced a trauma obvious to all, such as war or rape. Unfortunately, as in Lyle's case for twenty-seven years, even war may be overlooked as a trauma, and it is easy to overlook less obvious traumas such as chronic rejection. So to begin to define a diagnostic category by what is apparent to an outside observer of questionable skill is starting out on slippery ground.

The three additional clinical features one must have to earn this diagnosis are that one mentally reexperiences the traumatic event in one of a number of ways, such as flashbacks or nightmares; that one avoid some memories, thoughts, or feelings associated with the trauma; and that one have persistent symptoms of arousal such as insomnia, difficulty concentrating, or easy startling.

Lyle easily fit all of these criteria, but his most prominent symptoms were his profound depression, his irritability, and his intense anxiety. Further, the great majority of patients with PTSD have in addition other psychiatric diagnoses, such as alcoholism, antisocial personality, depression, and anxiety disorders. So this surgically clean, politically charged diagnostic category of PTSD now becomes messy and indistinct. I do not assert that obvious, "actual," overwhelming traumas may not affect a person differently from the less obvious, more insidious of life's traumas. Indeed, dissimilar traumas could be expected to affect people differently and to affect distinct groups of people (trained adults versus small children) differently, but we cannot be precise about this because there are too many unknown variables. For instance, we do not know precisely what the trauma meant to the person, precisely how well or how poorly he dealt with it, or precisely how many supports he had or didn't have. Lacking such precision, we can speak only in the broadest generalities.

Like many others, I do not feel that PTSD is a completely distinct syndrome. Bessel van der Kolk, a prominent psychiatrist at Boston University, and his associates describe "complex PTSD," which includes symptoms of emotional distress after the acute PTSD resolves when clinicians may not appreciate that the symptoms are the result of an earlier trauma. In fact, there have been elements of trauma (defined more broadly) underlying all the psychiatric symptoms that I have ever witnessed and treated.[2]

Lyle is now vastly improved. Except for occasions when he gets stirred up, he is calm and comfortable. His heart no longer races all the time, but now beats calmly and slowly. He smiles for the first time in decades. Although he continues to take several medications, he requires much less medication than when we started two years ago. I now prescribe sertraline, an SSRI antidepressant; clonazepam, a benzodiazepine for anxiety; and valproic acid, which was given to him as a mood stabilizer prior to my seeing him for a previous diagnosis of manic depressive illness. Although I have never diagnosed him with this condition, he feels this medication (which affects the same type of brain receptors as the benzodiazepines) helps to calm him, so we continue to use it. And he no longer relies on heavy doses of alcohol to supplement his prescribed psychotropic drugs.

The Pivotal Theoretical Importance of PTSD

PTSD is of pivotal theoretical and clinical interest because it bridges the gap between biological psychiatry and its sibling, dynamic psychiatry (an outgrowth of psychoanalysis). Some psychiatrists had asserted that disorders such as major depression and severe anxiety were generally the result of primary biological brain abnormalities, which they sought to discover. Dynamic psychiatrists held that such psychological problems were primarily the result of life experiences too painful and difficult to deal with.

Certain extreme and severe life experiences allow us to reflect on this debate. In World War II, with the ascent of psychoanalysis, it became widely recognized that there were vast numbers of psychological casualties from combat experience. Studies of Nazi concentration camp survivors indicate that 100 percent of survivors who were in camps for any length of time suffered substantial psychological symptoms of anxiety and depression. In a study of Vietnam veterans, psychologist Ghislaine Boulanger reported that about 36 percent of heavy- combat veterans suffered symptoms of PTSD. And in a more recent, comprehensive study led by psychologist Brian Engdahl of the Veterans Affairs Medical Center in Minneapolis, the research group found that among 262 veterans who had been prisoners of war during World War II or the Korean War, 53 percent had suffered PTSD. Among those held by the Japanese, who inflicted the most severe traumas, the lifetime rate of PTSD was 84 percent, of whom 59 percent continue to suffer the full syndrome. The authors concluded, "These findings indicate that PTSD is a persistent, normative, and primary consequence of exposure to severe trauma." By the term "normative," the authors mean that any ordinary person exposed to severe trauma can be expected to develop PTSD.[3] Psychiatrist William True and his associates assert that veterans who become ill are likely to be genetically more vulnerable to trauma, and psychiatrist R. K. Davies even asserted that victims of trauma may actually seek assaults because of possible neurologic or genetic abnormalities.[4]

Bessel van der Kolk reviewed the literature and described the physical effects of severe emotional trauma. His descriptions of the lasting physical effects of traumatic mental events were clear and striking and began to narrow the gap between the biological and dynamic approaches to the mind. Clearly, no longer could the mind and the body be considered separate, impenetrable worlds. From now on, the mind could affect the brain in substantial ways, and the brain could affect the mind. In other words, van der Kolk's work suggested that psychiatric syndromes were biologically induced by brain and hormonal abnormalities that were the consequences of traumatic life experiences. The solution, in Bessel van der Kolk's view, is biological because the defect is biological, but henceforth the biological defect has a new origin: the ethereal mind.[5]

There is no longer any doubt that psychological trauma can affect the body. A traumatic experience alters brain neurotransmitters, the immune system, and hormones as well. And there are psychological consequences to these physical changes. A new set of neurotransmitters will clearly affect one's view of the world. We see this whenever we take psychoactive chemicals, prescribed or illicit.[6] Lyle's persistent changes in body and brain resulted from his war experiences and were compounded by the disruption of his life by the resulting symptoms. These persistent biological effects can be treated psychologically, as Lyle's improvement through his psychotherapy demonstrates. In fact, Lyle and I made some original observations with the goggles that shed important light on the physical and the psychological nature of PTSD.

Lyle had been in treatment with me for about a year when I first thought of asking patients to limit their vision to one side. When he looked out of his left visual field (right brain), he said he didn't feel much anxiety. But his distress was palpable when he switched sides. When I asked what he was feeling, he said, "That plant [a large potted plant behind me] looks like the jungle." I asked him quickly to switch to the other side again, and he then, reported, "No, that's a nice-looking plant."

In some subsequent sessions, I tape-recorded his responses to the taped goggles. Here is the transcript of one of these trials.

(Without any glasses) "How much anxiety are you feeling right now?"

"Moderate."

"Pick one of the glasses. Okay, you're looking out the right side [left brain]."

"Yes . . . Just a little turbulence."

"How much anxiety are you feeling?"

"A little more."

"How would you rate it—none, mild; moderate, quite a bit, or extreme?"

"Quite a bit. More so than what it was."

"And how depressed do you feel; none, mild, moderate, quite a bit, or extreme?"

"I'm depressed quite a bit."

"Quite a bit. Do you have any physical feelings?"

"My heart rate seems to be at a higher rate."

"Does it seem very high? Is your heart racing or just a little bit fast?"

"Just fast. Worrisome."

"And how much stress do you feel: none, mild, moderate, quite a bit, or extreme?"

"Feel quite a bit, Doctor."

"Okay. And would you try the other glasses for me? (Thirty-second pause) So now you're looking out the left side [right brain]."

"How much anxiety do you feel now?"

"Moderate."

"And how much depression do you feel; none, mild, moderate, quite a bit, or extreme?"

"It's moderate; it's not extreme. I'm more at ease."

"And how about your heart?"

"I felt myself calm down."

"And how much stress are you under, none, mild, moderate, quite a bit, or extreme?"

"Moderate."

"Moderate stress? And how much difference is there between one side or the other?"

"On a scale of, say, one to ten, ten being extreme, one being nothing, from a nine to a four, easy."

"So you feel like a four on this side [right brain], and a nine on the other side [left brain]? And is that true for anxiety as well? How would you rate the anxiety?"

"Yeah, my entire . . . whole spectrum of things."

"How would you rate how you feel with these glasses on versus how you felt when you came in when you were sitting there without the glasses and I asked you how you felt?"

"Better."

"And on that scale between one and ten, how would you rate the difference between now and before you put on any glasses."

"Well, before putting any glasses on, I was about seven."

"And now?"

"Three or four, Doctor."

"So you feel less depressed on this side [right brain]?"

"Oh, most definitely."

"Now, can you let the other side look out this window [glasses allowing vision to the left visual field, which generally stimulates the right brain]? Can you let that other part of you see how calm the world looks out of this window, out this side?"

I am asking him if somehow (and I don't know how) he can let his troubled side look out and see the way the world looks to his healthier side.

"I understand what you're askin'. (One-minute pause) Well, he's balking. He don't really want to look. Let me concentrate here. They're so separate. (One-minute pause) Okay. I've got him over here."

"And can you let him see how calm and safe things are?"

"He's lookin'."

"And is he impressed?"

"I think he is."

"Can he see that the war's over?"

"Yes he can."

"How's he feel about that?"

"He feels good."

"Can he enjoy that?"

"He can. He can. He can see that side."

"Maybe he's not in danger anymore. Maybe he doesn't have to suffer anymore. Maybe he's safe now. Maybe it feels good to be safe."

"Oh, it does. He has to feel that way. He has to."

"And he can see it for himself?"

"Clearly now."

"Uh-huh. He doesn't have to trust me; he can look and see it for himself that the war's over."

"Yes, he can."

"He's done his duty; he can come home now."

"I think he can retire from the war, Doctor. And it's crazy; he feels he's tired, you know that. He's one tired veteran. He needs to rest. He can see that. He's calm now."

"Put your arms around him and bring him home. He's safe. He's done his duty. Now it's time for R&R; time to come home. Time to come home . . . to safety . . . to peace . . . to rest."

"He wants that. I know he does."

"And you'll protect him?"

"With all my strength and being, I will. I need him; he needs me."

"How's it feel now?"

"He's still lookin' in that window. I don't think he's looked through it long enough to see that clear-colored breeze—no bombs, no machine-gun fire. It's very quiet. He needs a lot of love and attention; he needs to be cared for. I don't think I've done my best. I feel stronger emotionally right now. I feel like I'm walkin' along beside him. He's battered and he's bruised. He's hungry for it. He's hungry for love."

"And he's gonna get it too."

"And peace."

"Let him have it. Let him have it."

(Patient sobs) "Nobody knows what the hell he's been through, Doctor. I gotta love him even though he's been a bad guy; but he's not really, just the way things happened to him. But he wants it; he wants it. He wants help. He's ready."

"You gonna bring him home?"

"I am. I am.

"How you feel?"

"I feel good."

"Good. First time I heard that in a long time."

"I don't recall ever saying it before."

Working with the goggles has shown us that Lyle does indeed still suffer from the experiences in Vietnam that he endured about thirty years ago. In his life before our work, he regularly suffered the symptoms of PTSD: angry outbursts, intrusive flashbacks and nightmares, avoidance of intimacy, pessimism, depression, and despair. The goggles helped us see that on one side (looking to the right), Lyle is much more symptomatic than when looking to the left. From our interview, we see that he too has two minds: one very troubled, still mentally living in Vietnam, and another mind much calmer and more realistic, living much more in his present reality.

Lyle's improvement did not come in one session by simply putting on a pair of glasses. It was a hard up-and-down struggle that only in the past two months has begun to show solid, reliable improvement that he can maintain between sessions. Essentially it took us two years, meeting weekly, often but not always using the goggles, to get his mature side to have the will and the courage to stand up to his then more energetic, more troubled side. We had to convince his troubled side that it too would profit by letting the mature side lead. We promised his troubled side that his mature side would nurture and protect him. His mature side and I imagined that we were rescuing his troubled side—a wounded soldier from the battlefield. We wanted to let the troubled part know that the war was over and that we were here to bring him home.

When a human mind is overwhelmed, it stops functioning at its highest level, suffering the effects of the traumatic experience in predictable ways. It will develop all of the symptoms of PTSD. These symptoms—disturbing thoughts and memories, emotional withdrawal, hyperactivity, anxiety, and depression—are the human mind's biological response to a sense of overwhelming danger and defeat. The important word here is "overwhelmed." The DSM-IV says that to have PTSD, the patient must have experienced an actual life-threatening event. I have not used the word "actual" in my clinical descriptions because what is experienced as catastrophic by one person may not be viewed in the same way by another. What is important, in regard to trauma, is that it causes injury when the mind is overwhelmed and stretched beyond its ability to cope. In an adult, it may take a war to overwhelm a mind, but in a small child, it may merely take sustained rejection or ridicule.

Lyle's mature-sided mind could better deal with the trauma and bring psychic resources to bear against the trauma and its memories. Lyle's recovery was aided by the goggles in two important ways. By isolating the troubled side, we became aware of the full extent of the psychological injury. His healthier side became stronger and thus able for the first time to teach his troubled side that both were finally safe. I described a third benefit in Chapter 3: the goggles provide the wearer a few moments to bask in the healthier aura of the more mature mind.

Abuse in Childhood

Kathleen was a forty-year-old, married, black woman who had been an executive at a leading Boston advertising firm until she was summarily fired, without obvious reason, two months earlier. That was nine months ago, when her primary care physician referred her to me because she seemed to be feeling periods of moderate depression. He put her on Prozac, which she felt didn't help her and caused her stomach distress.

In our first session, I learned that she came from a very intense dysfunctional family in which her mother alternately screamed at her and lavished love on her. Her father seemed a distant man who was prone to pathetic depressions. I attributed her depression to the pain of her job loss amplified by unresolved issues going back to her dysfunctional family. I pointed out that there might be another part of her that was more troubled by her past than she realized. I suggested she stop the Prozac, and I gave her a prescription for Zoloft, another SSRI antidepressant, because sometimes one SSRI will work when another does not.

Ten days later in her next session, she reported feeling much better, but neither of us understood why. She said, "I hope it isn't because of our discussing that inner part of me who had felt injured by my parents." On her own, she had begun to call that part of her Kathy because it seemed to relate to her childhood. She referred to her mature personality, the former advertising executive, as Kathleen. As with other patients I have described who have given names to the different aspects of their personalities, this was not a form of multiple personality disorder in which different parts of a person become autonomous and can have amnesia for other parts. With Kathleen, Kathy was merely a convenience to aid our discussions.

In the second session, Kathleen told me that she had decided not to fill the prescription for Zoloft. She expressed concern that I was not paying enough attention to her present life problems, but at the end of the session, when I described our task in her therapy as that of our teaching Kathleen how to be a good parent to Kathy, she suddenly broke into profound sobbing. Neither she nor I knew what my comment had touched.

Kathleen later called and asked for an urgent appointment, and I saw her two days after the second session. She had been feeling very upset since our last session. Essentially, she had been in a deep grief about her relationships with her mother and her father. We discussed the nature of grief and the process of handling it. She felt much better by the end of the session, but she felt a need to come in more often, and I began seeing her three times a week.

She continued to do well through her next three sessions, but in the following visit she reported that over the weekend, she had had a memory of her mother's holding her and slapping her so hard she thought her head would come off. She could still hear the sound of the slaps and remembers that she thought she would be killed. She had known that her mother hit her at times, but the vividness of the memory was new, as was the realization of the ferocity of the assault. During the session she began to have further memories, each new one revealing more shocking sadistic behavior involving both her parents. She recalled her father's beating her with a stick.

Her memories were detailed and consistent and were confirmed by a sibling who was also abused separately. The two had never discussed their abuse before. Over the following sessions, we struggled to deal with these emerging memories. She began to have vivid nightmares about the abuse, and began to require medication to sleep. Frequently I got calls from her in great distress. At times she became Kathy and would feel overwhelmed with terror and with actual physical pains in the different parts of her body that had been beaten. I struggled to arouse Kathleen, so that she and I could comfort Kathy. We were generally successful at this both over the telephone and in the sessions, but not infrequently her terror and despair would overwhelm her, and for the next few months the therapy took on the form of urgent rescues alternating with periods of composure in which Kathleen was in control. Overall, we were winning the struggle; Kathy was being comforted and reassured and calmed. But as more extensive, more cruel memories arose the battles kept repeating themselves.

Our strategy was simple. Kathleen and I needed to let Kathy know that this was the present and she was no longer in grave danger, and we needed to help both Kathy and Kathleen try to make some sense out of what had happened. How could her parents have acted so? How could other perpetrators in the world behave so sadistically? How could she have not known this before her therapy with me? Why did it not come up in an earlier treatment in her twenties? How did she survive and become such a successful wife, mother, and career woman?

The realization of her abuse brought up archaic inner feelings of defectiveness. Was she somehow responsible for her abuse? Did she in some way unwittingly provoke it? In Kathy, she felt great shame as well as terror. We pondered all of these and many other questions in our work together. Kathleen was very intelligent and mature and was able to be compassionate toward herself in the form of Kathy. The problem for us was that very often Kathy would take over, and the patient would spend the day in bed crying or planning a suicide. I pointed out that suicide would simply be Kathy's acting out ultimately her parents' sadistic impulses, and we would be able to gain control of the situation.

Several aspects of our treatment were helpful to Kathleen's recovery. First, she had established a trusting relationship with me. She believed I could help her and that I had her interests foremost, and she was able to use me as a valuable ally. She also had the help of a wonderful husband whose love, understanding, and support were without limit throughout months of nightmares, pain, and terror into which he threw himself without reserve and comforted her at all hours of need, in the middle of the night and the middle of his business day. Kathleen was also helped by her personal strength, courage, and intelligence.

In our strategy to get Kathleen to aid and lead Kathy, we found using a lateral visual technique to be helpful. Kathleen found the taped goggles frightening and oppressive, and so we couldn't use them. But I had developed a special pair of sunglasses; their effects generally less intense but otherwise similar to the taped goggles. A friend of mine, Robert Meyers, a professor of physics at Brandeis University, after hearing my description of my findings with the taped glasses, suggested that I might try using sunglasses that were tinted darkly on one side but gradually became clear on the other (see Figure 7.1). I took his suggestion and had an optometrist make a pair of sunglasses with round lenses so I could rotate the partially tinted lenses. Thus, one pair of glasses could serve as either left- or right-sided glasses. For some patients they have been very effective. Usually the sunglasses do not evoke as strong an emotional reaction as the tapped goggles on a given side, but they have the important advantage that they can be worn in public places and allow the patient free range of movement. I now have twelve patients who use the sunglasses in their daily lives. Kathleen is one of them.

For Kathleen the sunglasses were often helpful when she was trying

Figure 7.1

An illustration of sunglasses that are tinted more on one side of the lenses than on the other. The round lenses can be rotated to change the side that allows more light to pass through. These sunglasses have been found to have clinical responses similar to, though generally less intense than, those of the taped goggles and yet allow the wearer full vision and motion.

to calm Kathy. Unlike most other PTSD patients, Kathleen was comforted by looking to the right side (left brain). And as with other patients, the glasses by themselves without the context of psychotherapy would likely not have been of great value. Even within therapy, there were times when Kathy's distress was too great to be calmed by the glasses. Nevertheless, often the sunglasses were a significant help.

Gradually, over nine months, Kathleen and Kathy have worked well together, and generally Kathy feels safe and appreciated. Our work continues as Kathy gets stuck in a memory or in a nightmare and her terror and pain flare, but we are moving toward longer and more stable periods in which Kathleen leads and Kathy feels loved and safe.

The Essential Mechanisms of PTSD

Kathleen and Lyle are quite similar. Both primarily suffered symptoms of anxiety and depression, and in both, their symptoms were in response to overwhelming experiences. Both had their personalities overrun by an energized, immature part of themselves that tenaciously held on to the traumatic experiences. Both recovered by discovering and wisely using a mature part of themselves.

PTSD results when we are injured by that which confronts us and surpasses our capacity to cope—in spite of or because of all of our genes, all of our biochemicals, all of our life's experiences, and all of our efforts. Certainly dissimilar traumas will affect us differently and will affect us variously depending on our different resources. At the bottom of all that we suffer are the injuries we have not yet been able to recover from, not yet been able to grow from.

CHAPTER 8

Collapse

For a few weeks before being taken to the hospital by the campus police, Mark had been losing his contact with reality, Slowly and then rapidly he was slipping into a psychosis; he had been losing his mind, his rational mind. It began with some difficulty concentrating and studying, then feeling anxious most of the time. Most frightening was his not knowing why or what was happening to him. Soon he wasn't able to attend class because of his mental discomfort—his sense that he did not belong, did not fit in, could not make it—the constant sense of impending doom, the constant worry, the increasing inability to concentrate. More anxiety. Now a constant sense of impending humiliation. Ridicule. "You can't make it!" chants throughout his mind. He was becoming terrified. "Asshole, asshole" distantly rang in his ears. After two weeks, he could no longer leave his apartment; he was too disorganized, too confused, too terrified. He was immersed in an overwhelming pain that enveloped him without boundary. He was drowning. He felt he had no way out, but then a thought emerged—a simple thought, a thought that he might be superior. Perhaps he was mistaken, his suffering was exceptional, unique, misunderstood. Perhaps it was not he who was failing; it must be the world that was upside down, not him. There was a ray of hope, a relief from the storm. The *world* was crazy; *he* was safe. And so gradually he began to realize that he was Jesus. The parallels were all there: the misunderstanding, the misplaced ridicule, the false accusations, the lack of acknowledgment, the ultimate superiority and triumph, sustaining the success, love, and adulation he needed to assuage his anguish.

I met Mark a week after he was admitted to the hospital. He was referred to me for psychotherapy after he had settled down and was back to realizing that he was a broken man who had experienced a mental collapse. It was he who was crazy, not the world. He was embarrassed that he thought he was Jesus and avoided talking about those thoughts with which he tried to rescue his life.

We sat together, he mired in pain and confusion. I tried to let him know that he was not the first to become mentally undone. Sometimes when we feel overwhelmed with life, the fuses in our mind can blow.

He did not know what might have overwhelmed him. He was under some stress, especially by one professor whom he felt ignored him, but he wasn't feeling so much overwhelmed as undermined, as simply sinking into a mud hole, a pool of quicksand, in which the more he moved and tried to help himself, the more quickly he descended.

Growing up, Mark was constantly ridiculed and bullied by his peers. On the school bus from elementary school through high school, he endured chants of "Asshole, asshole." Panic filled him especially when he had to go to the cafeteria or gym class. He was chronically terrified, and the terror on his face was a signal to others to attack him with impunity, with taunts, insults, pushes, and punches. There was no escape, and there certainly was no understanding or help.

When Mark arrived at college, he was surprised to see that he was respected and included. For the first time in many years, he was treated without abuse, and for the first three years, he thrived in that environment. But in his last semester, he began to sink; he mentally reexperienced feelings of terror and helplessness, which in his therapy he could see resembled the chronic feelings of his earlier life.

Perhaps the uncertain prospects after graduation or the stress with the professor triggered his dormant memories to explode and overwhelm his mind. I presented this as simply a hypothesis, trying to offer some possible insight into what at first seemed chaotic and incomprehensible.

Mark and I seemed to make a good emotional connection, and he seemed eager to work with me. Since he was no longer having delusions that he was Christ, the staff felt he was safe to discharge a week after we began working together. Nevertheless, Mark was quite depressed and self-conscious, and he was suffering feelings of embarrassment and anxiety. He felt too distressed to return to his classes, and too disorganized and uncomfortable to concentrate on his schoolwork.

Upon admission, a medication psychiatrist initially diagnosed him with manic depressive illness and explained that this disorder was a genetic illness that, through a chemical imbalance in his brain, would cause him to have periods of psychosis. Fortunately, modern psychiatry offered medications that could help lessen the chance or the frequency of the recurrences of Mark's inherited, devastating problem. Mark felt beaten and couldn't see how he could ever climb out of the deep hole that he or his biology seemed to have dug for himself. He had been traumatized not only by his childhood tormentors, but also by his slip from reality, his official diagnosis, and his becoming a bona fide mental patient in a psychiatric hospital.

I told Mark that I did not share the view of the hospital psychiatrist; I felt he had had a psychotic episode largely because he somehow couldn't bear life as he saw it in a part of his mind. Given enough distress, any person could possibly become separated from reality. I agreed that he should be treated with the medications that the hospital had begun, valproate (a mood stabilizer like lithium) and risperidone (a new antipsychotic drug). After a few months together we decided to taper him off the risperidone.

At five months after his discharge, Mark showed a marked improvement. He was studying effectively and doing nicely academically. He remained shy-and ill at ease in social settings, but this area had always been difficult for him, and I didn't expect a rapid improvement there. Overall, I was pleased with Mark's progress. In his therapy, we continued to focus on helping him appreciate the pain and trauma he had experienced in childhood and as an adult, and then to teach a part of him we called the "little boy inside" that he was now safe and valuable.

Although we had a very good relationship, he at times admitted a fear that I might try to humiliate him. He thought perhaps that my interest in seeing him was to profit at his expense by taking his money under the false pretense of offering a service. A part of Mark knew that I had no interest in humiliating or exploiting him. We were able to see his fears of ridicule and abuse as coming from the "little boy inside" him, and by working on these ideas we were able to try to correct some of his archaic fears. Psychotherapists call this aspect of treatment "transference work." Freud discovered the concept of transference in which the patient would project his inner archaic ideas onto the therapist, offering an excellent opportunity to clarify the present reality. But transference work is a rather slow process that requires frequent repetition to achieve inner learning.

Then, at about a year and a half after his hospitalization, following an intense stress, Mark suddenly slipped into a disordered state of mind. It seemed to me as if the troubled little boy inside him had become distressed and energized, and was taking control of his mind. He could no longer concentrate or even attend classes. To look at him, one could easily see that he was not well. I worked with him to try to get the adult part of him to take control, and for short periods of time he would appear normal, but this healthy state would not persist for more than a few minutes. I markedly increased his medications.

At this time I had been working with the goggles with other patients. I was wary about trying them with Mark in his condition because I felt they might confuse him or make him more fearful. Finally, out of my feeling of urgency, I decided to use them with Mark in spite of my uncertainty about their safety. We had to take the risk.

Mark donned the goggles that activated his right hemisphere: "I don't trust you, Doctor!" I quickly urged him to try the other pair, allowing him to look out of the right side (left brain). He did this and almost immediately said with a very friendly smile, "Of course, I trust you." I was astonished. Looking out the right-sided goggles (left brain), Mark was absolutely normal, with no hint of a mental illness. He was relaxed and sociable, and he commented on how relaxed he felt. He realized that he was in a healthy mental state and seemed impressed and delighted by this sudden change in his condition.

I then asked him to try the other goggles again. Just as quickly as before, he became paranoid, tense, and angry. He lashed out that he didn't trust me and that he felt his roommates were abusing him, as the bullies of his childhood had done. Again I quickly asked him to switch back to the other side, and he immediately relaxed and said that he found me obviously trustworthy and that although he felt his roommates were not too likable, they were not bullying or abusing him.

Without removing the health-promoting goggles, we explored our observations of the "two" Marks. The goggles aided Mark to locate and arouse the two distinct personalities of his mind that we had long felt existed: one healthy and the other irrational, terrified, and suspicious. During the previous month, Mark's troubled mind was besting the healthy mind for control. Our task was to help the mature part learn to lead, protect, and comfort his frightened side, essential work because Mark's troubled side did not have the maturity or mental capacities to run his life in a safe, intelligent manner. We needed to let his troubled side see how safe the world appeared through his right-sided view (left brain) and see how well his life could go with his healthy side in the lead.

Mark and I were both delighted with this session's revelations and results. I gave him the health-inducing goggles to take home and suggested that he wear them as much as possible. On his own, Mark performed an experiment at home in which he wrote two descriptions of the session: one without the glasses on while he typed on his computer and one with them on.

Without glasses: I would say that the experience with Dr. Schiffer Friday night was fairly impressive, but who really cares? I feel like I need help right now just to get through anything in life. I'd like to get my hair cut, do not feel in control enough of my thoughts to do so. I just want to be able to control my thoughts.

With glasses: It's much harder to type with funny glasses on. Must persevere! I think the glasses experiment was phenomenal, and shows the power of the little boy inside (more like a petulant child at the moment). Our goal must be to make him sit down in his chair and let the adult part lead.

What I witnessed over the next several sessions was a remarkable struggle between these two aspects of his mind. He was not out of danger. When he was not wearing the goggles, his immature side still tended to dominate, though I could gradually see that we could more easily evoke his mature side. In each session we used the goggles, and his response to them remained robust and remarkable. We used them as a tool in our struggle to get his mature mind to lead and to teach his troubled side that it was safe and should no longer struggle for control. Over the next ten days, we were slowly winning, and for the first time in six weeks he was able to return to class.

Over the next month, he continued to make slow progress, first to about 50 percent of his usual capacity to study, then to about 65 percent, and by two months after we first used the goggles, he reported that he was now functioning at 100 percent of his capacity. Over this period, we continued to witness the same struggle. It seemed that the troubled part of his mind did not want to relinquish its power, even though it was clear that he would be better off with his healthier side leading. It was as if his troubled side was saying, "Yeah, but what do you want me to do—go on unemployment? Hell, no, I enjoy leading." Over time, with all our efforts, we succeeded in establishing the leadership of his mature side as we worked to discipline and comfort his troubled side.

It is now two years since we first tried the goggles, and Mark is functioning at a much higher level than ever before in his life. He is enrolled at a prestigious graduate school, where he is engaged in groundbreaking scientific work.

Dual-Brain Science and Psychosis

The dual-brain understanding of psychosis is that it can occurs when the mind of a less mature hemisphere becomes distressed, energized, and in a hyperaroused, disturbed state comes to dominate an individual's whole personality. Mark lost his mind—his mature mind, that is—to the powerful, disturbed, panicking immature personality of his right hemisphere. This troubled mind is "crazy" only if we expect to encounter the mind of a mature adult. But there is a method to its madness, reasons for its distressed state and behavior. Mark's troubled mind was upset because he had been ridiculed and abused severely in the past, and for some reason this old pain suddenly aroused and energized his troubled mind. Why did his troubled mind become active when it did? My conclusion was that his right-sided mind is a mind like all other minds, fully capable of responding and deciding. Apparently life, or the world as "this" part of Mark saw it, was becoming intolerably threatening, and this part of him apparently became energized. The human mind, whether adult or child, left or right, is unpredictable. It has its own capacity to make decisions and respond to the world.

Mark's right-sided mind did more than panic. It abandoned reality to create its own view of the world, a view in which he was no longer being ridiculed for being inferior, but rather one in which he was being attacked for being superior, for being Jesus Christ. I believe Mark's right-sided mind did this because it was seeking relief. Someone else might have thought of using alcohol or heroin or might have thought up a more creative and effective solution.

Another important factor led to Mark's psychosis. His more mature, left-sided mind collapsed under the pressure from his other side. The psychosis might not have materialized had his left-sided mind been able to hold its ground more effectively. But the relationship between two minds is difficult to predict, especially when they are engaged in a struggle for dominance. Did Mark's left-sided mind have to lose that struggle? I don't think so.

I don't believe that a psychotic disorder is entirely different from an anxiety disorder, a depressive disorder, or a posttraumatic stress disorder. In all cases, psychological problems stem from traumas that lead first to a sense of anxiety and then to defeat. Why trauma leads to anxiety, depression, and then a whole host of impairments goes back to our biological nature, our built-in defeat system.

A trauma model for psychosis is not new. Almost all psychological theories of psychosis have in a variety of ways seen the psychotic reaction as a response to some kind of trauma. For Freud, the trauma had to do largely with unbearable anxiety from conflicts between id impulses and ego and superego restraints. The eminent psychiatrist Harry Stack Sullivan, who devoted his career to working with psychotic patients, and a number of others prominent theorists, believed that psychosis had much to do with painful early relationships.[1]

Genetic Studies of Psychosis

Genetic studies of psychosis indicate that genetic factors are relevant, but they also clearly indicate that psychosocial factors are equally im-

portant. For example, in a large Finnish study of adoptees, when children whose mothers were diagnosed as schizophrenic were given up for
adoption and reared in healthy homes, none developed a mental illness. When such children were reared in unhealthy environments, a
number developed psychoses. Adopted children whose biological
mothers were apparently healthy did not develop serious mental illness
in either a good or a poor environment.[2]

Biological Theories of Psychosis

There are a number of theories about how chemical or neurological
defects could cause major mental illnesses, but the evidence does not
yet lead to a clear hypothesis. In patients with schizophrenia, there are
often structural brain changes. Whether these changes cause or follow
the psychological changes is not yet scientifically established. A number of neurotransmitter systems, such as norepinephrine, dopamine,
glutamate, and serotonin, have been found to be abnormal in these individuals, but some debate exists about whether these chemical
changes follow the structural brain alterations. Science has neither
discovered the primary causes of these severe mental disorders nor fully
understood the interactions between the psychological impairments
and the brain abnormalities.[3]

Theories of Hemispheric Abnormalities in Schizophrenia

Over the past thirty years, scientists have explored the possibility that
psychotic illnesses may involve one hemisphere more than the other.
Psychiatrist Pierre Flor-Henry found that a left hemispheric focus for
temporal lobe epilepsy was associated with schizophrenia and a right-
sided focus with manic depressive illness. Flor-Henry speculated that
schizophrenia was associated with a dysfunction of the left hemisphere
and that manic depressive illness was related to a comparable dysfunction in the right hemisphere. But the nature of such dysfunctions was
unclear, and whether findings from epilepsy can be extended to explain psychosis has not been supported over time.[4]

Nevertheless, a view that schizophrenia is somehow associated with an abnormality of the left hemisphere has persisted. In England, researcher John Gruzelier and his associates have used galvanic skin responses to measure the amount of electric current present in the skin of the hands. (Under stressful conditions, increased sweating generally increases electrical conductance.) Gruzelier found that under stress, patients with schizophrenia have greater conductance in their right hands, which are neurologically connectected to the left brains. In contrast, patients with depression had greater conductance in their left hands, suggesting an increased right brain activity.[5] In further studies, Gruzelier found that schizophrenic patients who manifested active symptoms, such as delusions and excitement, had a left hemispheric dominance, but schizophrenic patients who were withdrawn showed a right hemispheric dominance.[6]

Stuart Dimond, the psychiatrist who developed the contact lens for showing movies to one hemisphere or the other, along with his associate Graham Beaumont, did postmortem examinations of the brains of people who had been diagnosed as schizophrenic. They found that the corpus callosums from these patients tended to be enlarged. Dimond and Beaumont hypothesized that this enlargement was an attempt by the brain to compensate for poor communication between the hemispheres. In a follow-up study, they very briefly flashed stimuli to both the left and right visual fields simultaneously (going each to the opposite hemisphere) and asked subjects to try to determine if the stimuli were the same or different. Compared to a control group, the schizophrenic patients did poorly on this task, but they did just as well as control patients when both stimuli were sent to the same hemisphere. From these studies, Dimond and Beaumont concluded that the schizophrenic patients had difficulty communicating between their hemispheres.[7]

A more recent study from London's Institute of Psychiatry contradicts Dimond and Beaumont. Examining MRIs of forty-two patients with schizophrenia and forty-three normal control subjects, they discovered that the corpus callosum in the schizophrenic group was slightly smaller. They tested for how well the hemispheres communicated using a special neuropsychological test, and they could detect no differences between the two groups of subjects.[8]

Recent MRI studies from three different groups of scientists suggest an association between left hemisphere brain structural abnormalities in the temporal lobes in schizophrenic patients with auditory hallucinations. But the majority of imaging studies have failed to show physical differences between the two hemispheres in patients with schizophrenia.[9]

A large number of functional imaging studies have been performed on patients with schizophrenia. These studies use PET scans and other techniques to measure areas of brain activity at a given time. Unfortunately, overall these studies have given very inconsistent results. Karen Berman, from the National Institute of Mental Health Neuroscience Center, and her associates wrote:

> The notion that schizophrenia may involve disordered lateralization of brain activity has been explored for many years using a variety of methods. However, even among those studies that support the notion there is little agreement as to which hemisphere is implicated or whether the putative aberration may involve both hemispheres. Similarly, if there is an abnormality, it is unclear whether it consists of increased or decreased activity on the affected side or an increase on one side and a decrease on the other side. The existing functional brain imaging data concerning the question are relatively sparse and do little to resolve it.[10]

Treatment of Psychosis

I have always believed in the potential for psychological treatments to help people who have fallen into a psychosis. For many people, a mental collapse into a world of delusions wreaks a devastation they cannot recover from. From my 20-plus years of experience, I am convinced that the type of treatment a patient receives at the time of first illness will, more than any other factor, determine its eventual course. I have seen many people who came to me after years of being chronically ill, and I have often had more limited success in pulling them out than patients treated at the onset of their illness. It is urgently important, especially early on, before the condition multiplies upon itself, to offer the patient an intense effort with a high-quality psychological therapy as well as with drug therapy in order to attempt to effect an early, good recovery.[11]

New medications such as risperidone and olanzapine, alongside established antipsychotic and antimanic drugs, contribute to a powerful medicinal armamentarium aimed at psychotic disorders. When dealing with such a difficult and painful problem as psychosis, we need to apply effectively all available modalities.[12]

CHAPTER 9

Coca Compulsions

*L*enny's a little nervous. The big guy wants a cigarette. Lenny says, "Sure. Here—help yourself." The little guy rocks on his heels and looks around with eyes like searchlights scouring for enemy aircraft. "So you want the stuff or not?" the big guy wants to know.

"Sure I do. But your price is too high."

"Two hundred. Take it or leave it. This ain't an auction."

"Two hundred. Goddamn it. You're robbin' me."

The big guy turns to leave, and the little guy begins to follow. "Hey, don't call me no more," the big guy shouts as he moves down the street away from Lenny.

"Here. Here's two hundred."

Lenny's in a dangerous neighborhood. He's heard that people going to the grocery store have been shot there by stray bullets, and here he's buying cocaine—or some chemical he hopes is cocaine or at least resembles cocaine, but Lenny knows it could be talcum powder or a horse tranquilizer. He buys it anyway, even though he knows he'd be getting ripped off even if it were cocaine. And he could easily get arrested. For all he knows, the big guy could be under surveillance or he could be undercover. But Lenny has to buy. He has to do it, to go through this, to risk his life, go through the humiliation and terror, go through the risk of using whatever the hell he's taken possession of.

He took the two hundred from his wife's wallet. She'll see him when he comes in in the morning half baked, exhausted, spent, depressed. And she'll lay into him. He knows this because it always happens.

I met Lenny after he was admitted to the addiction unit at McLean Hospital in 1985, years before managed care arrived, when the program was for thirty days. At that time the hospital could act as a kind of dynamic air-bag, protecting the patient from himself and holding him long enough so that I could come in four times a week and mentally operate on his tortured psyche. At Lenny's discharge, our work was only beginning, but we had had enough time and psychic space to make an emotional bond, which would sustain our work, and thus his safety, even without the protection of the hospital. For two months after his discharge, we met twice a week, and over the next five years we saw each other weekly. Cocaine stopped the day Lenny was admitted to the hospital; it took another five years to repair the inner damage that had led to his addiction.

Lenny was one of nine cocaine abusers I treated in the mid-1980s with in-depth psychotherapy begun in the hospital program. Our breakthrough came when we realized that Lenny and the other cocaine abusers were addicted not only to the highs that the drug produced, temporarily relieving their everyday mental distress, but also to the lows that inevitably followed cocaine use. All of my patients had been emotionally denigrated as children. Some of their siblings were seen in their childhoods as future doctors or lawyers. But while my patients were still in diapers, they were usually identified as disappointments and expected to fulfill their parents' prophesy as they grew into adulthood. The disdain that they endured at home became unbearable but unavoidable. Nothing could gain the praise or even tacit approval for which they longed.[1]

I came to believe that these patients so strongly believed in their inevitable humiliation and so profoundly feared the pain of that eventuality that its anticipation became unbearable. Living in expectation of one kind of humilation or another, they would go to great lengths to bring it about, just to get the pain over with. For a short time after using cocaine, when they were "coming down," they experienced the anticipated profound humiliation and the "relief" that came from getting it over with. These patients seemed doomed to keep repeating the spiral of anticipated humiliation, relief through pain, and then after a brief respite, a new surge of anticipation.

Lenny revered his father, but his every action seemed to invite his father's criticism. When Lenny mowed the lawn, his father pointed to each area where the cut was imperfect. "You're just a fart in a cart," his father told him regularly. I helped Lenny see that although he had been mistreated as a child, he was as deserving of his parents' love and admiration as any other child. Over time, the lesson took hold; gradually Lenny grew able to appreciate and value himself. But even after five years of working together, we never really came to understand the reasons for his father's disdain; those answers remained locked inside his deceased father's unconscious mind.

Although I had been pondering my theories about two minds and two personalities for several years, I hadn't yet conceptualized the two minds of dual-brain science when I was treating Lenny. Those ideas came later. As part of our studies of the lateralized goggle effects, I called Lenny and some others I had treated in the 1980s, to invite them to participate informally in our program. Each had continued to do well since our last contact a decade earlier. With Lenny, we recorded my interview with him while he wore the different pairs of experimental glasses.

"So now you're not wearing any glasses. How much anxiety are you feeling on a scale of none, mild, moderate, quite a bit, or extreme?"

"I would have to say some, between none and mild."

"I would like you to pick one of those pairs of goggles. . . . So, you're looking out the right side [left brain]. How much anxiety are you feeling?"

(Within seconds) "Actually quite a bit. I'd rate it on a scale of zero to ten about an eight."

"On a scale of none, mild, moderate, quite a bit, or extreme?"

"Quite a bit."

"Is this feeling familiar?"

"I've felt this before. It would come when I would have the inability to converse and be with my dad. It's a feeling that I didn't have when I came in here today. It goes all the way to my legs and my feet. It's like a fight-or-flight feeling, an inability to get across to someone else."

"What comes to mind? Where does it take you?"

"It actually takes me to some of the physical fights that Dad and I used to have and not knowing why they started, but watching him get utterly frustrated and escalate that to the point where he would lose control. I asked my mom about that about a year ago. She doesn't remember any of that happening."

"Does this relate to any of the feelings with the substance abuse?"

"Yeah, to the acquisition of the substance. One of the things is that you would get a very anxious, paranoid feeling because it wasn't right; it wasn't legal. You didn't know when your so-called number was up. And you didn't know if the quality was good. You knew nothing about it, and every time you acted on it, you were taking a huge risk. As I look back on it, it was not worth it at all, but I would get this feeling, toward the end; I'd get such a feeling that I'd get diarrhea."

"And what would happen to this feeling when you'd use? Would using affect this feeling?"

"Don't know because the using confused the feeling, and maybe that's what's in abusing substances; maybe that's what the person's looking for in trying to confuse the feeling. So you really don't know what's going on. All you really know is that it's different. It may not be acceptable, but you do know that you've altered it."

"And after the substance is leaving your body, what's the feeling like?"

"Well, you're left right back where you began. You still have a feeling similar to this because you know you'll go out and acquire more, and it's just a matter of timing as to when. So this feeling is always there. It doesn't go away unless you alter it some way."

"And how do you feel about yourself in this condition?"

"You feel totally insecure. You feel out of control. Obviously you have no control over what's going on if you're acquiring."

"How do you feel about yourself as a person when you feel this way?"

"As a person, you feel pretty low about yourself because of what you're doing. You know what you're doing."

"Is this similar to or different from the way you felt about yourself when your father was upset with you?"

"It's similar."

"I want you to try the other goggles, if you would."

(Seconds later) "Now I'm looking out the left side [right brain].

I'm more calm. On a scale of zero to ten, it would have to be maybe a two or a three, which in your terms would be mild. Don't know why, but it's true. And it's a very calming effect. I no longer feel anxiety racing in my legs. That's all gone. This is very curious. It's a shame I can't wear glasses like this all the time."

"Can you remember when your father was angry with you?"

"Oh, I can remember."

"And how does that feel?"

"It would be the white noise of feelings—a total array of feelings from confusion, anxiety, panic, fight, flight."

"As you remember it right now, can you feel any of that? What are you feeling right now?"

"No, I don't feel any of that now. With this pair of goggles I have on, it's more like talking with my mom, who would always have a calming effect."

"Does the feeling that you have right now bear any relation to your drug use?"

"No, I would have to say not. I've acquired this type of feeling only in the last eleven or twelve years with the comprehensive understanding and acceptance of my problems with my father."

"And how did you acquire that?"

"Well, through four and half, five years of sessions with you, and actually grieving for my dad and the relationship we didn't have. Finding out about my dad through my brother, talking it over with my mom, and just basically putting it behind me. Getting rid of all the dark and the old feelings and remembering the good times, like my mom does."

"How do you feel about yourself right now?"

"Well, I feel confident."

"How do you value yourself? How do you feel about yourself as a person?"

"Well, I'm doing the most that I can in the best way that I can to exist on my own, to exist as a husband, and to exist as a father and to my family and doing the best job I can at work. There isn't really anything else that I can do to make my life better."

"What's the net result? How do you rate yourself? How do you rate yourself as a person?"

"Well, I'm a good person. I've made myself into a good person."

"I'd like you to switch glasses again."

"Can I buy these?" (Laughs)

"So now you're looking out the right side [left brain]."

"The right side. Tension is back into my legs and throughout my body. Still don't know why. Maybe I'll find out some day. I just feel the phrase, "torqued up," tight; expecting verbal abuse, quips, so to speak. One of the things that I've had to work on very hard is to try not to pass along to my boys what my dad passed along to me. And I'm not sure that he meant harm, but it came out to be that way. I don't want to pass it along. One of the instances that I think of is that when I would mow the lawn, when I was finished he would come out and show me what I didn't do, and I would feel like this."

"And what does this feel like?"

"This feels like a person who's never been rewarded, who never knows that he's an okay person, that he can and probably will never do right and always makes mistakes. It's a real lonely feeling."

"Let's try the other pair again."

"Let's not do these [the right-sided goggles] again. It [the left-sided goggles] immediately takes that away."

"So you're looking out the . . ."

"Left side [right brain]."

"This is the side you're feeling more comfortable on? Let's talk about how you felt when you had the other glasses on. Do you have any idea why you were using drugs? Do these glasses give you any insight into that?"

"I think I used drugs to alter the way that I felt about myself. I also used drugs as a way to gain friends. It got me acceptance into a wide group of people that I didn't really look at from a rational point of view; it was just a group of people who shared a substance abuse concept."

"Now the feeling that you had on the other side, was that related to the substance abuse, the torqued-up feeling?"

"Yeah, I would get that feeling. One of the reasons I sought help to end the cocaine abuse was because in the end, it started to accentuate the feeling I had looking out the right side. It was compounding my negative feelings about myself by a factor of about ten."

"Did you ever use to bring on that negative feeling?"

"That's a good question. Not in the beginning, but I think maybe by a year after the beginning, and then definitely from then on until the end."

"And how could you explain that? Could you elaborate on what you are saying?"

"You deceive yourself into thinking that it's going to give you what you want, but after a short period of time, you know it will never give you that. It will just give you negative feelings about yourself."

"Now when you came down from coke, did you feel the way you felt when your dad would yell at you, demean you?"

"Ah, yes, because that's the reason I took it in the first place to alter that feeling. But it wound up producing that feeling. In fact, it would accentuate the feeling by factors of five or ten. Finally it gets so out of control that you either stop or do something stupid. As they say jails, institutions, or death—that's the only place it'll take you."

"Looking from this perspective [right brain], how do you see your father and what he did?"

"I see my father as a product of circumstances. What he passed on to me was passed on to him by his parents. I've gotten some insight through my brother and through my mom. He probably tried not to pass on some things that were passed on to him. My mom also told me that by the time I came along as a fourth child, he was tired of kids and I did not get a lot of the consideration that the other three did. I understand that now."

"Do you understand that more now from this side [looking through the left-sided glasses]?"

"Ah, yes, because the other side produces clutter, and clutter does not produce clear thinking."

"It's more the way you felt as a child?"

"Right, the right side [left brain] is how I felt as a child. The left side [right brain] is how I feel now."

"Now with the glasses on, do you feel any different than if you have the glasses off?"

"Yeah. If I have the glasses off, I get a mixture of the feeling from the two glasses."

"Why don't you take them off?"

"And it's a constant battle to minimize those old feelings and keep them under control."

"But you've been able to win that battle so far."

"Yeah, I would never ever go back."

Lenny's visit and the use of the glasses confimed my belief that we had been treating the troubled mind in his left hemisphere all along. That troubled mind still exists, after years of therapy sessions and years of success in his career, marriage, and fatherhood. But what really matters was that it has given up its once-dominant role, perhaps finding comfort in the praise Lenny's mature side is able to obtain from the world in which he lives.

This extraordinary interview, ten years after Lenny completed his therapy, captured the unbearable pain Lenny felt as a child and young man criticized by his father. It was overwhelming in intensity and led directly to the torqued-up feeling he described. Although his cocaine use was a desperate attempt to alter that feeling, to bring relief, it brought along the criticism he anticipated and dreaded.

Freud found that many patients often retraumatized themselves by instigating situations similar to the initial traumatizing circumstance. Freud coined the phrase "repetition compulsion," to refer to the patient's unconscious attempt to master the trauma. I believe Lenny was caught in such a repetition compulsion. Notice the similarity between how he felt when he was criticized and how he felt when he acquired, used, and came down from his cocaine high. The most compelling observation was that Lenny could reexperience this pain simply by putting on the right-sided goggles, stimulating his left hemisphere. Lenny had apparently improved because the mind in his right brain grew stronger and capable of maintaining its leadership and healthier view of the world.[2]

A second patient, Reggie, had a similar history of cocaine abuse related to his father's chronic disapproval. Reggie agreed to return to my office to try out our goggles.

"Reggie, rate for me how anxious you feel sitting here [without goggles]: none, mild, moderate, quite a bit, or extreme?"

"Mild."

"Now I want you to put on either of those glasses. (Puts on glasses) Now you're looking out your right side [left brain]."

"Correct. My right side."

"How much anxiety are you feeling?"

"A decent amount."

"And on that scale—none, mild, moderate, quite a bit, or extreme—how much would you say?"

"Moderate."

"What are you feeling?"

"Anxious, 'cause I feel I can't see what might be comin' at me from the other side."

"Is this a new feeling or a familiar feeling?"

"Sort of familiar because I'm in business, and you never know what's about to happen. Definitely unknown."

"Would you try the other goggles? (Puts on goggles) How much anxiety are you feeling looking out the left side [right brain]?"

"I think less."

"How would you rate it?"

"Mild."

"Can you describe the difference between how you feel on this side versus the other side?"

"I'm more relaxed on this side. On the other side, I was a little more uptight."

"When we were working together before, did you feel generally in life more like this or more like the other side?"

"Generally in life, more like the other side. Now in my life, I feel more like this side."

"Let's put the other pair [left brain] back on. (Puts on goggles) How do you feel?"

"Same as before. Not as comfortable as the other side."

"Now how do you feel about yourself at this moment on this side versus the other side?"

"I feel more relaxed on the other side."

"Try the other pair again [right brain]. (Puts on goggles) Do you feel any differently about yourself on one side versus the other?"

"I feel better about myself on this side. I feel like a better person on this side: a little more caring, a little more sharing, open minded on this side, less anxiety, an easier walk on this side."

"And on the other side?"

"Uptight. The unknown."

"Let's put the other glasses on [left brain]. (Puts on goggles) Is this a familiar feeling?"

"Wow, this is an uneasy feeling. I don't want to go there. Just things about the past."

"Things you haven't felt for a while?"

"Yeah."

"What comes to mind?"

"Not a good sign here. I'm just thinking about things I did in the past and everything about me then. I don't really think about anybody but myself and the abuse, some of the things I've been through in life. This is not what I want to remember. Can I take them off now?"

"I just want to ask you one more question. Can you relate these uncomfortable feelings to your father?"

"I don't know. I was never comfortable around my father. With these glasses on, it's sort of like dealing with him again because it's always the unknown, and it's always a pressure and a problem."

"The way these glasses make you feel, is this related to the feeling you had when you'd want to use?"

"Yeah, you feel the unknown. You have the tension."

"After you'd come down from coke, did you have feelings like you have now?"

"Yeah, but not to the same degree. Bad. Why did I do it? Confused."

"Let's put the other glasses on [right brain]."

"More relaxed. More focused. Clearer."

"Now if you think of your father on this side."

"I can deal with him on this side. I know how to handle him now, and I don't think he'd get me upset, and I wouldn't do the counterproductive things if I looked at him out of this side all the time. I'd feel more pity for him and for the relationship, and I don't think I'd want to abuse myself by using drugs."

"What would someone have to do to you to get you to use drugs, feeling the way you do on this side?"

"I don't think it's an option on this side."

"Would they have to have a gun or something?"

"Oh, yeah, they'd have to do some extreme things."

"On the other side?"

"Yeah, I could see myself doin' it on the other side."

Although both Lenny and Reggie stopped using drugs over four-teen years ago, the right-sided goggles (stimulating their left brains) can elicit their old worldview. This is the disturbed view they devel-oped out of their traumatic relationships with their fathers that ulti-mately led to their substance abuse. And we see that the left-sided goggles offered a positive, healthy view of their worlds, views that have come to predominate in their lives.

Let's consider what this implies about the substance abuse in these two patients. It appears that a part of them, probably located in their left hemispheres, was traumatized by the rejection they experienced as children and young adults. That trauma led to convoluted, unsuccess-ful attempts to address their problems, which eventually led to their cocaine abuse. It appears that through their therapy, they were able to access or further develop a mind in their other hemisphere, a mind that could maturely guide them successfully to recovery and a success-ful life.

The Roots of Addiction

We are all creatures of habit. It is part of our human makeup that we develop habits. We brush our teeth and exercise, partly out of habit. An addiction is a habit or a compulsion to do something harmful. Lenny and Reggie both clearly had addictions. Both also had a more troubled hemisphere and a healthier hemisphere. As in most of my other patients who suffered significant psychological trauma, their troubled hemisphere is on the left. In these two patients, the compul-sion to use drugs clearly came from the troubled side, and I believe that within that troubled side, there existed a highly developed habit to use cocaine as a misguided solution to the psychologically agonizing maze in which that troubled side found itself.

Early psychoanalytic writers on addiction did not think of there

being two minds. But this classic psychoanalytic work is applicable because most patients behave as if they had only one mind—one very
troubled mind. The troubled side, as in my patients before they entered treatment, becomes so strong and dominant that it in effect runs
the patient's entire life. Sandor Rado, a contemporary and colleague of
Freud, saw the abuser's drug use as an attempt to relieve a depression by
inducing a state of "elation." He felt that when the elation wore off,
the patient would fall into an even deeper depression. Rado saw drug
use as autoerotic, resembling masturbation. The abuser's failures led to
heightened fears of punishment and destruction, which he and other
psychoanalysts called castration fears. Such anxieties then led to more
intense yearnings for the drug-induced pleasures.[3]

Edward Glover, another contemporary of Freud, focused on the
role of aggression in addiction. He thought that the drugs helped people lessen their intense, inner feelings of anger, which chronically
threatened to overwhelm their emotional lives. Thus, both Rado and
Glover saw addiction as a form of self-medication administered to help
deal with overwhelming feelings of anger, anxiety, and depression. In a
sense the drug addict was acting as his own psychopharmacologist, pre-
scribing a medication with many more side effects than benefits. Harvard psychiatrist Edward Khantzian, a contemporary analyst, has also
suggested this self-medication hypothesis. He and others have suggested that substance abusers suffer psychological traumas, which lead
to psychological deficiencies in development, for which the self-ad-
ministered drugs are intended, unwisely, to compensate.[4]

I agree that early trauma and subsequent psychological confusion
and pain are at the heart of addiction, and that self-medication is a
partial explanation for the unfolding of this condition. But I also think
that the role of self-abuse, copying and mentally incorporating the
early abuse, is an even more important factor.

In opposition to the psychological trauma theory of addiction is
the so-called disease model. This is the explanation developed by Al-
coholics Anonymous and supported by psychiatrist George Vallant,
among others. They propose that inner psychological issues generally
are unrelated to addiction. The causes of the addiction are the substances (alcohol and illicit drugs) themselves as they set in motion al-

tered brain states, causing abnormal mental states, which lead to the disease. The treatment of the disease is the elimination of the substance, which repairs the brain and ends the addiction. Psychological problems result from the brain effects of the substances that, once indulged in, by their inherent nature become irresistible. Smoking, for example, is difficult for anyone who has taken it up to quit. One smokes not because of a deep-seated psychological problem, but rather because nicotine is so physically addictive that once indulged in, it is hard to stop and leaves the person to endure the physical consequences of the compelling habit.

The disease model illuminates the degree to which substances themselves are destructive and have highly negative mental and physical consequences that add to the cycle of addiction. Removing the drug from the patient's life is essential to any attempt at recovery, and AA has a long list of superb techniques for helping people avoid using. Indeed, I recommend AA and other similar groups strongly to those who have addiction problems. But it is equally obvious to me that deep-seated psychological problems are also at the root of drug abuse. Repeatedly, I observed when my patients were discharged from McLean after being off drugs for their thirty-day stay, they were surprised to discover that they still felt depressed, anxious, and deeply troubled psychologically. Our work was only beginning when they were discharged. And the hospital detoxification was essential to any type of psychological treatment.

A third school of thought about addictions is an eclectic approach best represented by psychiatrists Bruce Rounsaville and George Woody. They see supportive psychotherapy as an adjunct to education and antidepressant therapy and tend not to explore deep-seated issues.[5]

I am convinced that a deep exploration of the psychological trauma and pain of patients with addiction is essential. It is unfortunate that fewer and fewer therapists are knowledgeable about how to conduct such an enterprise. People with substance abuse problems deserve to be understood deeply and to learn profoundly that they are worthy souls who have gotten lost in the psychological maze of their early abuse. I am not saying that people who abuse drugs have no responsibility to

help themselves; quite to the contrary, I know that if they don't discover and access some inner will (perhaps from their other hemisphere), then no one else will be able to be of assistance. It is essential
in such treatment to help to develop the person's more mature side and
to use it as an ally with which to help the more troubled side.

CHAPTER 10

Attack on the Heart

*F*rank and Cecil sit before Jordon in his oak-paneled corner office overlooking Boston Harbor. Cecil is pissed. Frank's trying to push his way past, and he lies—outright lies. He'll do anything to get ahead. All the times Cecil took Frank under his wing, protected him, taught him, showed him the business, and now he can't believe Frank's bold lies, dumping all the blame on his shoulders. He's talking hundreds of thousands of dollars, and Jordon believes him.

"I told him not to buy that shit. He knows it. I told him don't touch it," Cecil protests.

"Own up to it, C. You screwed up. It's your area. This is serious. You hurt the company." Jordon's not listening. His mind's made up. Frank must have gotten to him earlier.

"I didn't even know the fucker was buying. I told him not to."

Frank has the gall to cut in. "Don't curse at me. You don't have an answer, and you want to curse at me like we're in a school yard. Here's the memo, Cecil."

Cecil has been feeling tight in his chest since the meeting began twenty minutes ago; now it's crushing, and he's straining for air. Cecil doesn't want to quit and go down like a wounded warrior, so he's tried not to say anything about his chest pain, but it is now too great to ignore. He has no choice but to surrender. "Jordon, you better call an ambulance. I'm having chest pain."

In an instant, Cecil has become a patient. Jordon assists him to his couch and tells him to lie down. He calls an ambulance and asks Frank to leave. Cecil worries. What if it's nothing—just nerves or indigestion? But he's too tired to get up.

The EMTs arrive, and with mechanical efficiency have him IV'd, wrapped and strapped to the stretcher and wheeled out past the open offices, past his former compatriots to the elevator, out to the street where onlookers gawk, into the ambulance for a sirened, turbulent, terrifying ride to the emergency ward.

He's examined, ECG'd, X-rayed, and examined twice more. Then one of the doctors—he's not quite sure which one—says, "Mr. Rollins, you're having a heart attack. The circulation to your heart is blocked, and blood cannot get through to an area of your heart muscle. We want to take you upstairs and do an angioplasty. We will insert a catheter with a balloon on the end into the blocked artery, and we will expand the balloon to try to reopen your artery. We need you to sign here."

Cecil doesn't know whether to feel terrified or relieved. In fact, he feels both at the same time. The beeping of the heart monitors, the milling medical staff, the plastic-wrapped, ominous-looking medical equipment surrounding him confirm that he has become a cardiac patient. This like nothing else strikes terror in his heart. Yet, relieved to be in their hands, Cecil submits to their authority.

Cecil survived, and his internist, who knows me well, suggested that he consult with me after he came out of the hospital. It took a year before he allowed his wife to set up an appointment. Cecil, who was fifty-eight at the time, appeared robust and hardy. Although dressed as an executive in an expensive suit and tie, he had the air of a truck driver. He was back at work and very successful there; he had won back Jordon's loyalty and forced Frank out. Still, even after his angioplasty, cardiac rehab, and professional success, he seemed full of fury. He spoke slowly and pleasantly, yet I felt waves of anger and aggression just under his starched shirt and his Armani suit—like a grenade, sitting there harmlessly, but if the pin was pulled, all hell would break loose.

As a child, Cecil felt disregarded and unjustly criticized by his parents, especially his father. He had always inarticulately resented the fact that both parents favored his older brother. When I finally got Cecil to talk about it, he could feel his rage at the injustice rumbling around inside. We came to realize that one part of his mind tightly held on to this resentment, while another part had long before made peace with the unforgotten inequity.

In later sessions, we used the goggles. Looking out the left side, stimulating his right brain, he could feel his anger well up at the mere thought of his parents' doting praise of his brother. Switching to the right-sided goggles, stimulating his left brain, he felt calm and peaceful, even while we discussed the slights of his childhood. Cecil's troubled personality "lived" in his right brain, which experienced the past as if it were yesterday. At times of frustration, his feelings of outrage led to deep depressions. As with my other patients, we came to view his therapy as our teaching the troubled part of him that there was another way to view the world—a way to let go of the indignities and let the mature part of him love and appreciate the troubled part of him.

Cecil came to me a disgruntled, skeptical executive. He never expected to be helped by a psychiatrist, but he was the first to realize the great improvement he was experiencing in his life. Because of the dedication and seriousness with which he addressed the problem and his intense, lifelong but unarticulated search for a solution, he put his full power to the task. This was the same mental concentration he developed to fight business adversities, and within six months he was able to terminate dual-brain therapy with an excellent result.

In many ways, Cecil was a changed man. He no longer had an aggressive, ragged edge to his personality. He was, in fact, relaxed, and his relationships with his wife, children, and colleagues had all improved, because the relationship between his two minds had improved. The loss of his excess aggressiveness improved his work performance. Apparently he was no longer tripping over himself or provoking unnecessary struggles, but was learning how to work cooperatively. Cecil's follow-up exercise stress test, which had demonstrated abnormal ST segment changes (suggesting a heightened risk of another heart attack) shortly before he started his therapy, was now entirely normal.

Cecil discovered that Jordon's favoring Frank reverberated with his own childhood memories of his father's preference for his older brother. It dawned on Cecil that these memories energized the angry, frustrated, troubled part of him in his right brain. Once that part of him felt utterly defeated, it was somehow able to evoke a full-blown "defeat syndrome," complete with chest pain and a brush with death.

Cecil had seen quite a few cardiologists from the time he entered the emergency room, but none had any sense of how his mind was the force leading the attack on his heart. He was told when he left the hospital to try to reduce the stress in his life in the same breath in which he was told to reduce the fat in his diet, but neither he nor his doctors understood how complex the stress mechanisms were, or how difficult they would be to reduce if they were not understood.

Psychosomatic Medicine of the 1950s

In many ways medicine has improved over the years, but occasionally a piece of wisdom is left behind. In the 1950s and 1960s, psychosomatic medicine was a burgeoning young field. Psychoanalysts were at the forefront of the movement because they could appreciate the depth and complexity of the mind and its uncanny ability to affect the body, especially the heart. They produced a sophisticated literature filled with fascinating descriptions and theories on the relationship between the mind and the heart. But by the early 1970s, this literature had been relegated to the archives, as the field of psychosomatic medicine was taken over by leaders with a more pragmatic, experimental approach. This led to the popularization of the type A personality and a wealth of epidemiologic studies showing that stressful life events were associated with a significant increase in cardiac events. But for all its advances, this new approach lacked psychological depth. It established absolutely that stress was profoundly associated with heart problems, but it never attempted to understand the psychological nature of the connection, and few cardiologists were aware of or appropriately influenced by their findings.

And it was the cardiologists alone—not the epidemiologists, not the researchers, and certainly not the psychoanalysts—who treated and controlled the care of cardiac patients. The problem for cardiologists was that although they knew what smoking was and how to detect obesity and gender, they couldn't really grasp what stress looked like. It was too difficult to understand concretely, too messy. Also, the cardiac patients often held a view of psychology similar to that of their caretakers. The angry, aggressive, depressed, type A men were reluctant to touch their minds or have them touched. Like their cardiologists, they wanted their plumbing fixed. The last thing they wanted was to go off into that dark space where they inarticulately but intuitively knew death lurked. For a cardiac patient to be referred to a psychiatrist meant that his esteemed cardiologist regarded him as a mental case or a weakling or both, and such rejection and punishment were to be avoided, by both doctor and patient, at almost any cost.

By the early 1970s I determined to address these problems by enhancing the techniques of cardiology with the tools of depth psychology. I began by trying to integrate my cardiology training with my budding psychological ideas, ideas that were in harmony with the psychosomatic writings from the 1950s of Flanders Dunbar, Jacob Arlow, Franz Alexander, and Edward Weiss. Their various hypotheses were that cardiac patients would develop symptoms when they were unconsciously feeling defeated. To them, the cardiac dysfunctions had meaning: a heart attack was an attack on the heart from the unconscious mind. It was only later that I began to appreciate that the attack was coming from the troubled hemisphere.[1]

For instance, one of my patients was out to dinner with his business partner when he suddenly developed chest pain and was taken to the emergency ward and admitted to the hospital with a heart attack. What I learned in talking with him in the coronary care unit was that his father had died when he was ten years old, and as a consequence his mother would often lament her fate and complain desperately that she felt overwhelmed by life's problems. He learned then to say to her, "Don't worry; I'll take care of it," and he grew into adulthood with that credo. His wife had been very demanding, especially for expensive things they couldn't really afford, and he would respond to her urgent needs with, "Don't worry; I'll take care of it." In his business, his partner had been taking more and more time away from work, asking the patient to take ever-increasing responsibilities. Predictably he responded by accepting the added burden: "Don't worry; I'll take care of it."

In retrospect, in our interview in the coronary care unit, to the patient's surprise as we talked, he realized that at the meal at which he had his heart attack, his pain began shortly after his partner told him that he, the partner, was going on an impromptu Caribbean vacation and needed the patient to handle his overwhelming load at the office. The patient said to me, "I guess, I couldn't 'just take care of it' any more." I believe he had exceeded the limit of his troubled hemisphere and that all the pent-up worries and assumed overwhelming obligations finally burst their container and allowed to erupt the sense of dread and defeat that a part of him had felt since his father's early death. I believe that eruption precipitated his heart attack.

Another patient, a forty-year-old machinist, suffered a massive heart attack with severe complications that left him permanently impaired. He had been chronically harassed at work, and his heart attack occurred on a day when his boss ordered him to set up tedious, complex equipment. He dutifully completed his task, only to hear his boss growl, "Now take it all down." After my patient recovered, we learned in psychotherapy that his abusive, alcoholic father had ridiculed and rejected him throughout his childhood. It appeared that his boss's harassment, serious in and of itself, was greatly amplified by its resonance with his father's abuse. The similarity made the patient engage more fully emotionally with his boss's abuse. I speculated that the recent engagement intensified his agony, which led to his catastrophic coronary assault.

Mary Beth, a thirty-three-year-old executive, came to see me after her triple coronary bypass operation. She was referred to see me for severe depression which she was at a loss to understand. The heart surgery had been a few years earlier, and though she had a realistic concern about her health, she did not attribute her depression to her cardiac problems. We discovered that she lived with subliminal, unarticulated feelings of terror. Throughout her childhood, her mother had verbally abused and viciously beaten her with a hair brush. Although she was able to find some refuge at school and in her academic work, she was deeply scarred by her mother's behavior. Her childhood trauma, her constant anticipation and terror of violent physical and mental abuse, was causally related not only to her depression but also to her premature heart disease. Further, I hypothesized that her heart attack intensified her chronic, inarticulate anticipation of assault.

These patients and other cardiac patients I treated shared certain similar characteristics. They were relatively young for heart disease. None seemed to be very joyful or even simply content prior to the onset of their symptoms; in fact, each seemed to have suffered a sense of danger or defeat at that time. Several recent scientific studies have demonstrated that many heart patients die partially as a result of feelings of despair and defeat.

At the Montreal Heart Institute, 222 consecutive patients, one week after being admitted to the hospital for a heart attack, were given a commonly used depression scale, the Beck Depression Inventory. Over the following year and a half, the group, which initially showed higher depression scores, had eight times more cardiac deaths than the group having lower scores. After the authors statistically controlled for other coronary risk factors, the depressed group still had 6.6 times the cardiac mortality. Further, patients who had both depression and more than ten premature heart beats per minute died over this period at a rate twenty-nine times higher than those patients with neither depression nor that many premature beats.[2]

To try to put these results into some perspective, let's compare them with the findings on cholesterol from the Framingham Heart Study. Among 374 post–heart attack patients followed for an average of ten years, those with an initial cholesterol level over 275 mg/dL had 2.6 times the cardiac death rate of those with a level below 200 mg/dL.[3]

Another group of prominent researchers, led by Susan Everson, studied about twenty-five hundred apparently healthy men, ages forty-two to sixty, for six years. Those who were rated initially as feeling a high level of hopelessness had four times the rate of cardiac deaths over this period than the group rated as feeling a low level of hopelessness.[4]

A research group from Belgium reported findings in a study of three hundred heart patients, mostly males, who were in a cardiac rehabilitation program. Initially they gave the patients a number of personality tests and then followed the patients for about eight years. The researchers found that patients with a tendency to suppress emotional distress had four times more cardiac deaths than patients without that tendency.[5]

A group from Johns Hopkins studied over fifteen hundred people with no known heart disease who were evaluated for the presence of depression and then followed up thirteen years later. Those with mild depression had twice the rate of heart attacks as those without depression, and those with major depression had four and a half times the rate as those without depression.[6]

A Swedish study of over seven hundred men, all fifty years old and followed for six years, found that those with a lack of emotional support and social integration had four times the incidence of cardiac events as those with a high degree of social support.[7]

A study from Harvard led by research psychologist Laura Kubzansky found a strong correlation between worry, especially about social concerns, and the future incidence of coronary heart disease among seventeen hundred initially healthy men who were followed over twenty years.[8]

A study of about fourteen hundred cardiac patients followed for five years showed that those who were unmarried and without a significant relationship had over three times the rate of cardiac death as those patients with a significant relationship.[9]

Since the early 1980s, Jay R. Kaplan and his associates at the Bowman Gray School of Medicine have been studying heart disease in monkeys. It turns out that the species they studied resembles the human species in two important ways. First, they are socially very interactive, and, second, they get heart disease similar to their human kinsmen. Kaplan was working at a primate lab in the West Indies when he observed that when a new monkey was introduced to a group that had known each other, the new member seemed to get into a lot of confrontations. Kaplan then decided to use the stress of periodically changing the group in which a monkey was placed. A control group consisted of monkeys who remained in a stable, unchanged group. At the end of fourteen months, both groups were examined for coronary artery blockages.[10]

Kaplan also observed that some monkeys were dominant and some submissive. He looked at the effects of the psychological stress of being put in changing social groups on both dominant and submissive monkeys. He looked also at the effects of gender and diet (high fat and cholesterol versus low). His findings are nothing short of astounding. In the stable condition, submissive males had more coronary atherosclerosis than dominant males, and submissive females had more than dominant females. Males had more atherosclerosis than females with ovaries, but females who had their ovaries removed (taking away their estrogen protection) had increased atherosclerosis. When dominant males were put in the stressful, socially unstable condition, they more than doubled their amount of coronary artery disease, and that in-crease was not related to blood pressure, glucose levels, or blood lipids. The degree of coronary artery disease was greatly lessened when the monkeys were put on a low-fat diet, but even on the low-fat diet, the stressed monkeys still had five times the amount of coronary blockages as the unstressed. In a later study, neither high-stress nor low-stress male monkeys on a low-fat diet developed significant atherosclerosis, but those on a high-fat diet and with high stress had three times the amount of coronary blockages as those on the low-fat diet. Females housed in isolation, in single cages, had significantly more coronary atherosclerosis than females housed in stable social groups.[11]

All of these studies indicate that negative emotions such as depres-sion, hopelessness, loneliness, and intimidation are associated with car-diac disease. What becomes more interesting is why these associations exist. Meyer Friedman, one of the originators of the concept of the type A personality, is a cardiologist who, with an associate, Diane Ulmer, came up with a somewhat more sophisticated psychological theory from his many years of talking with cardiac patients in therapy groups at their cardiac rehabilitation program. Friedman and Ulmer proposed that the hard-driving type A individual was actually insecure and suf-fered a low self-esteem, which gave rise to the sense of time urgency and hyperaggressiveness, the hallmarks of the type A personality. From this they proposed that under stress, the persons's personality deteriorated and emotional exhaustion set in. They observed, but could not explain, that many type A patients seemed to possess a drive toward self-de-structive behavior, such as forgetting to file income taxes.[12]

From my early years as a researcher in cardiology, I began to form a hypothesis somewhat similar to Friedman and Ulmer's (which, in fact, seemed to build on the early psychoanalytic psychosomatic literature). Later, when I became interested in the cerebral hemispheres, I suspected that my patients' heart disease might relate to how their two hemi-spheres interacted. Instead of the immature side's creating psychological symptoms such as anxieties, depressions, or even compulsions, I now wondered if that side of the brain in addition might not, as seemed in Cecil's case, be able to affect the heart by creating so much distress that it overflowed into the body and initiated an extreme defeat syndrome, biologically linked to the heart and possibly other organ systems.

Freud proposed that people possess what he called a "death instinct," which he saw as the opposite of a "life instinct." For this concept, Freud has probably received more criticism than for any other of
his ideas, but I think he was on to something with his death instinct.
Freud never articulated his concept in this way, but I think that at the
bottom, he was really writing about the same biological drive to self-
destruction that I place in my cardiac patients.[13]

How the Mind Affects the Heart

The autonomic nervous system has two main divisions: one that
speeds things up and another that slows things down. The first is called
the sympathetic nervous system and the second, the parasympathetic
nervous system. Both systems, which originate in the brain, are affected by thoughts and feelings. Both affect the heart through nerves
that travel from the brain to the heart. Once the nerves reach the
heart, they release chemicals on the heart tissue. The sympathetic system releases adrenalin or noradrenalin (or both), the same chemicals
released under stress by the adrenal glands, situated on top of the kid-
neys. The parasympathetic system releases acetylcholine. Together
these two opposing systems can exert a finely tuned control over the
heart's rate and force of contraction.

The mind can affect the heart first by causing the brain to send
nerve impulses down the sympathetic or the parasympathetic systems,
which causes changes in the heart rate or heart rhythm. In extreme
conditions, such changes can cause the heart to fail to pump adequately. These conditions, called cardiac arrhythmias, are the likely
cause for many cases of sudden death.

Less proved is whether these nervous systems can cause or contribute to spasms of the coronary arteries. In the early 1970s, I set out
on a series of experiments to attempt to find out if emotional stress
could cause coronary artery spasms. At that time, coronary spasm was
not considered a common, significant factor in heart disease.

I studied patients with recurrent chest pain diagnosed as angina
pectoris. The coronary arteries are equipped with muscles, nerves, and
chemical receptors that could produce a temporary narrowing of these

critical blood vessels, and angina patients are often temporarily adversely affected by episodes of emotional distress.

I examined the patients while they experienced an emotional
stress and then while they underwent a physical stress. During an exercise test, such patients usually develop a change on their cardiogram,
which is monitored throughout the test. The change, called an ST-seg-
ment depression, can be measured. The depth of the depression of the
cardiogram wave correlates fairly well with the degree to which the
heart muscle is lacking sufficient blood to meet its needs, a condition
called coronary insufficiency, or ischemia. I reasoned that if a patient
had the same degree of ST depression during exercise as during emotional stress, but his heart was pumping much harder during the exercise, then one could infer that he had relatively less blood delivered
during the psychological stress, and this relative decrease in blood flow,
if it was temporary, would probably be due to coronary spasm.

To put the patients through a physical stress test was easy. Exercise
cardiac stress tests had been well established, and they were relatively
safe and easy to perform. To create an emotional stress, I wanted to
design a psychological stress test that would make the patient feel
somewhat defeated and would engage the patient emotionally. An
emotional stress had to grab the patient psychologically, or there
would be no stress. I settled on an imitation of an IQ test.

After the patient was wired for the ECG monitoring, I told him
that I had a brief IQ test to get a measure of his intelligence. The test
consisted of twenty questions, which I had earlier recorded on an au-
diotape. After each question on the tape, there was a pause during
which the patient had to give his answer. I stood before the patient in
a starched white coat with a clipboard in my hands and a scowl on my
face. I formulated the questions to appear easy, but in fact they were
nearly impossible, so the patient was being a bit defeated and embarrassed. As soon as the test was completed, I explained that the test was
intended only to see how his heart responded to emotional stress. Almost without exception, the patients responded by telling me that
they knew that all along, and they hadn't taken the test seriously. In
fact, the patients did know they were there to undergo an emotional
stress test and had given written consent. Nevertheless, the patients

almost uniformly had marked increases in their blood pressure and their heart rates. A number had ST depression, and a number had a marked increase in palpitations or premature heartbeats.[14]

In eleven patients, we found equal levels of ST depression on both the emotional and the exercise tests, and in these we found too that their hearts were working significantly less during the emotional stress than during the physical stress. This result was consistent with our hypothesis, and my colleagues and I suggested that the results supported the notion that emotional stress can cause coronary spasm. Eight years later, a group from the University of California at Los Angeles did a similar study using more sophisticated measures of cardiac ischemia and found similar evidence of coronary spasm during mental stress. A few years later, another group at Harvard did a study in the catherization laboratory where coronary angiograms are performed. They emotionally stressed patients during their angiograms and found that they could easily induce coronary spasms. Today it is generally accepted that emotionally induced coronary spasm is an important mechanism for disease in a number of cardiac patients.[15]

We do not know the specific mechanisms by which the mind induces the brain to induce coronary spasms or arrhythmias. The quickness with which they occur in response to an acute stress suggests that the autonomic nervous system is involved, but exactly how is not well understood. We do know that the autonomic nervous system is more connected to the right brain than the left brain, and that the left side of the sympathetic system (connected to the left brain) can cause an increase in dangerous cardiac rhythms. But we have only primitive evidence about whether the higher levels of the different hemispheres might play different roles in causing coronary spasms or cardiac arrhythmias. Werner Wittling and his associates, the German group that showed upsetting movies to one hemisphere at a time, found that people responded to stressful movies with greater increases in their blood pressures when the movies were shown to their right brains than to their left brains. And Kenneth Hugdahl and his colleagues found that when they flashed emotionally evocative pictures to the left visual field (right brain), they observed higher heart rate responses than when they flashed them to the right visual field (left brain).[16]

Wittling found in some of his experiments that the physiological responses were not always associated with the person's conscious sense of emotional distress. Research psychiatrists Richard Lane and Richard Jennings suggest that patients who get emotionally upset when their left hemisphere is dominant may be more vulnerable to serious cardiac arrhythmias. I wonder if their finding might relate to my observation that my PTSD patients had more psychological distress in their left hemispheres, but more studies need to be done to evaluate this possibility.[17]

The Benefit of Psychological Treatment for Heart Disease

Whatever the mechanisms turn out to be by which stress or depression contributes to heart disease, the good (but generally unappreciated) news is that there are effective psychological treatments for cardiac illnesses. The early psychoanalytic writers reported cases of cardiac patients successfully treated with individual psychotherapy, but they didn't have a large enough sample to do outcome studies.

The first controlled study to show a positive benefit of group psychotherapy was in 1974. In 1979, another group, led by renowned stress researcher Richard Rahe, reported a four-year follow-up of post–heart attack patients given brief group therapy after their heart attack. Rahe showed that among thirty-nine patients who were given the group therapy, none had another heart attack, and none died. Two of the thirty-nine did undergo a bypass operation. In a matched control group of twenty-two post–heart attack patients not offered group therapy, four had another heart attack, another four required bypass surgery, and another three died.[18]

The most impressive data come from Meyer Friedman's rehabilitation program in California. Friedman and his colleagues' aim was to change the personality of type A patients, to make them more easygoing. Friedman noticed that these patients had an underlying sense of insecurity, which led to their type A personality, and in ongoing group therapy sessions, this insecurity was addressed along with other issues. Over one thousand post–heart attack patients were enrolled in the rehabilitation program that emphasized the group counciling. These patient were followed for four and a half years and compared to a control group. The treated group had 44 percent fewer recurrent heart attacks over this period than the control group, and when the control group was eventually offered the group therapy, they too had a similar reduction in recurrent heart attacks.[19]

More recently, another group tried to replicate Friedman's work. They divided 265 post-bypass patients between an intensive cardiac rehabilitation treatment group resembling Friedman's program and a usual treatment group. At four and a half years after surgery, the control group had three times more cardiac deaths than the treatment group.[20]

In Finland, where there is a high incidence of coronary heart disease, 275 post–heart attack patients were given a comprehensive three-month cardiac rehabilitation program with a strong psychological component. Over the following ten years, they had half the rate of sudden cardiac deaths as a matched control group.[21]

Dean Ornish and his colleagues studied forty-eight cardiac patients divided so that half received his intensive cardiac rehabilitation program, which included a strong dose of group psychotherapy, and the other half received routine care. They found that the patients in the program had an average 9 percent decrease in their coronary artery blockages determined by coronary catheritization and visualization, while the control group had a 24 percent increase. They also found an improvement in coronary blood flow in the treatment group but a decline in the control group.[22]

These impressive results remind me of an advertisement played on the radio during one summer in the late 1950s in Atlantic City. Referring to Duke Hazlett, a singer who imitated Frank Sinatra when he was at the height of his popularity, the announcer said, "If you like Duke Hazlett, you'll love Frank Sinatra." My feeling is that if group therapy can get impressive results, then intensive individual therapy, such as I offered Cecil, might get overwhelming results if it could be offered to enough patients to do a controlled study. My new idea of proper treatment harkens back to the kind of work the psychoanalysts did with cardiac patients in the 1940s and 1950s.

The problem is that cardiac patients and cardiologists have an antipathy to intense psychological work. If the patient is sent to a rehabilitation program that includes a stress reduction component, then that is usually acceptable, but many such programs do little in the way of effective psychological treatment. A recent study surveyed sixty-five cardiac rehabilitation programs and found that forty offered stress reduction programs, but only three of those were considered by the authors to be at a level that could be expected to give a benefit. The rest were judged useless in terms of stress reduction.[23]

I think part of the problem is that cardiac patients, like their cardiologists, tend to be left brained in the popular sense. That is, many tend to avoid the ethereal and the poetic, as they attend almost exclusively to their external lives, trying to ignore their inner psychological pain and insecurity. One patient in his thirties came to see me for episodes of chest pain and palpitations, which his cardiologist felt might be aggravated by some underlying, hidden stress. I found that the patient grew up in a war zone in which he was constantly exposed to artillery fire. The alarm he felt when he had his cardiac symptoms seemed to me to be remarkably similar to what one might feel if he were exposed to shellings. I offered an interpretation to the patient that related his symptoms to his early experiences, and he had an immediate resolution of his cardiac problems. They stopped cold. The patient called me to cancel our next appointment because he had found that the cause of his symptoms was something he had been eating. He consciously denied that my interpretation was related to his symptoms or their relief, but nevertheless he maintained his improvement. I think that unconsciously he was able to use what I had offered him, but he was too terrified to face consciously how frightened he was on another level.

If patients like Cecil can get past their initial fear and reluctance, they can do excellent psychological work in the right setting. I believe that younger patients especially would have substantial physical benefits.

CHAPTER 11

Dual-Brain Therapy to Discover
and Assist Your Troubled Mind

Through the course of this book, I have demonstrated the essential principle of the dual-brain model. We are, I believe, of two minds, each associated with one cerebral hemisphere. Dual-brain therapy is the application of this principle toward helping people better understand and repair their psychological distresses. The lateralized glasses assisted me in my quest to understand how the mind works, and in those patients who had a robust response to them, they were of enormous therapeutic value. But whether a particular patient had a reaction to the glasses, he was almost always aided greatly by the principles that they helped establish about how the mind functions.

In this chapter I will gather together the therapeutic ideas of dual-brain psychology and show how you can apply them yourself, to improve your emotional health and life. First, each patient I described came to me because of a symptom that was bothering him. Your first step is try to identify what problems or symptoms you would like to work on. Are you depressed, anxious, insecure? Do you procrastinate or avoid relationships? Do you feel unfulfilled? Do you deal poorly with current stresses? These are some of the many problems that can be helped with dual-brain therapy.

After you have a clearer idea of the symptoms or problems you would like to address, consider how you understand these difficulties. Why do you think you feel depressed or insecure or overstressed or underrelated to? How do you now understand yourself?

199

The patients I have described had problems typical of patients I see. Usually they had little insight into their problems when they entered treatment. I asked them to describe their problems for me, as I am asking you to describe yours to yourself. Try to elaborate your description of your difficulties. When did they begin? What has seemed to aggravate them? To help them?

Next, I asked my patients to describe their childhoods. I wanted to know about the quality of their relationships with their parents, siblings, and other significant people. What was your general feeling about the past? What were some of the more significant events?

As you have seen, I encourage patients to try to relate the feelings associated with their symptoms to any feelings from their past. All this may sound like typical therapy stuff, but it is very useful.

You may have noticed that my patients have more similarities than differences. Even in their most different aspect, their individual symptoms tended to overlap. This is typical of the hundreds of patients I have treated. The causes for their symptoms were always related to past insults, injuries, or traumas, usually in the form of neglect, derision, or overt abuse. None was injured by excessive love, admiration, or consideration, although often they were treated alternately derisively and lovingly. Sexual abuse is often rationalized as love by the perpetrator, but it is in fact an expression of ultimate disregard for the child.

It is often difficult for patients to appreciate that their early life involved mistreatment. This acknowledgment, when it is true, often feels like a shameful cop-out. Joe told me, "You shrinks always want to lay all the blame on the parents," when he described for me how his father beat him with a belt as he verbally excoriated him. Children are made to feel responsible for their ridicule, neglect, or other mistreatment, and when they grow into adults, they often retain the same attitude and feel guilty when I ask them to face what was done to them by the people who were supposed to love and protect them.

The Essence of Dual-Brain Therapy

Dual-brain therapy can conceptualize how past traumas might still affect you. The idea is that there exists an actual mind in one of your hemispheres that is still living in the past, still seeing the world as you saw it earlier in your life. This part of you may be your dominant personality, as it was in the cocaine addicts before their treatment, or in Mark when he became psychotic, or in Carol or Ryan when they were in their initial distress.

As in Harold, if you have a troubled hemisphere, it might operate behind the scenes, creating inexplicable behaviors, compulsions, or inhibitions. Or perhaps like Joe, you might have an intense anxiety that on the surface has no reasonable explanation. But beneath the surface, inside his left hemisphere, was a part of him living in the past and waiting for his father's mental and physical abuse.

Dual-brain therapy begins with the realization that there is an intact troubled person in one hemisphere. Some people may not have a troubled mind in either hemisphere, but these people usually aren't symptomatic. If you are troubled by anxiety, unexplained sadness, inhibitions, or any other of a long list of problems, then you likely have a troubled hemisphere.

The idea of a troubled hemisphere is intended to be clarifying, not frightening. The troubled part is hurting and will be appreciative of help. If you come to recognize that your symptoms are the expressions of a troubled part of you—a part of you that you can, with effort, compassionately understand—then you will achieve a tremendous insight into the nature of your symptoms. You will also be given a blueprint for how to work yourself out of your problem.

In some patients, it is rather easy to identify the two intact minds that exist within. With Carol, because her distressed state was a radical change from her usual mature personality, I found it relatively easy to help her recognize the two parts of her. In other patients, because one side is so dominated and repressed by the other, as in Cecil (the executive with the heart attack), the task of getting the patient to appreciate that there is another significant part to his personality is more of a challenge. In a few others, perhaps because both sides are troubled, as I believe may be the case in some of my chronically ill patients, I have not succeeded in locating two separate minds.

For years before I discovered the glasses, I worked successfully with this concept of two autonomous minds in my patients, but in patients who respond to them, the glasses are remarkably helpful. Dorothy, a woman in her sixties, a victim of horrendous childhood abuse, came into my office wheezing as she had been since being awakened by a nightmare in the middle of the night. I had her cover her left eye with her left hand and the middle half of her right eye with her other hand and within seconds her wheezing stopped, as did her emotional distress. I had her look out the other side, and she immediately felt great distress, and we quickly returned to the other side. She said, half jokingly, "This makes me so mad. I can't stand this. It means it's all in my head, doesn't it?"

"Well, yes," I said, "in half your head."

I don't want to give the impression that dual-brain therapy is simply having someone put on a pair of glasses. Quite the contrary. The glasses or the hand covering is only a tool to assist in the true task of the treatment: recognizing the troubled part and helping it. Patients who do not respond to the glasses can still succeed by working with the concept of two minds and then discovering and working with their troubled mind. The glasses are helpful in clarifying these principles, but they are by no means necessary for a full recovery.

The first part of dual-brain therapy is the recognition and experience of a troubled personality within. I help my patients to experience the actuality of this part of them, and this discovery is always clarifying and helpful. If you have already considered what your symptoms are and how they may relate to your life's difficult experiences, then you are ready to feel around inside yourself for your troubled mind. Your troubled part may be childlike, or it may simply be a terrified adult, but it almost always is somewhat impulsive or reactive because it is usually on guard. It has a tendency to catastrophize—to see the worst in everyone and everything. It does this because it expects an old abusive situation to be repeated, and often it successfully sets things up to fulfill that expectation. Harold could have lost Jane through his hesitancy, and he would likely have seen that in his troubled mind as proof that Jane, like his mother, was destined to reject him, confirming the wisdom of his reluctance.

Sometimes the troubled mind attacks the person, as we saw in Earl (the troubled part of Don). Often when we are depressed, our troubled side is attacking us. Recognizing this situation when it is occurring is extremely helpful in resolving the depression.

Almost all of my patients easily recognize the troubled aspect of themselves after they have delineated their symptoms and deeply considered the subtleties of their life experiences. Usually when a patient can't discover his troubled part, he is too repressed. Over time, within the safety of therapy, the troubled part becomes apparent as it either emerges from its hiding place or is permitted to surface by a dominating side that has learned to relax its grip.

Often I use the lateralizing glasses, or simply the patients' hands, to restrict vision to one side or the other, in order to assist the patient in discovering his troubled mind. As an exercise, you can try this now. (If you believe you have experienced significant trauma that you aren't able to work through alone, you may want to find professional help. The information in this book may be a good adjunct to your therapy, and your therapist a good adjunct to the book.)

Trying a Technique for Lateralizing Your Vision

Choose your left or right side to look out of first. (I begin with a description of how to look to your right, but you may begin on your left side. It does not matter which side you choose.) Cover your left eye with your left hand, then cover the middle half of your right eye with your right hand. You should cover your right eye so that you can see out of only its right half. You can move your hand slightly to cover more of your eye and see if that changes any effects. Remain still for about a minute before measuring your level of anxiety, using the scale from zero to five (none, mild, moderate, quite a bit, or extreme). Switch to the other side, and cover your entire right eye with your right hand and the middle half of your left eye with your left hand, just as you did on the other side. Again, wait a minute before rating your level of anxiety.

Did you notice a difference? What was your rating for your left side? Your right side? Were you more distressed on one side and calmer on the other? If you felt a difference between sides, did the experiences feel familiar?

Many of my patients do not respond to this technique. Usually over the course of therapy, the technique does work at least enough to give them the experience of having two separate views of the world. I have found that to a degree, patients are more responsive when they are more symptomatic, although this is not always the case. Frequently patients who do not respond initially can later have robust responses.

But again I emphasize that patients who do not respond to lateralized vision still appreciate and greatly benefit from the concept and inner experience of having two minds. That is, the experience of two minds does not depend on the lateralizing techniques, although it can be aided by them. Recall that I used this dual-brain concept in my work with my patients well before I discovered the lateralized glasses.

If you did experience a response to this technique of lateralized vision, did you recognize a familiar anxiety or insecurity? If you noticed a distinction between sides, this may have been your first experience of your two minds as separate, distinct entities. Move back and forth, and repeat the exercise several times. Become familiar with how each side feels and how you feel as you activate and isolate the hemispheres. Feel the novelty of having contrary views of the world. Which view is more familiar? Which view seems to dominate? Which feels more realistic?

For many patients who have a robust response and feel distress on one side and calmness on the other, the experience is literally mind boggling. Patients will laugh and say, "What is this? This is strange. What does this mean?" I never intended this technique as a mere curiosity. I apply it to the primary aim of every patient's treatment: the education and assistance of the troubled part of the patient.

What is most important in the course of therapy is the relationship between the healthier and the more troubled mind. Only after a patient has been able to experience and appreciate the existence of these two minds does the work of therapy really begin. Psychotherapy, in this context, resembles couples therapy in which one partner is more troubled. I use the glasses or the hand covering to facilitate that relationship. As an example, here is a transcript of a session with a patient in which we used the hand-covering technique, not so much to recognize the two parts, but to facilitate a healthy dialogue between them—to improve their relationship and assist the troubled part to appreciate that his world had greatly improved since the past.

Abe is a thirty-five-year-old patient of mine, a single man who had been in therapy for a year before I discovered the lateralizing techniques. Abe had an unusual story to tell. As a child of five he was abducted by his estranged father, who tended to treat him over the ensuing years with an unexplained contempt, and at times would terror-ize Abe with cruel stories of evil creatures lurking in the dark.

Abe had been diagnosed with severe anxiety and depression. In spite of his symptoms, he was very successful in his field, yet this success didn't help him conquer his deep and chronic pangs of insecurity. Over the course of the year, we used traditional psychotherapy to help him gain insight, and he achieved periodic symptomatic relief. He took Prozac, but as far as we could tell, it had little effect on his symptoms.

In the following session in which we used his hands to block his vi-sion, we achieved a dramatic breakthrough, and since this session, which occurred four months earlier, he has remained symptom free. The session shows how lateralized vision can be used to improve the relationship between his two minds.

Abe came into the session feeling an intense despair and, in fact, had been having some passing thoughts of committing suicide. After I asked Abe to use his hands to block his vision so that he could see out of the right side (enhancing his left brain), he immediately began to feel relief. With his permission, I tape-recorded the remainder of the session.

"Do you feel differently from before you covered your eyes [looking to the right, the left brain]?"

"I don't feel any despair, though I still feel a heaviness."

"How sad are you feeling?"

"Mildly sad."

"How about loneliness?"

"It's there, but it's not unmanageable. It's very familiar."

"Would you try switching to the other side [looking out his left side (right brain)]?"

(One-minute pause) "Very different. Distinctively different. Very very profound sadness. I feel extreme sadness."

"How does this compare with before, when you first came in?"

"It's about the same."

"How much anxiety?"

"Extreme."

"And loneliness?"

"Extreme."

"So this is what you've been living with? What comes to mind about this feeling? What's it remind you of?"

"There's this great fear that I don't know how to get out of it. It has its clutches in me, and I don't know how to fight it. Just leaves me feeling quite vulnerable and alone—the way I used to when I was a little boy."

"And helpless? Not sure where to turn?"

"Exactly."

Abe's crying interrupted our dialogue for about a minute.

"Try looking out the other side."

He again moves his hands so that he's looking to his right side (left brain).

(After a minute) "Again a very distinct sort of shift of emotions. It's manageable. On your scale, it's moderate, but I'm still aware there is something that isn't right."

"Tell me."

"Well, this lack of energy and desire to perform my simple everyday tasks is due to all this stuff that's going on right now."

"How does the world look now?"

"It's gray, but I know that what's happened to me is surmountable, that it's not hopeless."

"That's important. This isn't something you knew as a child?"

"No."

"Something you learned somewhere as an adult?"

"Right."

"And it seems there's another part of you that doesn't know this."

"That's right."

"And we need to tell that part that there is hope and that the vulnerable position that you were actually in is different today. Today you are a powerful person."

"That's right. I can make choices today where I couldn't as a child."

"And you can protect yourself today, whereas you couldn't as a child, when you were frightened as a child. Today you're not threatened except for what's coming from inside."

"Yes."

"And can you let the other side look out this side?" There is a pause of about a minute.

"He's not used to this."

"What's that feel like?"

"It's a little scary."

"Tell me."

"He's so used to feeling helpless. To see that it doesn't have to be this way, that's quite a revelation, but it's a whole new—what's the word I want to use?—sort of a whole new frontier for him."

"He has to learn how to live in a different world."

"Right. And change is scary for a little boy."

"Even good change."

"Yeah. He needs to learn to trust that I'm not here to hurt him, that I'm here to help him."

"Try looking to the other side."

He again looks to his left side (right brain), which had initially stimulated his distress. After a pause, he continues.

"Well, the levels of anxiety and sadness don't feel the same anymore."

"And can this side remember what it looked like on the other side?"

"Yes."

"How did it look on the other side?"

"A lot calmer, manageable."

"And was there someone present to protect you?"

"Yes."

"Different from the past?"

"Very different."

"And was there someone there to abuse you?"

"No."

"That's different."

"Yes, it is."

"And can you see that?"

"Yes, I can."

"On this side too?"

"Yes. It's been a long road, and it's been hard to trust that you won't be crushed down. And that even though all this tragedy is present, there are people out there who care and want to help and nurture for that condition."

"And one of those people is the other side of you?"

"That's right."

"Seems like a lot of protection."

"Yeah. When I bring this side [the distressed side] with the other side, this one can look in there and extrapolate and take and see what's going on, and I can bring it together with the other side with feeling. It neutralizes a lot of the pain that's been here on this side. It becomes clearer and a lot more obvious as the adult comes together with the child and is able to clarify and help understand why those feelings are the way they are, where they're coming from. And in a way as important as they are today, they're also things that happened in the past and don't have any bearing on the reality of what's happening in the present."

"And also it's not as dangerous."

"Right."

Abe has been able to get his two sides not only to communicate but even to share their views of the world. When one side of the brain is stimulated to become dominant, the other side is still active and present. The two minds are in this sense co-conscious, even though only one may be the active dominant mind at the time.

Imagine you and I are in a room with a third person. When I direct my conversation to you and you engage in the conversation with me, we may lose sight of the fact that for a few moments, we are ignoring the third person. But this third person still exists and observes and thinks even when he is not actively engaged in the conversation. This is my vision of how the two minds generally work. When one side is stimulated, the other still exists and functions. We look at the brain wave changes with the glasses and see a clear, measurable shift in the power of the EEGs over each hemisphere, but it is a relative shift. We do not see one hemisphere light up and the other become dark.

The two hemispheres relate to each other as two people do. Both listen, talk, and consider. Both have feelings and attitudes toward the other. In addition, these two minds exist in the same skull, and they are connected through the corpus callosum and other connecting fibers. I believe it is through these neural connections that the mind of one hemisphere can actually feel directly what the other side experiences. When Abe says that he is letting his troubled side look out the view of his healthier mind, I believe that this is actually what is happening. Abe's two minds are relating to one another, and his healthier mind is working to comfort his troubled mind.

I then asked Abe to switch again to his more comforting right side (left brain).

"The emotions are less. I'm still in a moderate place, but it feels different. The intensity of that moderate level is less. I'm still feeling a certain sadness and a certain amount of loneliness and anger but it's not . . ."

"Is there any sense of well-being?"

"Yes, there is. There's a sense that I can handle this, that I can make it better."

"That there's some hope?"

"Yes."

"What do you make of that?"

"Well, it's an exercise that I need to be very much aware of and practice, so I have a lot more balance and control over what stirs inside."

"There's another view?"

"Yes. It's not all that bleak. There's hope."

"Is there a future?"

"Yes, there is."

"How's that look?"

"Challenging but good."

"Why don't you put your hands down. How do you feel?"

"Remarkably better than I did when I walked in through this door. I'm exhausted, but I feel much lighter. It's amazing what we do to ourselves. Honestly, when I walked though these doors today, I was just ready to give up. I sat in my car earlier wondering if I was even going to make it up the stairs."

Essentially, what Abe's session teaches us is that he has two distinct minds—two distinct ways of viewing the world. One perspective is that the world is extremely dangerous and that he is almost certainly going to be injured and humiliated. This view is complete and internally consistent. The other view is also complete, though at variance with the first. Here, he sees himself as safe, powerful, and successful; his world is, for the most part, under his control.

Both views are his views. Depending on which side he looks out, Abe will see one view or the other. The experience of changing one's view of the world by changing one's lateral vision is remarkable and striking, and it challenges the dogmatic stance of his negative view.

Abe is also helped by our talking to his troubled right brain and our encouraging it to look out his healthier side. We are actively trying to teach his troubled side that there is another view of the world—a view that Abe is safe, strong, and well regarded. During the session, it seemed to us that we succeeded in reaching his troubled side. We saw his anxiety melt away. By the end of the session, even looking out of the troubled side (encouraging his right brain) did not evoke anxiety. The lesson his right brain learned through this exercise has lasted eight months so far, and I believe that the longer it lasts, the stronger it will grow.

Abe's healthier side is also strengthened by its alliance with me. I encourage this side to believe in itself, as well as to assist his other side. As in Abe's case, there are often defining moments in therapy when the troubled mind gets the message and learns that it is truly safer and more valued than it had believed. Further, even when the troubled side forgets what it was taught, it becomes easer to teach it the next time (and the next). Teaching the troubled mind, the heart of therapy, generally requires great patience and repetition. Abe's enduring response was exceptional but not rare.

So if you get a response as you look from one side or the other, begin a conversation between the two aspects of yourself. Let each part of you notice the way the other part of you sees the world. Then you must think about this and work to teach your more troubled side that there is another more realistic view.

Another technique I have used with patients is to talk directly to the troubled mind. I described this in the chapter on depression, when I talked with Don's troubled side. The most surprising thing about talking to a troubled part of a person is that it listens. I know this because frequently I have asked a troubled part of a person to stop attacking the other part of him, and suddenly the person feels remarkable relief.

I suggest that once you have a sense of your troubled self, talk with it, even talk out loud (not in a public place). Tell it you care and want to help it. I have a patient who silently tells his troubled part to go sit on the bench while he plays tennis. His troubled part liked to take control during the games but had a tendency to swing wildly. To my patient's amazement, when he asked that part of him to sit on the bench and watch the game, he could feel that this was happening, and his game improved dramatically.

More important, I have taught patients like Don to talk firmly with their troubled minds when it is attacking them and causing intense anxiety or depression. It is an amazing experience to talk very firmly with your troubled self and tell it to stop attacking you, much as I spoke with Don's troubled side, and find that you suddenly feel better. I have had many patients succeed at this. It relieves distressing symptoms, clarifies the existence of the troubled mind, and improves the communication and relationship between the two sides.

Another technique I have found helpful in my practice is what I call "focusing." I ask patients to look at an object in the room—perhaps a plant or their shoe. I ask them to attend to it actively, paying strict attention to it, to try to see the details of it—in essence, the reality of it. If a patient can focus attention on the object in this way, the process pulls him out of his own head and into the external reality of the room. When this exercise works, the person's contact with reality increases and can lead to a sudden calmness and clarity, quite similar to the effect some people have with the lateralized vision. For people with whom this works, I encourage them to focus by looking, for example, at their shoe if they are in a meeting and feeling stress and anxiety. Pulling the mind into close contact with reality often has a calming, grounding effect.

For people who are calmed by the glasses, I encourage them to use their hands to block their vision before (or after) a stressful meeting. Some patients have made a pair of goggles (taped to evoke calmness) and put them on as a kind of meditation or respite for a half hour before they go to sleep each night.

General Principles for Enhancing Communication Between the Two Minds

The troubled mind often clings to its old views. We have difficulty getting it to hear us, let alone seriously consider our opinion or change its

mind. Psychotherapists have a term that describes a troubled mind's reluctance to change: resistance. When a patient has difficulty getting in
touch with his feelings or cooperating with the therapeutic enterprise,
the psychotherapist says the patient is resistant. Although the term
can be used pejoratively, it shouldn't be. Freud understood that much
of the benefit of therapy had to do with the constructive working
through of the resistances that continuously came up in treatment.

I see resistance as the troubled side's distrust of anything that challenges what it believes to be true. Often it was traumatized or disturbed
by some past events, and it remains vigilant, even many years later,
against the anticipated recurrence of the disturbing situations. Sometimes this side will influence situations so that they end up recreating
the feared circumstance, just as Harold almost did before dual-brain
therapy. It is not that the troubled side wants to repeat the trauma;
rather, it is highly motivated to avoid repeating the painful experience.
This mind believes that it knows the traumas will be repeated, and it
anticipates the repetition of the trauma. When the trauma does not
occur, the troubled mind feels not relief but more anxiety because it
"knows" the trauma will recur and becomes even more expectant as
the anticipated trauma gets "delayed."

If this mind believes that the recurrence of an unbearable pain is
inevitable, it will remain preoccupied with it, and any effort to reassure
it will be seen as imprudent advice, to be avoided at all costs. Getting
this troubled side to reconsider what it believes it "knows," getting it to
trust someone else (a mature-sided mind or a therapist), letting it consider that what happened in the past need not be repeated in the future—all this is extremely difficult, but it is the essential task in
helping troubled minds.

To convince your troubled mind to change, you need to use the
same techniques of persuasion you may use to change other peoples'
minds. You need to demonstrate that you are trustworthy, that you
care, and that you are responsible and intelligent. In a sense, you need
to be a good leader or a good parent to your troubled mind.

Strengthening your more mature mind is perhaps the first step in
learning how to talk with your more troubled mind. The more mature
mind needs to be a healthy leader who guides the other side, while
being strong enough to listen to and consider that side's troubled

thoughts and feelings. Thus, the mature side is the executive. This mind should be more mature, more grounded, more responsible, and less impulsive.

Like any executive, the mature mind can be strengthened by receiving encouragement and education, by using determination and perseverance, by forming alliances, and by paying attention to information. A strong, mature side has a large capacity to bear pain and other feelings, as well as the restraint or temperance required to reach prudent judgments.

Perhaps the greatest strengthener of any mind is success. I believe that as animals, we have inherited a biological system whereby when we perceive ourselves as successful, a whole set of helpful organic mechanisms is released. It is a success syndrome, if you will, the opposite of a defeat syndrome, in which our bodies and minds sabotage ourselves.

As an example of the success syndrome, let's say you are playing tennis against someone you are not supposed to beat, and you find yourself closing in or taking the lead. Suddenly you might find yourself playing better than you had ever played before. Your body is pumped up, and every part of you feels and functions superbly. Mentally you are focused and clear, and in both your mind and your body, you have a great sense of well-being.

Now your opponent might feel *his* success syndrome and rally. He might start to ace his serves or come to the net and destroy you. You then realize that you are going to lose. The situation seems hopeless. Your mind sees this, and suddenly, just as quickly as you entered the success syndrome, you now find yourself in the midst of the failure syndrome. No part of you works any longer as it was intended. You feel fatigued. Your timing is off, as is your concentration. Mentally you feel a depression settling in. You can't wait to get off the court. Your body, which not long ago felt new and lubricated, now feels pained and decrepit.

What happened? Your perception of your situation along a continuum of success-failure released intense, innate, biological responses commensurate with your view. If you want to see how profoundly important these innate responses are to well-being, just notice the number of illnesses that bear a relationship to a person's having a sense of defeat: depression, ulcers, colitis, coronary artery disease, and hypertension, just to begin the list. There are no illnesses that result from a sense of success; in fact, such perceptions promote wellness.

What does this have to do with the mature side? I was discussing how to strengthen this side, and an important way to strengthen it is to increase its real power in the world. Success breeds success. To strengthen the mature side, we need to find encouragement from our relationships with friends, mentors, lovers, colleagues, and families. Encouragement should also come from ourselves; in fact, self-encouragement is probably the most important source. We need to believe in ourselves.

Education can help empower the more mature mind. We need to be familiar with and open to the ideas of others. Yet we also need to retain our ability to challenge intelligently those ideas by processing them through our own judgment.

Making wise decisions strenthens our more mature mind by increasing its power and circumstance and our trust in its decisions. That is, the better our decisions, the better our circumstances become, and the more we will learn to trust ourselves.

To begin to help our more troubled minds, it seems we need to have a mature side as strong as Schwarzenegger, as wise as Lincoln, and as temperate as a saint. But the first problem is that the mature side's most important source of strength and wisdom is the other side. To improve ourselves, we must strive to get both parts of us to participate constructively.

In any relationship, whether between two people or between two minds in one person, both sides must respect the other and be about equally influenced by the other in a cooperative, harmonious manner. Unfortunately, many relationships are such that one person overpowers the other. One person may always have to be right and may be able to influence the other person unduly and dominate him or her. In some relationships, the participants may covertly attempt to sabotage each other.

There is a relationship between your two minds, and that relationship, like all other relationships, follows certain principles. First, in any relationship, one party can influence another. Second, relationships vary along a continuum of cooperation-antagonism and dominance-submission. Third, any relationship can be modified by changes in the power of the individuals relative to one another. In order to achieve the highest level of mental well-being, we must develop a loving human relationship between our two minds, and the issues that apply to any relationship will apply to the one within us.

Work on the relationship between your two minds. When you are in a focused frame of mind, decide if you are willing to direct your energies toward becoming better able to tolerate distressing feelings or memories, impulses, and urges without taking immediate action. You will need to make a conscious effort to try to be more mature and wise. Toward your troubled side, you will need a very caring, patient attitude. If you can help your more troubled mind become a strong, healthy ally, then your life will be remarkably improved.

To be truly healthy, you must have a fit mind on both sides, with a constructive relationship between them. If we as individuals become deeper and wiser and develop more harmony between the disparate parts of ourselves, we will become more able to identify, and address with effort and compassion the serious problems of those around us. In this small way, we can contribute in our attempt to make this human endeavor succeed, to permit our species to achieve its full meaning and its magnificent potential.

Notes

CHAPTER 1. INTRODUCTION

1. Mischel W: *Introduction to Personality.* 2nd ed. New York, Holt, Rinehart and Winston, 1976.
2. Dennett DC: The origins of selves. *Cognito* 1989; 2:163–173.
3. Eccles J, Robinson DN: *The Wonder of Being Human: Our Brain and Our Mind.* New York, Free Press, 1984.
4. Radden J: *Divided Minds and Successive Selves: Ethical Issues in Disorders of Identity and Personality.* Cambridge, MA, MIT Press, 1996.

CHAPTER 2. A NEW LOOK AT SPLIT-BRAIN STUDIES

1. Bogen JE, Vogel PS: Cerebral commissurotomy in man. *Bull Los Angeles Neurol Soc* 1962; 29:169–172.
2. Dennett DC: *Consciousness Explained.* Boston, Little Brown, 1991.
3. Schiffer F, Zaidel E, Bogen J, Chasan-Taber S: Different psychological status in the two hemispheres of two split-brain patients. *Neuropsychiatry, Neurospsychology, and Behavioral Neurology;* in press.
4. Bear DM, Fedio P: Quantitative analysis of interictal behavior in temporal lobe epilepsy. *Arch Neurol* 1977; 34:454–467.

   Fedio P, Martin A: Ideative-emotive behavioral characteristics of patients following left or right temporal lobectomy. *Epilepsia* 1983; 24 (Suppl 2):S117 S130.
5. Zaidel E: A technique for presenting lateralized visual input with prolonged exposure. *Vision Res* 1975; 15:283–289.

   Sperry RW, Zaidel E, Zaidel D: Self recognition and social awareness in the disconnected minor hemisphere. *Neuropsychologia* 1979; 17:153–166.
6. Zaidel E: Personal communication.
7. Zaidel, E: Personal communication.
8. Ferguson SM, Rayport M, Corrie WS: Neuropsychiatric observations on behavioral

consequences of corpus callosum section for seizure control. In: Reeves A G, ed. *Epilepsy and the Corpus Callosum*. New York, Plenum Press, 1985.

Sperry RW: Brain bisection and mechanisms of consciousness. In: Eccles JC, ed. *Brain and Conscious Experiences*. New York, Springer-Verlag, 1966.

Gazzaniga MS: *The Bisected Brain*. New York, Appleton-Century-Crofts, 1970.

Geschwind N: The perverseness of the right hemisphere. *Behavioral Brain Sci* 1981; 4:106–107.

Joseph R: *Neuropsychology, Neuropsychiatry, and Behavioral Neurology*. New York, Plenum Press, 1990.

9. See Joseph: *Neuropsychology*.
10. See Joseph, *Neuropsychology*.
11. Diamond SI: *Neuropsychology*. London, Butterworths, 1980.
12. Gazzaniga MS: *The Social Brain*. New York, Basic Books, 1985.
13. Gazzaniga, *Social Brain*.

Gazzaniga MS: Right hemisphere language following brain bisection: A 20-year perspective. *Am Psychol* 1983; 38:525–537.

Gazzaniga MS, LeDoux JE: *The Integrated Mind*. New York, Plenum, 1978.

14. LeDoux JE, Wilson DH, Gazzaniga MS: A divided mind: Observation on the conscious properties of the separated hemispheres. *Ann Neurol* 1977; 21:417–421.
15. Sperry RW: Forebrain commissurotomy and conscious awareness. In: Trevarthen C, ed. *Brain Circuits and Functions of the Mind*, Cambridge, Cambridge University Press, 1990.
16. Bogen JE: Partial hemispheric independence with the neocommissures intact. In: *Brain Circuits and Functions of the Mind*.
17. Zollinger R: Removal of left cerebral hemisphere. *Arch Neurol Psychiatry* 1935; 34:1055–1064.

Crockett HG, Estridge NM: Cerebral hemispherectomy. *Bull Los Angeles Neurol Soc* 1951; 16:71–87.

French LA, Johnson DR, Brown IA, Van Bergen FB: Cerebral hemispherectomy for control of intractable convulsive seizures. *J Neurosurgery* 1955; 12:154–164.

Hillier WF: Total left cerebral hemispherectomy for malignant glioma. *Neurology* 1954; 4:718–721.

Smith A: Speech and other functions after left (dominant) hemispherectomy. *J Neurol Neurosurg Psychiatry* 1966; 29:467–471.

Gott PS: Language after dominant hemispherectomy. *J Neurol Neurosurg Psychiatry* 1973; 36:1082–1088.

18. Wigan AL: *A New View of Insanity: The Duality of the Mind Proved by the Structure, Functions, and Diseases of the Brain and by the Phenomena of Mental Derangement, and Shown to Be Essential to Moral Responsibility*. Originally published Longman, Brown, Green, and Longmans, London, 1884; Reissued by Joseph Simon Publisher, 1985.

19. Myers RE, Sperry RW: Interocular transfer of a visual form discrimination habit in cats after section of the optic chiasm and corpus callosum. *Anat Record* 1953; 115:351–352.

20. For more details of the divided field studies on faces, see: Patterson K, Bradshaw JL: Differential hemispheric mediation of nonverbal visual stimuli. *J Exp Psychol* 1975; 1:246–252.

    Suberi M, McKeever WF: Differential right hemispheric memory storage of emotional and nonemotional faces. *Neuropsychologia* 1977; 15:757–768.

    Bradshaw, Taylor, Bradshaw JL, Taylor MJ, Patterson K, Nettleton NC: Upright and inverted faces, and housefronts, in the two visual fields: A right and left hemisphere contribution. *J Clin Neuropsychol* 1980; 2:245–257.

    Bradshaw JL, Sherlock D: Bugs and faces in the two visual fields: Task order, difficulty, practice, and the analytic/holistic dichotomy. *Cortex* 1982; 211–225.

    For discussions of the relative capacities of the hemispheres see: Kolb B, Whishaw IQ: *Fundamentals of Human Neuropsychology*. W. H. Freeman, New York, 1996. Also Iaccino, JF: *Left Brain–Right Brain Differences: Inquiries, Evidence, and New Approaches*. Hillsdale, NJ, Erlbaum, 1993.

21. Wada JA, Rasmussen T: Intracarotid injection of sodium amytal for the lateralization of cerebral speech dominance: Experimental and clinical observations. *J Neurosurgery* 1960; 17:266–282.

22. Risse GL, Gazzaniga MS: Well-kept secrets of the right hemisphere: A carotid amytal study of restricted memory transfer. *Neurology* 1978; 28:950–953.

23. Ahern GL, Herring AM, Trackenberg J, Seeger JF, Oommen KJ, Labiner DM, Weinand ME: The association of multiple personality and temporolimbic epilepsy: Intracarotid amobarbital test observations. *Arch Neurol* 1993; 50:1020–1025.

24. Bogen JE: The other side of the brain II: an appositional mind. *Bull Los Angeles Neurol Soc* 1969; 34: 135–162.

CHAPTER 3. LOOKING RIGHT (AND LOOKING LEFT)

1. Schiffer F, Teicher MH, Papanicolaou AC: Evoked potential evidence for right brain activity during the recall of traumatic memories. *J Neuropsychiatry Clin Neurosci* 1995; 7:169–175.

    Schiffer F: Cognitive activity of the right hemisphere: Possible contributions to psychological function. *Harvard Rev Psychiatry* 1996; 4:126–138.

2. Wittling W: Brain asymmetry in the control of autonomic-physiologic activity. In: Davidson RJ, Hugdahl K eds. *Brain Asymmetry*. Cambridge, MA, MIT Press, 1995.

    Wittling W, Roschmann R: Emotion-related hemisphere asymmetry: Subjective emotional responses to laterally presented films. *Cortex* 1993; 29:431–448.

    Wittling W, Schweiger E: Neuroendocrine brain asymmetry and physical complaints. *Neuropsychologia* 1993; 31:591–608.

3. Dimond SJ, Farrington L, Johnson P: Differing emotional response from right and left hemispheres. *Nature* 1976; 261:690–692.

4. See Wittling, Brain asymmetry, for his explanation.

For discussions of the likelihood that one hemisphere can suppress the other, see: Iaccino JF: *Left Brain*.

Kinsbourne M: The control of attention by interaction between the cerebral hemispheres. In: Kornblum S, ed. *Attention and Performance* II. New York, Academic Press, 1973.

Kinsbourne M: The mechanisms of hemisphere asymmetry in man. In: Kinsbourne M, Smith WL, eds. *Hemispheric Disconnection and Cerebral Function*. Springfield, IL, Charles C. Thomas, 1974.

Levy J: Regulation and generation of perception in the asymmetric brain. In: Trevarthen C, ed. *Brain Circuits and Functions of the Mind*. Cambridge, Cambridge University Press, 1990.

Schiffer, Cognitive activity.

5. Kinsbourne's studies of lateral vision stimulating the opposite hemisphere are described in Kinsbourne M: Lateral input may shift activation balance in the integrated brain. *Psychologist* 1983; 38:228–229,

Lempert H, Kinsbourne M: Effects of laterality of orientation on verbal memory. *Neuropsychologia* 1982; 20:211–214.

The idea that one hemisphere could inhibit or stimulate the other has been suggested from studies from a number of authors such as; Kinsbourne, Mechanisms of hemisphere asymmetry.

Galin D: Implications for psychiatry of left and right cerebral specialization. *Arch Gen Psychiatry* 1974; 31:572–583.

Levy J, Regulation.

Ross ED, Homan RW, Buck R: Differential hemispheric lateralization of primary and social emotions: Implications for developing a comprehensive neurology for emotions, repression and the subconscious. *Neuropsychiatry, Neurospsychology, and Behav Neurol* 1994; 7:1–19.

Schiffer, Cognitive activity.

6. Drake RA, Bingham BR: Induced lateral orientation and persuasibility. Brain Cognition 1985; 4:156–164.

Gross Y, Franko R, Lewin I: Effects of voluntary eye movement on hemispheric activity and choice of cognitive mode. *Neuropsychologia* 1978; 16:653–657.

Walker E, Wade S, Waldman I: The effect of lateral visual fixation on response latency to verbal and spatial questions. Brain Cognition 1982; 1:399–404

Casey SM: The influence of lateral orientation on cerebral processing. *Cortex* 1981; 17:503–514.

Tressoldi PE: Visual hemispace differences reflect hemisphere asymmetries. *Neuropsychologia* 1987; 25:636–644.

7. Fouty HE, Otto MW, Yeo RA, Briggs CR: A novel contact-lens system to assess visual hemispheric asymmetries. *Percept Motor Skills* 1992; 74:567–575.

8. Levick SE, Lorig T, Wexler BE, Gur RE, Gur RC, Schwartz GE: Asymmetrical visual deprivation: A technique to differentially influence lateral hemispheric function. *Percept Motor Skills* 1993; 76:1363–1382.

9. Schiff B, Lamon M: Inducing emotion by unilateral contraction of hand muscles. *Cortex* 1994; 30:247–254.

10. Schiffer F: Affect changes observed with right versus left lateral visual field stimulation in psychotherapy patients: Possible physiological, psychological, and therapeutic implications. *Comp Psychiatry* 1977; 38:289–295.

11. See Ross ED, Edmondson JA, Seibert GB, et al: Acoustic analysis of affective prosody during right-sided Wada test: A within-subjects verification of the right hemisphere's role in language. *Brain Language* 1988; 33:128–145; Ross et al, Differential hemispheric lateralization; Sackeim HA, Gur RC: Lateral asymmetry in intensity of emotional expression. *Neuropsychologia* 1978; 16:473–481.

Schwartz GE, Davidson RJ, Maer F: Right hemisphere lateralization for emotion in the human brain: Interactions with cognition. *Science* 1975; 190:286–288.

Tucker DM, Roth RS, Arneson BA, et al: Right hemisphere activation during stress. *Neuropsychologia* 1977; 15:697–700.

Tomarken AJ, Davidson R, Henriques JB: Resting frontal brain asymmetry predicts affective responses to films. *J Personality Soc Psychol* 1990; 59:791–801.

Ladavas E, Nicoletti R, Umilta C, et al: Right hemisphere interference during negative affect: A reaction time study, *Neuropsychologia* 1984; 22:479–485.

Tucker DM, Stenslie CE, Roth RS, et al: Right frontal lobe activation and right hemisphere performance: Decrement during a depressed mood. *Arch Gen Psychiatry* 1981; 38:169–174.

Schiffer, Cognitive activity.

12. Wittling W: Psychophysiological correlates of human brain asymmetry: Blood pressure changes during lateralized presentation of an emotionally laden film. *Neuropsychologia* 1990; 28:457–470.

Wittling W, Pflüger M: Neuroendocrine hemisphere asymmetries: Salivary cortisol secretion during lateralized viewing of emotion-related and neutral films. *Brain Cognition* 1990; 14:243–265.

Wittling W, Roschmann R: Emotion-related hemisphere asymmetry: Subjective emotional responses to laterally presented films. *Cortex* 1993; 29:431–448.

Wittling W, Schweiger E: Neuroendocrine brain asymmetry and physical complaints. *Neuropsychologia* 1993; 31:591–608.

13. See: Tomarken AJ, Davidson R, Henriques JB: Resting frontal brain asymmetry predicts affective responses to films. *J Personality Psychol* 1990; 59:791–801.

Davidson RJ: Cerebral asymmetry, emotion, and affective style. In: Davidson RJ, Hugdahl K, eds. *Brain Asymmetry*, Cambridge, MA, MIT Press, 1995.

14. For the report from Davidson's group, see Lane RD, Reiman EM, Ahern GL, Schwartz GE, Davidson RJ: Neuroanatomical correlates of happiness, sadness, and disgust. *Am J Psychiatry* 1997; 154:926–933.

For other PET studies in which negative emotions were provoked, see: Pardo JV, Pardo PJ, Raichle ME: Neural correlates of self-induced dysphoria. *Am J Psychiatry* 1993; 150:713–719.

George MS, Ketter TA, Parekh PI, Horowitz B, Herscovitch P, Post, RM: Brain activity during transient sadness and happiness in healthy women. *Am J Psychiatry* 1995; 152:431–351.

For a review, see Schiffer, Cognitive activity.

15. See Schiffer et al, Evoked potential evidence.

For PET studies, see Rausch SL, van der Kolk BA, Fisler RE et al: A symptom provocation study of posttraumatic stress disorder using positron emission tomography and script-driven imagery. *Arch Gen Psychiatry* 1996; 53:380–387.

Shin LM, Kosslyn SM, McNally RJ, Alpert NM, Thompson WL, Rauch SL, Macklin ML, Pitman RK: Visual imagery and perception in posttraumatic stress disorder: A positron emission tomographic investigation. *Arch Gen Psychiatry* 1997; 54:233–241.

For an overview of PET studies, see Rausch RL, Shin LM: Functional neuroimaging studies in posttraumatic stress disorder. *Ann NY Acad Sci* 1997; 821:83–98.

For a general overview see: van der Kolk BA, Burbridge JA, Suzuki J: The psychobiology of traumatic memory: Clinical implications of neuroimaging studies. *Ann NY Acad Sci* 1997; 821:99–113.

16. See Teicher MH, Ito Y, Glod CA, Schiffer F, Golbard HA: Neurophysiological mechanisms of stress response in children. In: Pfeffer CR, ed. *Severe Stress and Mental Disturbance in Children*. Washington, DC, American Psychiatric Association Press, 1996.

Teicher MH, Ito Y, Glod CA, Andersen SL, Dumont N, Ackerman E: Preliminary evidence for abnormal cortical development in physically and sexually abused children using EEG coherence and MRI. *Ann NY Acad Sci* 1997; 821:160–175.

17. See Asbjornsen A, Hugdahl K, Bryden M P: Manipulation of subjects' level of arousal in dichotic listening. *Brain Cogn* 1992; 19:183–194.

Gruzelier J, Phelan M: Stress-induced reversal of a lexical divided visual field asymmetry accompanied by retarded electrodermal habituation. *Int J Psychophysiol* 1991; 11:269–276.

Gerhards F, Yehuda R, Shoham M, Hellhammer DH: Abnormal cerebral laterality in posttraumatic stress disorder. *Ann NY Acad Sci* 1997; 821:482–485.

18. See Ross 1994.
19. Iaccino, *Left Brain*.

    Joseph Bogen, personal communication.
20. See Teicher et al, 1997; Galin, Joseph, Implications.
21. See: Davidson RJ, Schaffer CE, Saron C: Effects of lateralized presentations of faces on self-reports of emotion and EEG asymmetry in depressed and non-depressed subjects. *Psychophysiology* 1985; 22:353–364.

    Schweinberger SR, Sommer W, Stiller RM: Event-related potentials and models of performance asymmetries in face and word recognition. *Neuropsychologia* 1994; 32:175–191.

    Lavine RA, Jenkins RL: Hemispheric asymmetry in processing visual half-field pattern-reversal stimuli assessed by reaction time and evoked potentials. *Intern J Neurosci* 1989; 44:197–204.

    Tressoldi PE, Cusumano S: Visual evoked potentials related to behavioral asymmetries during foveal attention in the two extrapersonal hemispaces. *Brain Cogn* 1992; 18:125–137.

    Greeberg JH, Reivich M, Alavi A: Metabolic mapping of functional activity in human subjects with the [18F] fluorodeoxyglucose technique. *Science* 1981; 212:678–680.
22. Schiffer F, Anderson CM, Teicher MH: EEG evidence of hemispheric activation with contralateral visual field stimulation. *Am Psychiatr Assoc New Res Program Abstr* 1997; 218.

    Schiffer F, Anderson CM, Teicher MH: Affect changes and EEG and bilateral ear temperature evidence of hemispheric activation with contralateral visual field stimulation. In submission.
23. Boyce WT, Higley JD, Jemerin JJ, Champoux M, Suomi SJ: Tympanic temperature asymmetry and stress behavior in rhesus macaques and children. *Arch Pediatr Adoles Med* 1996; 150:518–523.
24. Schiffer F, Anderson CM, Renshaw PF, Maas LC, Teicher MH: Baseline asymmetry in right temporal lobe blood flow by fMRI correlates with EEG and affect responses to lateral visual field stimulation. *Am Psychiatr Assoc New Res Progrm Abstr* 1998; 175.

CHAPTER 4. DUAL-BRAIN PSYCHOLOGY

1. Sperry RW: Hemisphere deconnection and unity in conscious awareness. *Amer Psychologist* 1968; 23:723–733.
2. Akelaitis AJ: Studies on the corpus callosum. IV. Diagnostic dyspraxia in epileptics following partial and complete section of the corpus callosum. *Am J Psychiatry* 1945; 101:594–599.
3. Levy J, Trevarthen C: Metacontrol of hemispheric function in human split-brain patients. *J Experimental Psychol* 1976; 2:299–312

Ahern GL, Herring AM, Trackenberg J, et al: The association of multiple personality and temporolimbic epilepsy: Intracarotid amobarbital test observations. *Arch Neurol* 1993; 50:1020–1025.

4. Galin D: Implications for psychiatry of left and right cerebral specialization. *Arch Gen Psychiatry* 1974; 31:572–583.

Galin D: Conceptual and methodological issues in neuropsychological studies of depression. In Kinsbourne M, ed. *Cerebral Hemisphere Function in Depression.* Washington DC, American Psychiatric Press, 1988.

Joseph R: *The Right Brain and the Unconscious* New York, Plenum, 1992.

Schiffer F: Cognitive activity of the right hemisphere: Possible contributions to psychological function. *Harvard Rev Psychiatry* 1996; 4:126–138.

Watt DF: Higher cortical functions and the ego: Explorations of the boundary between behavioral neurology, neuropsychology, and psychoanalysis. *Psychoanal Psychol* 1990; 7:487–527.

Levin FM: *Mapping the Mind.* Hillsdale, NJ, Analytic Academic Press, 1991.

5. For a review of PMS, estrogen, and neurotransmitter systems, see: Fink G, Summer BE, Rosie R, Grace O, Quinn JP: Estrogen control of central neurotransmission: Effect on mood, mental state, and memory. *Cell Molec Neurobiol* 1996; 16:325–344.

6. For discussions of MPD, see Henninger P: Conditional handedness: Handedness changes in multiple personality disordered subject reflect shift in hemispheric dominance. *Consciousness Cog* 1992; 1:265–287.

Stringer AY, Cooley EL. Divided attention performance in multiple personality disorder. Neuropsychiatry, Neuropsychol & Behav Neurol 1994; 7:51–56.

For a discussion of MDI and laterality, see: Gruzelier J, Davis S: Social and physical anhedonia in relation to cerebral laterality and electrodermal habituation in unmedicated psychotic patients. Psychiatry Res 1995; 56:163–72;

Bruder GE, Stewart JW, Towey JP, et al: Abnormal cerebral laterality in bipolar depression: Convergence of behavioral and brain event-related potential findings. Biol *Psychiatry* 1992; 32:33–47.

7. Janet P: *L'Automatisme psychologique.* Paris, Alcan, 1889; cited by Ellenberger HF: *The Discovery of the Unconscious: The History and Evolution of Dynamic Psychiatry.* New York, Basic Books, 1970.

8. See Schiffer, Cognitive activity.

9. Hilgard ER: A neodissociation interpretation of pain reduction in hypnosis. *Psychol R* 1973; 80:396–411.

10. Erdelyi MH: *Psychoanalysis: Freud's Cognitive Psychology.* New York, Freeman, 1985.

11. See Teicher et al, 1997.

12. Goleman D: *Emotional Intelligence.* Bantam, New York, 1995.

13. LeDoux J: *The Emotional Brain: The Mysterious Underpinnings of Emotional Life.* New York, Simon & Schuster, 1996.

14. For evidence of close neural connections within each hemisphere between the cortex and amygdala, see Amaral DG, Insausti R, Cowan WM: The commissural connections of the monkey hippocampal formation. *J Comp Neurol* 1984; 224:307–336.

Mesulam MM, Mufson E: The insula of Reil in man and monkey: Architectonics, connectivity and function. In Peters A, Jones EG, eds. *Cerebral Cortex*, vol. 4. New York, Plenum Press, 1985.

15. See Gloor P: Role of the human limbic system in perception, memory, and affect: Lessons from temporal lobe epilepsy. In: Doane BK, Livingston RE, eds. *The Limbic System: Functional Organization and Clinical Disorders*. Raven Press, New York, 1986.

16. See Bremner JD, Randall P, Scott TM, et al: MRI-based measurement of hippocampal volume in combat-related posttraumatic stress disorder. A J Psychiatry 1995; 152:973–981.

Gurvits TG, Shenton MR, Hokama H, et al: Magnetic resonance imaging study of hippocampal volume in chronic, combat-related posttraumatic stress disorder. Biol *Psychiatry* 1996; 40:1091–1099.

Bremner JD, Randall P, Vermetten E, et al: MRI-based measurement of hippocampal volume in posttraumatic stress disorder related to childhood physical and sexual abuse: A preliminary report. *Biol Psychiatry* 1997; 41:23–32

17. Munroe R: *Schools of Psychoanalytic Thought: An Exposition, Critique, and Attempt at Integration*. New York, Holt, 1955.

18. Freud S: (1923) *The Ego and the Id. Standard Edition*, vol. 22. London, Hogarth, 1963.

Freud S: (1917) *Introductory Lectures on Psychoanalysis. Standard Edition*, vols. 15, 16. London, Hogarth, 1961, 1963.

19. Freud S: (1915) *Repression. Standard Edition*, vol. 14. London, Hogarth, 1957.

Breuer J, Freud S: (1895) *Studies in Hysteria. Standard Edition*, vol. 2. London, Hogarth, 1955.

Freud S: (1896) *The Aetiology of Hysteria. Standard Edition*, vol. 3. London, Hogarth, 1962.

Freud S: (1926) *Inhibitions, Symptoms, and Anxiety. Standard Edition*, vol. 20. London, Hogarth, 1959.

Freud S: (1939) *Moses and Monotheism: Three Essays. Standard Edition*, vol. 2. London, Hogarth, 1955.

CHAPTER 5. APPREHENSION

1. Torgersen S: Twin studies in panic disorder. In Ballenger J, ed. *Neurobiology of Panic Disorder*. New York, Liss, 1990.

Crowe RR, Noyes R, Wilson F, et al: A linkage study of panic disorder. *Arch Gen Psychiatry* 1987; 44:933–937.

Crowe RR, Noyes R Jr, Samuelson S, et al: Close linkage between panic disorder and α haptoglobin excluded in 10 families. *Arch Gen. Psychiatry* 1990; 47:377–380.

Wang ZW, Crowe RR, Noyes R Jr.: Adrenergic receptor genes as candidate genes for panic disorder: A linkage study. *Am J Psychiatry* 1992; 149:470–474.

CHAPTER 6. DESPONDENCY

1. Spitz RA: *The First Year of Life*. New York, International Universities Press, 1965.
2. See Goleman, 1995.
3. Horney K: *Neurosis and Human Growth*. New York, Norton, 1950.

   Rado S: *The problem of melancholia. Int J Psychoanal* 1929; 9:420–438.

   Bowlby J: Process of mourning. *Int J Psychoanal* 45:317, 1961.

   Kohut H: *The Analysis of the Self: A Systematic Approach to the Psychoanalytic Approach of Narcissistic Personality Disorders*. New York, International Universities Press, 1971.

   Zetzel E: Depression and the incapacity to bear it. In: Schur M, ed, *Drives, Affects and Behavior*, vol. 2. New York, International Universities Press, 1965.

   Brenner C: A psychoanalytic perspective on depression. *J Am Psychoanal Assoc* 39:25, 1991.
4. Freud S: *Mourning and Melancholia. Standard Edition*, vol. 14. London, Hogarth Press, 1963.

   Abraham K: Notes on the psycho-analytical investigation and treatment of manic-depressive insanity and allied conditions. In *Selected Papers of Karl Abraham, M.D.* New York, Basic Books, 1953.
5. Beck AT, Rush AJ, Shaw BF, Emery G: *Cognitive Therapy of Depression*. New York, Guilford, 1979.
6. Nathan KI, Musselman DL, Schatzberg AF, Nemeroff CB: Biology of mood disorders. In: Schatzberg AF, Nemeroff CB, eds. *Textbook of Psychopharmacology*. Washington, DC, American Psychiatric Press, 1995.

   Janowsky DS, El-Yousef MK, Davis JM, et al: A cholinergic-adrenergic hypothesis of mania and depression. *Lancet* 1972; 2:573–577.

   Prange AJ Jr., Wilson IC, Lynn CW, et al: l-Tryptophan in mania: Contribution to a permissive hypothesis of affective disorders. *Arch Gen Psychiatry* 1974; 30:56–62.
7. Ries Merikangas K, Kupfer DJ: Mood disorders: Genetic aspects. In: Kaplan HI, Sadock BJ, eds. *Comprehensive Textbook of Psychiatry/VI*, 6th ed. Baltimore, Williams and Wilkins, 1995.
8. Von Knorring AL, Cloninger CR, Bohman M, Sigvardsson S: An adoption study of depressive disorders and substance abuse. *Arch Gen Psychiatry* 40:943, 1983.
9. Cadoret RJ, O'Gorman TW, Heywood E, Troughton E: Genetic and environmental factors in major depression. *J Affective Disord* 9:155, 1985.
10. Egeland JA, Gerhard DS, Pauls DL, et al: Bipolar affective disorders linked to DNA markers on chromosome II. *Nature* 325:783, 1987.
11. Kelsoe JR, Ginns EE, Egeland JA, et al: Re-evaluation of the linkage relationship be-

tween chromosome 11p loci and the gene for bipolar affective disorder in the old order Amish. *Nature* 16:238, 1989.

12. Kinsbourne M: Hemisphere interactions in depression. In: Kinsbourne M, ed. *Cerebral Hemisphere Function in Depression.* Washington, DC, American Psychiatric Press, 1988.

Tucker DM: Lateral brain function,emotion, and conceptualization. *Psychol Bull* 1981; 89:19–46.

Flor-Henry P: Lateralized temporal-limbic dysfunction in psychopathology. *Ann NY Acad Sci* 1976; 280:777–797.

13. See Wittling, 1995.

Arato M, Frecska E, Duncan J, et al: Serotonergic interhemispheric asymmetry: Neurochemical and pharmaco-EEG evidence. *Prog Neuro Psychopharmacol Biol Psychiatry* 1991; 15:759–764.

Kemali D, Galderisi S, Maj M, Mucci A, DiGregorio M: Lateralization patterns of event-related potential and performance indices in schizophrenia: Relationship to clinical state and neuroleptic treatment. *Int a Psychophysiol* 1991; 10:225–230.

Ingum J, Bjorklund R: Effects of flunitrazepam on responses to lateralized visual stimuli: Evidence for cerebral asymmetry of execution of manual movements to targets in contralateral and ipsilateral visual space. *Psychopharmacology* 1994; 114:551–558.

Baxter LR Jr., Schwartz JM, Bergman KS, et al: Caudate glucose metabolic rate changes with both drug and behavior therapy for obsessive-compulsive disorder. *Arch Gen Psychiatry* 1992; 49:681–689.

Swedo SE, Pietrini P, Leonard HL, et al: Cerebral glucose metabolism in childhood-onset obsessive-compulsive disorder: Revisualization during pharmacotherapy. *Arch Gen Psychiatry* 1992; 49:690–694.

14. Stark R, Hardison CD: A review of multicenter controlled studies of fluoxetine vs. imipramine and placebo in outpatients with major depressive disorder. *J Clin Psychiatry* 1985; 46:53–58.

Appleton WS: *Prozac and the New Antidepressants.* New York, Penguin, 1997.

CHAPTER 7: EXTREMES

1. Boulanger G: Post-traumatic stress disorder: An old problem with a new name, in Sonnenberg SM, Blank AS, Talbott J A, eds. *The Trauma of War: Stress and Recovery in Viet Nam Veterans.* Washington, DC, American Psychiatric Press, 1985.

2. van der Kolk BA, Pelcovitz, D, Roth S, Mandel FS, McFarlane A, Herman JL: Dissociation, somatization, and affect dysregulation: The complexity of adaptation to trauma. *Am J Psychiatry* 1996; 153 (Supplement):83–93.

Keane TM, Kaloupek DG: Comorbid psychiatric disorders in PTSD: Implications for research. *Ann NY Acad Sci* 1997; 821:24–34.

3. Lewis ND, Engel B: *Wartime Psychiatry,* New York, Oxford University Press, 1954.

Hocking F: Extreme environmental stress and its significance for psychopathology. *Am J Psychother* 1970; 24:4–26.

Eaton WW, Sigal JJ, Weinfeld M: Impairment in Holocaust survivors after 33 years: Data from an unbiased community sample. *Am J Psychiatry* 1982:139:773–777.

See Boulanger, Post-traumatic stress disorder.

Engdahl B, Dikel TN, Eberly R, Blank A Jr.: Posttraumatic stress disorder in a community group of former prisoners of war: A normative response to severe trauma. *Am J Psychiatry* 1997; 154:1576–1581.

4. True WR, Rice J, Eisen SA, et al: A twin study of genetic and environmental contributions to liability for posttraumatic stress symptoms. *Arch Gen Psychiatry* 1993; 50:257–264.

Davies RK: Incest: Some neuropsychiatric findings. *Int J Psychiatry Med* 1979; 9:117–121.

5. van der Kolk, B: *Psychological Trauma.* Washington, DC, American Psychiatric Press, 1987.

6. Murburg MM, McFall ME, Veith RC: Catecholamines, stress and posttraumatic stress disorder. In: Giller EL, ed. *Biological Assessment and Treatment of Posttraumatic Stress Disorder* Washington, DC, American Psychiatric Press, 1990

Watson IP, Muller HK, Jones IH, Bradley AJ: Cell-mediated immunity in combat veterans with post-traumatic stress disorder. *Med J Australia* 1993; 159:513–516.

Yehuda R, Southwick SM, Perry BD, Mason, JW, Giller EL: Interactions of the hypothalamic-pituitary-adrenal axis and the catecholaminergic system in posttraumatic stress disorder. In: Giller, EL *Biological Assessment.*

CHAPTER 8. COLLAPSE

1. Meyer A: *Psychobiology: A Science of Man.* Springfield, IL, Charles C Thomas, 1957.

Freud S: On the history of the psycho-analytic movement. *Standard Edition of the Complete Psychological Works of Sigmund Freud,* vol. 14. London, Hogarth Press, 1957.

Federn P: *Ego Psychology and the Psychoses.* New York, Basic Books, 1952.

Hartmann H: Contributions to the metapsychology of schizophrenia. In: *Psychoanalytic Study of the Child VIII.* New York, International Universities Press, 1953.

Sullivan HS: *Clinical Studies in Psychiatry.* New York, Norton, 1956.

Segal H: *Introduction to the Work of Melanie Klein.* New York, Basic Books, 1973.

Fairbain W: *On Object-Relations Theory of Personality.* New York, Basic Books, 1954.

Bateson G: The group dynamics of schizophrenia. In: Appleby L., ed. *Chronic Schizophrenia.* New York, Free Press, 1960.

Lidz T: *Schizophrenia and the Family,* New York, International Universities Press, 1965.

Wynne LC: Thought disorders and family relation of schizophrenics, IV: Results and implications. *Arch Gen Psychiatry* 1965; 12:201–212.

2. Tienari P, Sorry A, Lahti I, et al: The Finnish adoptive family study of schizophrenia. *Yale J Biol Med* 1985; 58:227–237.

3. Knable MB, Kleinman JE, Weinberger DR: Neurobiology of schizophrenia. In: Schatzberg AF, Nemeroff CB, eds. *Textbook of Psychopharmacology*. Washington, DC, American Psychiatric Press, 1995.

   Wyatt RJ: Neurodevelopmental abnormalities and schizophrenia: A family affair. *Arch Gen Psychiatry* 1996; 53:11–15.

   Weinberger D. Implications of normal brain development for the pathogenesis of schizophrenia. *Arch Gen Psychiatry* 1987; 44:660–669.

   Waddington J: Schizophrenia: Developmental neuroscience and pathobiology. *Lancet* 1993; 341:531–536.

4. Flor-Henry P: Schizophrenic-like psychosis associated with temporal lobe epilepsy: Etiological factors. *Am J Psychiatry* 1969; 26:400–403.

   Flor-Henry P: Psychosies and temporal lobe epilepsy: A controlled investigation. *Epilepsia* 1969; 10:363–395.

   Flor-Henry P: Lateralized temporal-limbic dysfunction and psychopathology. *Annals NY Acad Sci* 1976; 280:777–795.

5. For a review of articles supporting a connection between the left hemisphere and schizophrenia, see Nachshon I: Hemispheric dysfunctioning in schizophrenia. *J Nerv Ment Dis* 1980; 168:241–242;

   Gur RE: Left hemisphere dysfunction and left hemispher overactivation in schizophrenia. *J Abnormal Psychol* 1978; 87:226–238;

   Walker E, McGuire M: Intra- and interhemispheric information processing in schizophrenia. *Psychol Bull* 1982; 92:701–725.

   For a review of Gruzelier's work in this area, see: Gruzelier J, Hammond N: Schizophrenia—a dominant hemispheric temporal lobe disorder? *Res Comm Psychol, Psychiatry, Behav* 1976; 1:33–72.

6. Gruzelier JH: Hemispheric imbalance in schizophrenia. *Int J Psychol* 1984; 1:227–240.

7. Beaumont G, Dimond S: Brain disconnection and schizophrenia. *Br J Psychiatry* 1972; 123:661–662.

8. Woodruff PW, Phillips ML, Rushe T, Wright IC, Murray RM, David AS: Corpus callosum size and inter-hemispheric function in schizophrenia. *Schizophrenia Res* 1997; 23:189–196.

9. Barta PE, Pearlson GD, Powers RE, Richards SS, Tune LE: Auditory hallucinations and smaller superior temporal gyral volume in schizophrenia. *Am J Psychiatry* 1990; 147:1457–1462.

   Shenton ME, Kidinis R, Jolesz FA, et al. Abnormalities of the left temporal lobe and thought disorder in schizophrenia. *N Engl J Med* 1992; 327:604–612.

Bartley AJ, Jones DW, Torrey EF, Zigun JR, Weinberger DR: Sylvian fissure asymmetries in monozygotic twins: A test of laterality in schizophrenia. *Biol Psychiatry* 1993; 34:853.

Berman KF, Daniel DG, Weinberger DR: Schizophrenia: brain structure and function. In: Kaplan HI, Sadock BJ, eds. *Comprehensive Textbook of Psychiatry/VI*. Baltimore, Williams & Wilkins, 1995.

10. See Berman et al, Schizophrenia.

11. Fenton WS, McGlashan TH: We can talk: Individual psychotherapy for schizophrenia. *Am J Psychiatry* 1997; 154:1493–1495.

Schwartz RC, Cohen BN, Grubaugh A: Does insight affect long-term impatient treatment outcome in chronic schizophrenia? *Comp Psychiatry* 1997; 38:283–288.

12. Daniel DG, Whitcomb SR: Treatment of the refractory schizophrenic patient. *J Clin Psychiatry* 1998; 59(Suppl) 1:13–19.

Marder SR, Davis JM, Chouinard G: The effects of risperidone on the five dimensions of schizophrenia derived by factor analysis: Combined results of the North American trials. *J Clin Psychiatry* 1997; 58:538–546.

Hamilton SH, Revicki DA, Genduso LA, Beasley CM Jr: Olanzapine versus placebo and haloperidol: Quality of life and efficacy results of the North American double-blind trial. *Neuropsychopharmacology* 1998; 18:41–49.

CHAPTER 9. COCA COMPULSIONS

1. Schiffer F: Psychotherapy of nine successfully treated cocaine abusers: Techniques and dynamics. *J Substance Abuse Treat* 1988; 5:131–137.

2. Freud S: (1920) *Beyond the Pleasure Principle*. In: Strachey J, ed. and trans. *The Standard Edition*, vol. 18. London, Hogarth Press, 1959.

3. Rado S: The psychoanalysis of pharmacothymia. *Psychoanalytic Q* 1933; 2:1–23.

4. Glover E: On the etiology of drug addiction. In: *On the Early Development of Mind*. New York, International Universities Press, 1970. Khantzian EJ, Khantzian NJ: Cocaine addiction: Is there a psychological predisposition? *Psychiatric Ann* 1984; 14:753–759.

Khantzian EJ: The self-medication hypothesis of addictive disorders: Focus on heroin and cocaine dependence. *Am J Psychiatry* 1986; 142:1259–1264.

Wurmser L: Psychoanalytic considerations of the etiology of compulsive drug use. *J Am Psychoanal Assoc* 1974; 22:820–843.

Krystal H, Raskin HA: *Drug Dependence: Aspects of Ego Functions*. Detroit, Wayne State University Press, 1970.

Wieder H, Kaplan EH: Drug use in adolescents: Psychodynamic meaning and pharmocogenic effect. *Psychoanal Study Child* 1969; 24:399–431.

Spotts JV, Shontz FC: Drug-induced ego states. I. Cocaine: phenomenology and implications. *Int J Addict* 1984; 19:119–151.

Adams JW: *Psychoanalysis of Drug Dependence: The Understanding and Treatment of a Particular Form of Pathological Narcissism.* New York, Grune & Stratton, 1978.

5. Rounsaville BJ, Gawin F, Kleber H: Interpersonal psychotherapy adapted for ambulatory cocaine abusers. *Am J Drug Alcohol Abuse* 1985; 11:171–191

Woody GE, O'Brien CP, Rickels K: Depression and anxiety in heroin addicts: A placebo-controlled study of doxepin in combination with methadone. *Am J Psychiatry* 1975; 132:476–450.

CHAPTER 10. ATTACK ON THE HEART

1. Dunbar F: *Psychiatry in Medical Specialties.* New York, McGraw-Hill, 1959.

   Arlow J: Identification mechanism in coronary occlusion. *Psychosom Med* 1945; 7:195–209.

   Alexander F: *Psychosomatic Medicine: Its Principles and Applications.* New York, Norton, 1950.

   Weiss E, English OS: *Psychosomatic Medicine.* 3rd ed., Philadelphia, Saunders, 1957.

2. Frasure-Smith N, Lesperance F, Talajic M: Depression and 18-month prognosis after myocardial infarction. *Circulation* 1995; 91:999–1005.

3. Wong ND, Wilson PW, Kannel WB: Serum cholesterol as a prognostic factor after myocardial infarction: The Framingham Study. *Ann Intern Med* 1991; 115:687–693.

4. Everson SA, Goldberg DE, Kaplan GA, et al: Hopelessness and risk of mortality and incidence of myocardial infarction and cancer. *Psychosom Med* 1996; 58:113–121.

5. Denollet J, Sys SU, Stroobant N, Rombouts H, Gillebert TC, Brutsaert DL: Personality as an independent predictor of long-term mortality in patients with coronary heart disease. *Lancet* 1996; 347:417–421.

6. Pratt LA, Ford DE, Crum RM, Armenian HK, Gallo JJ, Eaton WW: Depression, psychotropic medication, and risk of myocardial infarction. Prospective data from the Baltimore ECA follow-up. *Circulation* 1996; 94:3123–3129.

7. Orth-Gomer K, Rosengren A, Wilhelmsen L: Lack of social support and incidence of coronary heart disease in middle-aged Swedish men. *Psychosom Med* 1993; 55:37–43.

8. Kubzansky LD, Kawachi I, Spiro A III, Weiss ST, Vokonas PS, Sparrow D: Is worrying bad for your heart? A prospective study of worry and coronary heart disease in the Normative Aging Study. *Circulation* 1997; 95:818–824.

9. Williams RB, Barefoot JC, Califf RM: Prognostic importance of social and economic resources among medically treated patients with angiographically documented coronary artery disease. *JAMA* 1992; 267:520–524.

10. Kaplan JR, Manuck SB, Clarkson TB, Lusso FM, Taub DM: Social status, environment, and atherosclerosis in cynomolgus monkeys. *Arteriosclerosis* 1982; 2:359–368.

    Kaplan JR, Manuck SB, Clarkson TB, Lusso FM, Taub DM, Miller EW: Social stress and atherosclerosis in normocholesterolemid monkeys. *Science* 1983; 220:733–735.

11. Hamm TE Jr, Kaplan JR, Clarkson TB, Bullock BC: Effects of gender and social be-

havior on the development of coronary artery atherosclerosis in cynomolgus macaques. *Atherosclerosis* 1983; 48:221–233.

Kaplan JR, Manuck SB, Clarkson TB: Psychosocial stress and atherosclerosis in cynomolgus macaques. In: Beamish RE, Singal PK, Dhalla NS, eds. *Stress and Heart Disease*. Boston, Martinus Nijhoff, 1985.

Kaplan JR, Manuck SB, Adams MR, Williams JK, Register TC, Clarkson TB: Plaque changes and arterial enlargement in atherosclerotic monkeys after manipulation of diet and social environment. *Arteriosclerosis Thromb* 1993; 13:254–263.

Shively CA, Clarkson TB, Kaplan JR: Social deprivation and coronary artery atherosclerosis in female cynomolgus monkeys. *Atherosclerosis* 1989; 77:69–76.

12. Friedman M, Ulmer D: *Treating Type-A Behavior and Your Heart*. New York, Knopf, 1984.

13. Freud S: (1920) *Beyond the Pleasure Principle*. *Standard Edition*, vol. 18. London, Hogarth, 1955.

14. Schiffer F, Hartley LH, Schulman CL, Abelmann WH: The quiz electrocardiogram: A new diagnostic and research technique for evaluating the relation between emotional stress and ischemic heart disease. *Am J Cardiol* 1976; 37:41–47.

15. Schiffer F, Hartley LH, Schulman CL, Abelmann WH: Evidence for emotionally induced coronary artery spasm in patients with angina pectoris. *Br Heart J* 1980; 44:62–66.

Rozanski A, Bairey CN, Krantz DS, et al: Mental stress and the induction of silent myocardial ischemia in patients with coronary artery disease. *N Engl J Med* 1988; 318:1005–1012.

Yeung AC, Vekshtein VI, Krantz DS, et al: The effect of atherosclerosis on the vasomotor response of coronary arteries to mental stress. *N Engl J Med* 1991; 325:1551–1556.

16. Hugdahl K: *Psychophysiology: The Mind-Body Perspective*. Cambridge, MA, Harvard University Press, 1995.

Wittling W: Brain asymmetry in the control of autonomic-physiologic activity. In: Davidson RJ, Hugdahl K, eds. *Brain Asymmetry*. Cambridge, MA, MIT Press, 1995.

Wittling W: Psychophysiological correlates of human brain asymmetry: Blood pressure changes during lateralized presentation of an emotionally laden film. *Neuropshchologia* 1990; 28:457–470.

Hugdahl K, Franzon M, Andersson B, Walldebo G: Heart rate responses (HRR) to lateralized visual stimuli. *Pavlovian J Biol Sci* 1983; 18:186–198.

17. Hugdahl, *Psychophysiology*.

Lane RD, Jennings JR: Hemispheric asymmetry, autonomic asymmetry, and the problem of sudden cardiac death. In Davidson, Hugdahl, *Brain Asymmetry*.

18. Ibrahim VA, Feldman JG, Sultz HA, et al: Management after myocardial infarction: A controlled trial of the effect of group psychotherapy. *Psychiatry Med* 1974; 5:253–268.

Rahe RH, Ward HW, Hayes V: Brief group therapy in myocardial infarction rehabilitation: Three- to four-year follow-up of a controlled trial. *Psychosom Med* 1979; 41:229–242.

19. Price VA, Friedman M, Ghandour G, Fleischmann N: Relation between insecurity and type A behavior. *Am Heart J* 1995; 129:488–491.

    Friedman M, Thoresen CE, Gill JJ, et al: Alteration of type-A behavior and its effect on cardiac recurrences in post myocardial infarction patients: Summary results of the Recurrent Coronary Prevention Project. *Am Heart J* 1986; 112:653–665.

    Friedman M, Powell LH, Thoresen CE, et al: Effect of discontinuance of type-A behavioral counseling on type-A behavior and cardiac recurrence rate of post myocardial infarction patients. *Am Heart J* 1987; 114:483 490

20. Burell G: Behavior modification in secondary prevention of coronary heart disease: A treatment model that can prolong life after myocardial infarction and coronary artery bypass graft surgery. Paper presented at the III Congresso Nazionale, Societa Italiana Di Cardioneurologia, Pavia, 1993.

21. Hamalainen H, Luurila OJ, Kallio V, et al: Long-term reduction in sudden deaths after a multifactorial intervention program in patients with myocardial infarction: 10-year results of a controlled investigation. *Eur Heart J* 1989; 10:55–62.

22. Ornish D, Brown SE, Billings JH, et al: Can lifestyle changes reverse coronary atherosclerosis? Four-year results of the Lifestyle Heart Trial. *Circulation* 1993; 88:I–385.

    Gould KL, Ornish D, Scherwitz L, et al: Changes in myocardial perfusion abnormalities by positron emission tomography after long-term, intense risk factor modification. JAMA 1995; 274:894–901.

23. Campbell NC, Grimshaw JM, Ritchie LD, Rawles JM: Outpatient cardiac rehabilitation: Are the potential benefits being realized? *J Roy Coll Physicians London* 1996; 30:514–519.

Index